WEST E
POLITI

WEST EUROPEAN POLITICS TODAY

Geoffrey Roberts
Jill Lovecy

Manchester
University Press

Manchester and New York

Distributed exclusively in the USA and Canada by St. Martin's Press

Copyright © Geoffrey Roberts and Jill Lovecy 1984

Reprinted 1988 (with revisions)

Published by Manchester University Press
Oxford Road, Manchester M13 9PL, UK
and Room 400, 175 Fifth Avenue,
New York, NY 10010, USA

Distributed exclusively in the USA and Canada
by St. Martin's Press, Inc.,
175 Fifth Avenue, New York, NY 10010, USA

British Library cataloguing in publication data

Roberts, Geoffrey
 West European politics today
 1. Europe—Politics and government—1945 –
 I. Title   II. Lovecy, Jill
 320.94   JN94.A2

Library of Congress cataloguing in publication data

Roberts, Geoffrey K.
 West European politics today.
 Bibliography: p. 252
 Includes index.
 1. Europe—Politics and government—1945 –
I. Lovecy, Jill   II. Title
JN94.A2R6 1984   320.94   83–18702

ISBN 0 7190 0909 X paperback

Printed in Great Britain by
Biddles Ltd., Guildford and King's Lynn

CONTENTS

PREFACE

West European Politics Today has been written for use by sixth-forms and by students in higher education who are undertaking introductory courses in politics or European Studies. Though the main emphasis of the book is on the political systems of Britain, France and West Germany, deliberately and necessarily frequent reference has been made to the political arrangements and experiences of other west European countries, especially where these illustrate the *variety* of forms of democratic politics: Swiss federalism, for example, the Irish electoral system, Belgian party divisions, or Spain's recent transition from dictatorship to democracy. The importance of the European Community in contemporary western European affairs has been acknowledged not only by the inclusion of a chapter dealing with the institutions and problems of the Community, but also by appropriate references to the Community in other chapters.

It is hoped that the book will explain the intricacies of west European politics, demonstrate the importance of comparing and contrasting the political arrangements of different countries in order the better to understand them, and also serve as a reference source for those requiring up-to-date information on the states of western Europe.

The authors gratefully acknowledge the valuable advice of the staff of Manchester University Press in the preparation of the book, and the assistance of Carole Webb, whose expertise was especially useful in preparing the chapter on the European Community.

Geoffrey Roberts   Jill Lovecy

1

PATTERNS OF POLITICS
IN WESTERN EUROPE

Liberal democracy

Despite obvious and important differences in the patterns of politics of the states which comprise western Europe, they all possess the attributes of 'liberal democracy' as their state form, or else they hope and intend to acquire those attributes. From Iceland and Eire in the west to Italy, Greece and Austria in the east, from Finland in the north to Spain in the south, there is a common basis of political organisation which is distinctly differentiated from the aristocratic regimes which preceded western democratic development, the monolithic so-called 'people's democracies' of eastern Europe, or the dictatorships (which increasingly involve the military) to be found especially in non-European countries today.

But precisely what is to be understood by this label: 'liberal democracy'? How does it differ from other forms of democracy? How did it develop historically? Other chapters in this book will explore in detail, and by comparative reference to a number of west European countries, the central features of liberal democratic politics. This chapter will preface those detailed comparisons by considering the elements of a general definition of liberal democracy, and how it contrasts with other patterns of political organisation to be found elsewhere or at other historical periods. Then will follow a survey of west European political development, essential to an understanding of how and why the states of western Europe acquired the political organisations which they have today, and the chapter will conclude with a consideration of the challenge which the development of international organisations, particularly in defence and economic affairs, have posed to the nation-state as a unit of political organisation, and the impact of ideals of a supranational or 'federalist' development of Europe, which some west European politicians have nurtured.

What is liberal democracy? – and what is it not?

One authority on west European politics has claimed that liberal democracy exists when the political organisation of a state includes three essential features:

mechanisms of political choice;
balanced political structures;
a stable political system.[1]

This involves some system of competing political parties, an electoral system by means of which the public can indicate their choice of candidate or party in an effective manner, mutually limiting institutions of an executive and legislative nature (including the possibility of legitimate opposition in the system), and stability based primarily on a measure of acceptance by the public of the rules of the political game rather than on coercion by the military or secret police. To these, one might well add other features, implied by those minimum conditions:

(*a*) The rule of law and an independent judiciary – for this acts as a barrier to the manipulation of democratic political procedures by those hostile to liberal democracy;

(*b*) A free and varied range of mass communications media, such as newspapers, books, journals and broadcasting facilities – for this preserves the possibility of criticism of those in power and allows the public an *informed* choice at elections;

(*c*) An economic system which is not monopolised by state authorities, in ownership or planning – because liberal democracy seems to be associated with the attainment of a relatively high degree of economic development. Though there is room for dispute concerning how much economic planning is compatible with the preservation of political freedom (the Scandinavian countries demonstrate that a substantial degree of economic planning *can* co-exist with liberal democracy), an economic system which leaves no place for unplanned and uncontrolled enterprise would seem to require severe restrictions on political freedom also.

Clearly, there is now a wide variety of actual political arrangements which qualify as liberal democracies by possession of these qualities. Equally, many political systems in the past have not met these requirements, and many states today have regimes which do not meet the conditions of liberal democracy.

The liberal democratic pattern, involving a degree of national political organisation based on government responsible to an elected legislature and subject to opposition, criticism and replacement, is not the *only* possible model of democratic politics. Similarly, many non-democratic forms of regime have also been tried in the past.

1. Although the twentieth century has seen the emergence of democratic forms of government as replacement for the aristocratic regimes which had previously existed, not every west European state acquired – or, if acquired, retained – a democratic political system. Several states have experienced *monarchical rule*. In some cases (such as the United Kingdom, Belgium and the Netherlands) this has been progressively tempered by the co-existence of democratic institutions, and thus has been transformed into *constitutional monarchy*. In contrast, both Germany before the first world war and Spain provide examples of monarchical rule of a more autocratic type, and Greece has also intermittently experienced such a monarchical regime. Even today, the Spanish monarchy retains – after the long interludes of the republic, the civil war and the dictatorship of Franco – a high degree of political significance and authority, as the background to the 1981 attempted coup by the military demonstrates.[2] In addition to Spain, several west European countries today still have a monarch as a head of state, but confined principally to ceremonial, rather than political powers: the United Kingdom, the Netherlands, Belgium, Sweden, Norway, Denmark and Luxemburg.

2. Forms of *autocracy* have also been tried in twentieth-century western Europe, in which power and authority have been concentrated in the hands of one man, aided by a small circle of supporters, unrestricted by the constraints of elections or of legitimate opposition. The regimes of Salazar in Portugal, Franco in Spain, Mussolini in Italy and Pétain in Vichy France during the second world war, are the chief examples, together with the *military autocracy* of Papadopoulous in Greece (the 'rule of the colonels' 1967–74). In the more distant past, *theocracies* (the rule

of priests) have existed in Europe, but today only the minute Vatican City state falls into this category in Europe, though, as the example of Iran illustrates, it is not unknown in other parts of the world.

3. Totalitarian regimes offer a more complex set of contrasts to liberal democracy. Such regimes can be categorised as *totalitarian dictatorships* (the Hitler regime being the most obvious example, though many political scientists would include the Stalinist period in the Soviet Union in this category also), and *totalitarian democracies*, such as the USSR and its east European satellite states today. Unlike other dictatorships, in which rulers have been content to exercise unchallenged power, with opposition and criticism muted and ineffective, and obedience secured, totalitarian regimes demand active support, conviction, participation. Their claims to the exercise of power rest on the imperatives of an ideology, such as Marxism or Nazism; in order to realise the demands of that ideology, total control of economic, social and cultural, as well as of political matters is sought. Autonomous institutions cannot be tolerated, for these might eventually challenge the omniscience and omnipotence of the regime. To enforce control, such a regime requires a large-scale coercive apparatus of police, informers, prison-camps and armed forces. In totalitarian democracies, it is claimed that power is exercised in the name of the people and through a single mass party which is the democratic embodiment of the people's wishes (the vanguard of the proletariat, for instance). In totalitarian dictatorships the need for such linkages to organised expressions of the will of the masses is absent; the leader or the elite party 'incorporate' the national will. However, whether of the left or the right, whether claiming to be democracies or not, the effects of such regimes on the public are not easily to be distinguished.

The development of liberal democracy has not occurred without criticism of some of its aspects, such as the partisan attitudes nourished by political parties to the detriment of national unity, or without the questioning of some of its assumptions, such as the extent to which parties or legislatures are really 'representative', the reality of popular control of executive government and its entrenched bureaucracies, or the responsiveness of government to the demands and needs of the electorate. Such criticism has led to rejection of liberal democracy by, for instance, Franco and his supporters in Spain, the Nazis in Germany, and by fascist-style movements in many European states before and during the second world war. Other critics have wished to retain democracy as the basis of government, but have sought alternative modes of political organisation in order to avoid what they see as the drawbacks of liberal democracy.

1. Many who are impatient with the limitations of liberal democracy see its 'linkage organisations' (parties and pressure groups) as barriers between the people and government, or, at least, as inefficient, self-serving and distorting channels for the popular will. Many point to the simplicities of *direct democracy* as their ideal: the people taking decisions, by majority vote, for themselves. In a large, complex, modern society direct democracy is impractical, except perhaps at the local level (it is used in some smaller Swiss cantons, for instance). There have been suggestions that viewers will soon be able to 'vote' by pressing a button on their television sets, but even when this becomes technically feasible, it raises all kinds of practical difficulties: how is one to know that the voter pressing the button is eligible to do so, and not a child or a foreigner, for example? Others have proposed greater use of the referendum, but that is a costly device, to be used, at best, only sparingly (see below, chapter 4).

2. One alternative to liberal democracy which has been tried is democracy based on *local councils of workers*. In the USSR, this was the model which the communists proposed to follow after the Bolshevik revolution in 1917 – democracy through soviets (councils) of workers, at which every member would be entitled to attend, speak and vote (so it would be, at that level, direct democracy). These councils would elect delegates to higher-level councils and committees, right up to the level of the national government. Political parties as agencies of representation would be superfluous. The distinction between legislative institutions and executive authority would disappear. Experiments with this form of government were made in Germany after the downfall of the monarchy in 1918–19, but the failure of the so-called German 'revolution' brought them to an end. It is still nominally the pattern used in the USSR, but the system has become overlain

with the ideology of Marxism-Leninism and by the dominant role assumed, according to that ideology, by the Communist Party in political and administrative affairs.

3. Another variant is *corporatist democracy*, in which the agencies of political representation and decision would not be parties or local councils but functional groups based on industries or other social organisations, such as the churches, the military, perhaps, and the professions. This would link the economic, cultural and political aspects of society into an integrated unit, in a way that 'normal' parliamentary politics cannot and does not. This was, to some extent, the intention of Mussolini's original fascist state organisation in Italy, though corporatism of that type was really part of a tradition of anti-democratic ideals (see below, chapter 3). Some have suggested that the modern state in complex, industrialised societies is moving .in the direction of corporatist representation because of the power and responsibility of certain groups, such as business and commercial organisations, trade unions, churches and the professions, and because of their close relationship with government (see below, chapter 6). It is interesting, also, to note that proposals have been made to introduce a system of functional representation into, or in place of, the House of Lords in the United Kingdom, and functional representation of groups is the basis of membership of the Economic and Social Committee of the European Economic Community (see below, chapter 11).

4. Some observers have claimed to perceive a process underway by which liberal democracy is being transformed into *mass politics*, in which elites manipulate the general population through the use of mass parties, mass media and mass organisations, such as trade unions. In such 'mass society', institutions are national in scale, and tend to be so uniform and bureaucratic that local or sectional distinctions are ignored, people lack a feeling of identification and a sense of belonging, and are easily swayed by demagogic, and perhaps artificial, appeals and causes. Democratic choice is reduced, in effect, to a periodic visit to the polling booth to select one or other of competing – but in many ways similar – teams to act as the government, and thus liberal democracy becomes only formally, and not in actuality, 'government by the people'.

The survival of liberal democracy in western Europe is constantly under challenge. It is threatened by the ambitions of those who would replace its uncertainties and compromises by the simplicity of dictatorship or the certainty of totalitarianism. It is threatened by social and economic developments, which may transform it into 'corporatist' or 'mass' democracy. It is threatened by public discontent at its failure to solve *all* the problems of society, its failure to prevent interruptions in the progress toward an ever-improving standard of living, its failure, sometimes, to protect itself from its internal or external enemies. Because it is essentially an 'open' form of political organisation, because it encourages criticism and tolerates opposition, it is necessarily a fragile institution.

West European political development

The fundamental problem of politics is concerned with the question of how members of a community are to live together peaceably and resolve their differences in an acceptable manner. The liberal-democratic model is one – but not the only – response to this problem. Liberal democracy is a relatively modern form of political regime, which has come about as the result of processes of historical development. This development has been very much affected by both national and cross-national events in Europe.

Europe in the eighteenth century was a Europe of empires, ruled by the *ancien régime* of emperors, kings and aristocrats, in which the political role of the masses was that of subjects, not participants. Moreover, although the boundaries of territories changed from time to time, because of wars, treaties and royal marriages, this traditional style of government had remained relatively unaltered and unchallenged, if not unquestioned, for centuries. Three significant and interrelated developments changed the situation: the industrial revolution, the French revolution, and the spread of literacy.

The industrial revolution led to the growth of an urbanised middle class, which possessed wealth and economic power, and laid claim to a comparable degree of political power. The French revolution gave impetus to the claims of *nationalism* – the idea that each 'people' should rule themselves, not be ruled by others; of *liberalism* – the idea that political authority should be justified by consent rather than by heredity, and should be limited by law and a constitution; and of *equality* – the idea that political participation should not be confined to an aristocratic elite, but be open to all citizens (however citizenship might be defined). The spread of literacy, stimulated by the needs of an industrialising society, allowed the dissemination of liberal and radical political ideas that challenged the claims of the upper classes to exercise unrestricted authority. The pamphlets of the Chartists in the United Kingdom, the proclamations of the German liberals in 1848 and the manifestos of the Paris Commune in 1871 were produced because, by then, many people could *read* them and could be influenced by them.

So the nineteenth century became the century of political transition in Europe from traditional dynastic autocracy to modern liberal democracy. Some states – the United Kingdom, Sweden, the Netherlands and Switzerland – were relatively unscathed by revolutionary developments, and offer examples of continuity and political adaptation. Others were subject to quite violent discontinuities and to revolutionary change: France, Italy, Spain and Germany, for instance. The aftermath of the Napoleonic wars and the nationalism which the French revolution and Napoleonic conquests had provoked, resulted in the creation of nation-states either by a process of separation (Belgium seceded from the Netherlands and became an independent state in 1830; Norway proclaimed its independence of Sweden in 1814) or of amalgamation (Italy and Germany were both created by a process of unification of previously separate states) to join those already in existence. The first world war – which can, from this point of view, be considered to mark the climax of nineteenth-century developments – set a seal on this process of political transition by eliminating monarchical rule in Germany and Austria as well as in Russia, and by creating a pattern of independent states in place of the Austro-Hungarian empire.

The nineteenth century was also the period in which many features of modern democracy were first established. The suffrage was extended in most countries, first to the middle classes, then to the proletariat, so that universal suffrage – for men at least – was more or less attained by the end of the first world war. By then, almost every country had an elective legislative assembly. Parties developed, in terms of their importance in politics and society, their membership and their organisational complexity. Responsible government, dependent upon the support of a parliamentary majority (based on a single party or a coalition) replaced government based on monarchical fiat. Pressure groups such as, for example, trade unions, church-related groups in continental states, and the women's suffrage organisations in the UK, became more common and more active.

The twentieth century, on the other hand, has been a period in which liberal democracy has either been consolidated – as in the UK – or subject to disruption – most notably in Spain, Italy and Germany. The political arrangements of many countries of western Europe have been disturbed by challenges from within, involving revolution, civil war and dictatorship, or from without, through war and occupation, and their development has been very much affected by those disturbances.

These historical trends can be better appreciated by examining the contrasting cases of the UK, as an example of continuity of development, and France, Italy, Germany and Spain as examples of more discontinuous development.

The United Kingdom
The continuity of political development in the UK has had much to do with the fact that – the persistent matter of Ireland apart – questions of national identity have not intruded as major political issues. The existence of the British empire acted as a stabilising factor; even its dissolution in the years following the second world war was managed in a way that avoided the internal tensions that, for instance, so plagued French politics when it had to abandon many of its overseas possessions.

Parliamentary supremacy had been established in the United Kingdom by the gradual elimination of monarchical political power in the eighteenth century. This supremacy of parliament has meant that 'so much British history is parliamentary history'.[3] Attempts by radical groups (of which the Chartist movement in the 1840s was the most famous) to achieve a thoroughly democratic system of government stimulated, but did not pre-empt, the gradual process by which the right to vote was extended. Following the first comprehensive reform of constituencies and the suffrage in 1832, other legislation in 1867 and 1884 increased greatly the percentage of male adults entitled to vote until, with the Acts of 1918 and 1928, all men and women were enfranchised. The Ballot Act of 1872 made voting secret, thus eliminating much improper pressure and corruption from elections. The crisis of 1909–11 over Lloyd George's radical budget resulted in a reduction of the power of the House of Lords, confirming the primacy of the elected House of Commons and the decline of aristocratic rule in the political system of the UK. The growth in power of the trade unions and the formation of the Labour Party at the turn of the century, did much to make effective the nominal political power of the working-class voter which had been conferred by the franchise. By the end of the first world war, Labour had replaced a divided Liberal Party as the main challenger to the Conservatives. Lacking a written constitution, the UK has never needed to 'start again' by drafting one – though it has helped its former imperial possessions to do so as they achieved independence. Neither of the two world wars resulted in occupation or revolution, and not even the general strike in 1926 proved a serious threat to the pattern of political adaptation which has existed, under the aegis of a constitutional monarchy, since 1688.

France

The course of political development in France has been marked by a series of changes of regime. Although the question of national identity has not been of political importance (except for the mid-1950s, with regard to Algeria), the form of regime has frequently been in dispute. The revolution of 1789 became transformed into the plebiscitary regime of Napoleon. Following Napoleon's overthrow in 1815, the monarchy was restored, though in 1830 popular uprisings led to a transfer of the Crown from the Bourbon to the Orleans branch, with some limitations on the role of the monarchy being imposed. In 1848, another revolution led first to a republic, then to a restoration of the Napoleonic dynasty under the Emperor Louis Napoleon. His reign was terminated by defeat in the Franco-Prussian war and by uprisings in France itself. The Third Republic lasted from 1871 to its capitulation to German occupation forces in 1940. Part of France was then subjected to the direct rule of the occupying German forces; part – 'Vichy France' – was ruled as a puppet state by Marshal Pétain and his head of government, Pierre Laval.

After the second world war, a Fourth Republic was established in 1946. This suffered from chronic governmental instability, with twenty-five governments in twelve years before the end of the Fourth Republic in 1958, when De Gaulle, France's wartime hero, was brought from retirement to act as the country's leader. He introduced a new regime, the Fifth Republic (see chapter 12). His domineering style of leadership was challenged in May 1968 by street demonstrations and strikes, but he survived, and the Fifth Republic has proved to be an essentially stable form of regime.

Despite, or perhaps because of, these discontinuities, and the many conflicts over forms of government for France, the country has been in the forefront of democratic development, in terms of the rights of the individual (linked to the Declaration of the Rights of Man adopted by the original revolutionaries), the attainment of male universal suffrage, the development of parties and popular political participation, including the use of the plebiscite and the referendum.

Italy

Italy became a unified state comparatively late in the nineteenth century. Not until 1870 was the process of unification completed, following a long period of diplomatic and military struggle. The new Italian state was a monarchy, and progress toward democratic institutions was very slow before the first world war. After the war, the shift to constitutional monarchy with the rather sudden introduction of parliamentary government, based on the competition of a multiplicity of parties, acted as a destabilising force, compounding economic and social problems and resulting in the increasing resort to violence in politics. In 1922, Mussolini led his extreme right-wing fascists on a 'march on Rome', to challenge the government. He was successful to the extent that the King asked him to form a government, and gradually he imposed a fascist dictatorship on Italy. During the second world war, Mussolini joined Hitler in the Axis pact, but was overthrown by the Italian military in 1943 and executed by partisans in 1945. After the war, following a referendum in June 1946, a republican regime was established in 1948 to replace the monarchy. Though democratic in terms of its constitution and political institutions, Italy has many problems of a special nature to cope with: its very uneven economic development – the contrast between the industrial north and the agrarian south is particularly marked; its failure, compared to France, for example, to modernise its economy or its social structures; the dominance of one party, the Christian Democrats, in its political system, and the endemic crises of government formation caused by unstable legislative majorities; the frequency of the resort to violence by extremists of the right and of the left; all these factors contribute to a continuing instability of the political system in Italy even today.

Germany

The empire of Germany was formed only in 1871, from an assortment of smaller states ranging from the kingdoms of Prussia and Bavaria to a variety of small dukedoms and independent city-states. The process of unification, instead of being completed according to the plans of liberals through a voluntary union of Germanic states, resulted instead from the diplomatic skills of Bismarck, who achieved a united Germany under the hegemony of the Prussian state whose King he served. The conservatism of Prussia set the tone for the whole German empire, and progress toward responsible and democratic government was slow. After the defeat of Germany in the first world war, the Emperor (*Kaiser*) abdicated and a republic was proclaimed. This republic (called the Weimar republic, after the town in which the new constitution was drafted) adopted a system of government which sacrificed effective rule for the forms of total democracy. Germany had a democratic regime, but few democrats to lead the nation or support the new republic. External pressures following the Versailles peace treaty, economic weaknesses and political deadlock destroyed all hope that the Weimar republic could survive and develop. Instead, Hitler came to power by constitutional means, but, once appointed Chancellor by President Hindenburg, he proceeded to institute a fascist dictatorship, buttressed by the Nazi Party. All forms of democratic freedom or constitutional constraint disappeared. The defeat of Hitler in the second world war was followed by a period of occupation by the UK, France, the USA and the Soviet Union, in which Germany was divided into four separate zones. By 1948, the 'cold war' had led to the *de facto* division of Germany into the three western zones on the one hand, and the Russian-occupied eastern zone on the other. In 1949, the western occupying powers therefore allowed the Germans of their zones to introduce a German Federal Republic with a democratic constitution. This new state has flourished as a democracy, and has become one of the most stable of all west European states.

Spain

The political history of nineteenth-century Spain is one of continuous conflict between conservatives and liberals, in which monarchical rule was twice interrupted and many times threatened by revolts and uprisings. Following the restoration of the monarchy in 1874 after a brief period of republican government, a constitution – liberal in design but oligarchic in operation – was accepted by the King in 1876. An inflexible pattern of government resulted, in which the Catholic church and the military preserved their privileges, social tensions went unrelieved, and regional claims to autonomy went unregarded. Because of strains resulting from unemployment after the first world war, military disaster in Morocco and the growth of nationalism in Catalonia, monarchical rule was replaced by the dictatorship of Primo de Rivera in 1923. After Rivera's retirement in 1930, opposition to this form of government grew, and a republic was established based on a new constitution and a democratically elected assembly. Social tensions continued, however: landowners, the military and the church all felt their privileged position to be threatened by the new regime. The fragmentation of the party system (as in Weimar Germany) and the polarisation of the political conflict between the conservative forces on the one hand and the left-wing 'Popular Front' of socialists and communists on the other, enfeebled the government, and civil war broke out in 1936 following an attempted military coup led by General Franco. Franco's victory in 1939 was followed by a period of unrelieved military dictatorship. Only near the end of his life did Franco make plans for the restoration of the monarchy and, in 1967, he permitted a measure of popular election for the legislature – but under severe limitations and with, in fact, only a low level of popular participation. Franco died in 1975, and, as he had planned, was succeeded as head of state by King Juan Carlos. Since then, democracy has gradually been restored and regional problems have, to an extent, been resolved (see below, chapters 8 and 10). A military coup in 1981 was intended to receive the blessing of the King, but instead was condemned by him, and failed: a sign that democracy in Spain is now fairly well established.

The post-war challenge

Europe in 1945 was in a state of political shock. The hopes that the first world war had been the 'war to end all wars' and that the peace settlements then had provided secure foundations for democracy, national self-determination and – through the League of Nations – international co-operation, had been rudely shattered by, first, the assumption of power by dictators in Italy, Spain and Germany, and, second, by a new world war. Democracy had proved to be weak, national self-determination merely provocative of new conflict, and international co-operation a chimera. What form, then, should political reconstruction take after the second world war?

In fact it took the form of international integration, but according to two very different patterns. In eastern Europe, integration was under the patronage of the Soviet Union, and meant, in effect, a uniform system of one-party communist states, totally controlled state-socialist economies linked together through the COMECON agreement, and a military alliance – the Warsaw Pact – directed against the western powers. In western Europe (except for neutralist or neutralised states such as Sweden, Switzerland and Austria), it meant a slow process of economic integration in, first, the Coal and Steel Community, then the European Economic Community (see below, chapter 11); in defence, an alliance – the North Atlantic Treaty Organisation – promoted by the United States and directed against the eastern bloc; but, politically, a diverse pattern of regimes, not all of which, all of the time, have been liberal democracies.

In western Europe, the ideal of integration which ultimately led to the creation of the European Community seemed especially attractive to those who blamed the nation-state for the wars that had twice devastated Europe.[4] Even before the first of those wars, internationalism had appeared to some to be an attractive way of securing peace; the Inter-Parliamentary Union had been created in 1887, and the International Court of Justice at the Hague in 1899, for instance. The League of Nations between the wars had failed, but it was felt that the structure of its post-war successor, the United Nations Organisation, would enable it to avoid the errors and weaknesses of the League. This internationalist perspective suggested that European federalism would remove sources of conflict in western Europe and that the nation-state would decline in importance.

Nearly four decades later, assessment can be ventured of the successes and failures of these challenges to the nation-state. The internationalism of the United Nations Organisation and ideas of 'world government' or even of European political union have not made much progress. The European Economic Community has had considerable success as a customs union; its benefits have attracted six new members since the original six countries signed the Treaty of Rome in 1957, and other countries have expressed interest in joining (though France, in particular, has expressed doubts about the ability of the Community to absorb these additional members). But the experiences of the EEC have served to emphasise the *persistence* of national interests and the difficulties of moving toward political integration, even though, conversely, Community membership has imposed new constraints on national governments. Indeed, not only has the nation-state remained strong: loyalties have rather sought a more localised, not more international focus: in Scotland and Wales, in Corsica and Brittany, in Catalonia and in Greenland, for instance.

Post-war fears for the future of liberal democracy within the context of the nation-state have also proved unfounded. In western Europe, the trend has been toward, not away from democratic regimes. West Germany has not, as was feared, succumbed to neo-Nazism; France, since 1958, has shown a remarkable degree of stability and – in 1981 – an ability to survive a major change in political direction; Greece, Spain and Portugal have returned by different routes to democratic forms of government. Even Italy, despite its continual political crises, remains in the democratic camp. The advent of Eurocommunism (see below, chapter 3) has greatly reduced the risk that any west European country will, except perhaps by external intervention, be transformed into a one-party state.

Liberal democracy is vulnerable because of its openness, its reliance on compromise and its toleration of opposition. But its strength lies in its flexibility; it can adapt swiftly to changing political circumstances (for example, the UK in the second world war); it can change its formal structures (as in France in 1958, when a majority voted to adopt a new constitution – that of the Fifth Republic); and it can survive challenges to its authority (as in West Germany, during the Baader–Meinhof terrorist campaign, or Spain in 1981, when threatened by a military coup). It is a complicated, and often frustrating social invention. This book is intended to be a guide to the way liberal democracy operates in western Europe today, some of the problems it faces, and the different forms its institutions can take.

Notes

1. Gordon Smith, *Politics in Western Europe* (London, Heinemann, 2nd edn. 1976), p. 1.

2. In March 1981 a group of officers invaded the Spanish parliament at gunpoint and in Valencia a general brought tanks out on to the streets, in expectation that the King and other generals would support a coup to reimpose military rule. They were disappointed in their ambitions, for the King re-emphasised his commitment to democracy. The participants in the coup were tried and sentenced by a special military court in June 1982.

3. J. M. Roberts, *Europe 1880–1945* (London, Longman, paperback edn. 1972), p. 125.

4. D. W. Urwin, *Western Europe since 1945* (London, Longman, 2nd edn. 1972), p. 4.

2

THE DEMOCRATIC
POLITICAL PROCESS

What is 'a liberal democracy'?

In the first chapter of this book, it was argued that a central, shared feature of contemporary western European states has been their claim to be liberal democracies, a claim that distinguishes them from political systems based on dictatorship, whether civilian or military, from totalitarian autocracy, and from the pre-twentieth-century regimes based on the rule of an aristocracy or an absolutist monarch. However, although it is not difficult to understand the way in which democracy is different from non-democratic political systems, there have been many attempts to define democracy and these different conceptions of what democracy is have been used to legitimise widely divergent methods of government in the modern period.

In ancient Greece, Plato and Aristotle rather scathingly equated democracy with unstable 'mob rule', a form of government based on envy and susceptible to the blandishments of demagogues. In the middle of the last century, Abraham Lincoln summed it up as 'government of the people, for the people, by the people', while more recently Churchill termed it the worst possible form of government – except for all others! The regimes established after 1945 in eastern Europe have followed the example of the Soviet Union in using the term to describe the unchallenged rule of the Communist Party as the vanguard of the working class. Clearly, a label that can be used to describe the USSR as well as the United Kingdom, the German Democratic Republic as well as the German Federal Republic, must require more careful and precise definition if it is to be a useful term, if it is to distinguish one type of political system or one method of government from others.

In this book the concept of *liberal democracy* is our specific concern, for it is on this ideal that contemporary western

European states have drawn to legitimise the range of domestic political arrangements operating in their countries. As was argued in the first chapter, the concept of liberal democracy has itself been subject to reinterpretation over time. It is a complex concept, combining several distinct, but nevertheless related political principles. It is therefore not surprising to find that at any given time in each of these countries a number of different tendencies exist, within organised public opinion and among the political parties, as to the relative importance to be accorded to the constituent elements of liberal democracy.

A first principle is that of representative government. The liberal democratic ideal seeks, through certain political procedures, to maximise the extent to which governments will be both representative of and responsive to the wishes of the citizens of that state. At the same time, the liberal democratic tradition inherited, from previous historical struggles to curtail absolutism, a concern to limit the unrestrained use of executive power by providing in government a system of mutual checks and balances among the different institutions of government – the legislature, the executive and the judiciary. Taken together, these principles of liberal democracy give rise to a number of issues which continue to arouse controversy, concerning, for example, the extent to which most ordinary citizens should be actively involved in the political process and the forms which their participation should take, the role of political parties as representatives of public opinion, the relationship between the opinions and interests of the majority and those of minority groups and the proper scope of governmental intervention in society and the economy.

Traditionally, considerable importance has been attached to establishing freedom of opinion and freedom of expression for the individual. More recently, liberal democratic theorists have stressed the need for a plurality of competing parties and organised groups to be involved in policy-making, in order to defend the divergent and conflicting interests present in society. However, it is important to note that liberal democracy is based on the premise that the existing state institutions do correspond to viable, national political communities, in which internal divisions and conflicts of interest may be considerable. However, these should not be so radical as to undermine the possibility of achieving a consensus (at least as regards the *procedures* by which such differences of interest should be publicly represented and expressed, and binding policy decisions be made).

It is within this framework that the protection of the right of the people to choose and change governments in a peaceful, fair and effective manner, at regular intervals, has come to be an obvious distinguishing feature of liberal democracies. The right of the people to choose and change governments is protected in such a political system either by constitutional provision or by law. It does not depend only on the whim of the rulers and is not confined only to an elite. In a liberal democracy the franchise is given to the whole of the adult population, with only a few very specific exceptions (such as aliens resident in the country, or those whose civic rights have been withdrawn by legal process). It is a right to choose: this implies open competition among different parties, for example, and fair competition at that. If a one-party state, where other parties are banned by law, cannot be a proper democracy, there are also problems in determining whether the competition between parties is indeed fair and effective. The introduction of measures to ensure secrecy of the ballot and to eliminate corruption or improper pressure was of particular importance, but questions remain concerning the source and scale of resources available to different political parties, and how far the state should intervene to regulate the terms of competition in these respects.

The peaceful exercise of this right to choose will be effective where the protection of the state extends to all participants in the election campaign and where there is some degree of consensus regarding the procedures by which policies are arrived at, and a sense of identification with the national political community. Peaceful electoral competition has been sustained in the contemporary period in western Europe, even though significantly different assessments of the value of liberal democracy have been held by sections of the community, for' example in France, Italy and Spain where substantial communist parties exist; whereas Northern Ireland, the Spanish Basque province and, in less acute form, Corsica, all demonstrate the limited viability of the peaceful exercise of effective choice where adherence to the established nation-state institutions is itself under challenge.

Finally the regular exercise of the right to choose and change governments can be ensured through laws providing for elections at maximum intervals. The different electoral systems in use in western Europe are described in chapter 4, but all meet the fundamental requirements of being methods of free, secret and direct election (as required for instance, in Article 38 of the West German constitution).

An effective democracy must have efficient processes of communication both at election times and between elections, and such communications must flow from the people to government, as well as from government to the people. (TV, an important feature of political communication, is considered in chapter 12.) Only through such communication can the government explain and defend what it is doing, opposition parties criticise the government and propose alternative policies, and the electorate make informed judgements and press on the government its wishes and needs. Liberal democracies therefore require the existence of a variety of uncensored channels of communication: broadcasting agencies, daily newspapers and periodicals, poster sites, book publishers and numerous other means of expression, while the introduction of censorship and the creation of any monopoly of control raise issues of particular concern.

This chapter will now explore these features of liberal democratic politics in western Europe in three ways. First, the basic pattern of their *political systems* will be analysed in terms of the inter-relationship between institutions, the mutual checks and balances involved, and the responsiveness of the authorities to the popular will. Second, *the democratic political process* will be examined as a process through which multiple interests are expressed and conflicts resolved through agreed procedures, rather than through authoritarian dictate or the anarchy of the unrestrained force. Thirdly, the dependence of democracy on *popular participation* will be emphasised as being at once its most characteristic feature and yet, in practice, one which is frequently contested by different groups. Participation by the mass of the people in a democratic process requires appropriate channels and resources, and a belief that these are adequate for the achievement of political goals. Increasingly, throughout western Europe, the extent and pattern of political participation are being taken as indicators of the health and stability of a democratic political system.

Political systems

The political systems of the United Kingdom, France and West Germany are all classified as liberal democracies. The three share many common features: competing parties, a free press, a wide range of pressure groups, the rule of law, free elections, responsible government. Yet they differ in other ways: the West German state is, as its official title reveals, a federal republic; the United Kingdom is a monarchy; the President of France is elected directly by the people, and is politically powerful, whereas the President of the German Federal Republic is elected by a special electoral college, and is politically almost impotent; the UK has a non-elected second chamber of hereditary and life peers; the three countries have different electoral systems; and so on.

The problem, then, is how to compare these liberal democracies, how to comprehend their political systems so that the similarities and differences become apparent.

Just as a scientist might build a model to explore a problem, so a political scientist can, similarly, use an abstract model or framework to uncover the fundamental features of political processes. Some frameworks have been extensively used, their 'images' of political activity and even their vocabulary widely adopted. One such framework is that devised by an American political scientist, David Easton. He makes use of very direct and essentially simple imagery to convey the nature of political systems. Easton sees political systems being composed of *processes* through which the wishes and needs of people (in a democracy) are *converted* by government action, for better or worse, into *outputs*. In outline, this view of politics envisages a two-way process of communication and responses linking governments to electorates. Easton's concept of a political process can be presented diagramatically, as in figure 1.

It would be wrong to interpret Easton's framework too literally. The apparently mechanical process of inputs, conversion, outputs and feedback is more disjointed and less tidy in real life. Easton's view of the relationship between inputs and outputs is not shared by everyone. Nevertheless his framework does make it possible to identify certain key elements in the political process. First of all, political systems are concerned with *demands* from the public. These are generally diverse, often rather vague, sometimes

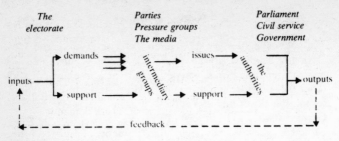

Figure 1

self-contradictory, and in any case will be extremely numerous.
People want the government to do all sorts of things: to 'ban the
bomb', reform the electoral system, take the United Kingdom out
of the Common Market, nationalise the banks, reduce
unemployment, build more hospitals, lower income tax rates. If
everyone communicated all their demands directly to the
government, as they have a right to do in a democracy, the mere
task of opening all the mail and answering the telephone would be
impossible. So *intermediary groups* – parties, pressure groups, the
mass media – filter and collect together demands, make them
coherent, give certain matters priority, and then transmit them as
issues to the authorities in parliament, in the cabinet room and in
the ministries. The authorities assess these demands, analyse
them, decide what to do about them, and eventually act upon
them by passing laws, making rules, taking action, signing treaties,
calling elections or, indeed, choosing to do nothing, and so on.
These are the *outputs* of the system. For example, the budget is
one, usually very important, set of outputs, and the pre-budgetary
period is a time when the Chancellor of the Exchequer or the
Minister of Finance is the target for numerous demands from
individuals or groups concerning what should be included in or
excluded from the budget. A speech on television by the head of
government, a discussion with a foreign diplomat, a new law
making the wearing of seatbelts compulsory, a decision to close a
military base: these are examples of other forms which outputs
might take. But the story doesn't end there. The effects of those
outputs are communicated to the electorate in the form of
increased taxes, as announcements in the press, through
restrictions on their freedom of action, through changes in their

job security, and in many other ways. Outputs are not always welcomed. Opposition parties may criticise government action. Other groups and individuals may support, oppose or remain indifferent. The government will both publicly and via organised private channels justify and defend their decisions. This process of *feedback*, through the various channels of political communication, influences the shape of future demands.

If the authorities succeed in satisfying most of the people most of the time, they gain *support*; if not, they will lose it. If support for one set of authorities declines sufficiently, then the next election will bring about a change of government. If support for the whole *method* of government (called the *regime*) declines too much, then there is the danger that it will be overthrown, and a new system introduced, possibly by revolution (see chapter 12). This happened in Germany in 1933, when Hitler took power, and in France in 1958 when de Gaulle's Fifth Republic replaced the discredited Fourth Republic. It happened twice in 1917 in Russia. Since the second world war it has happened in Greece, in Spain and in Portugal. Support can also be communicated to the authorities through intermediary groups, and through election results and opinion poll data.

The political systems of the United Kingdom, France and the Federal Republic of Germany will now be outlined briefly in terms of this comparative framework. Details of each part of the system will be discussed at more length in later chapters.

The political system of the United Kingdom

The political system of the UK is a constitutional monarchy, though there is no codified written constitution and the political – as opposed to the ceremonial – powers of the monarchy are now minimal.

Political demands are voiced and mediated through a variety of groups, including the well-established political parties and pressure groups and a range of smaller, often more transient organisations. There are four main political parties: the right-wing Conservative Party, a left-wing Labour Party (to which most of the important trade unions are affiliated), a moderate Social Democratic Party founded by former members of the Labour Party, and a Social and Liberal Democratic Party. There are also regionally-based Welsh and Scottish nationalist parties, and a variety of small parties peculiar to Northern Ireland. Extremist parties, whether of the left or the right, are very small in terms of voting support. The major pressure groups are concerned with economic and labour-related issues: the trade unions, most of which are affiliated to the Trades Union Congress; the Confederation of British Industry; the National Farmers Union; and the professional organisations, such as the British Medical Association. The churches play a very limited role in politics, confined mainly to ethical and moral issues.

Pressure groups, to be effective, need to be tuned to the interests and preoccupations of their members (who may, in some groups, reflect a surprisingly wide spectrum of opinions) and to be able to press these issues on to the authorities. The larger the group, the more diverse the set of interests, the greater the problem for the group's representatives to settle on demands appropriate for political action. National party and pressure group conferences provide one kind of filter, reducing a diffuse set of demands into a more manageable package which can be adopted as party policy or be turned into a pressure group 'campaign'.

The authorities in the UK consist of the government of the day (made up of the leading figures of the party which has a majority in the House of Commons) and parliament, to which the government is answerable, and which debates and criticises government proposals. In an extreme situation, the House of Commons can overturn a government by voting in favour of a motion of censure or defeating some major proposal of the government. (This happened, in effect, in 1979, when the Labour government was defeated in the House of Commons and the Prime Minister, Mr Callaghan, was compelled to call a general election.) The House of Lords has the right to debate all legislative proposals, but has only a limited power to delay or veto legislation passed by the Commons. The monarch must give approval to all bills passed in parliament. The work of the government is heavily dependent on the administration, advice and ideas of the civil service, which in the UK is deliberately non-partisan in terms of party politics. The Prime Minister chooses, and, if necessary, dismisses members of the government, but major decisions are taken collectively in the cabinet, which is a committee of the twenty or so senior ministers. Most ministers (and always including the Prime Minister and the Chancellor of the Exchequer) sit in the House of Commons. Others sit in the House of Lords. Should a minister exceptionally be appointed without a seat in parliament, efforts are made to obtain a seat as soon as possible.

Some classes of decision are delegated to local authorities: county, district and parish councils. Scotland, and, to a lesser degree, Wales, also have regional powers devolved to their own Secretaries of State. There is also a Secretary of State for Northern Ireland, but efforts are made from time to time to restore a limited form of self-government to the province. However, whatever powers are delegated or devolved to other levels of government, parliament always retains the right to recall or change such powers at any time.

The outputs of the authorities are publicised on radio and television, through the British Broadcasting Corporation (a public authority, though independent of the government) and commercial broadcasting agencies. Newspapers and magazines of varying styles and political sympathies also devote much space to news of governmental activity and to commentaries upon it. This feedback process then leads, through local party or pressure group discussions, through letters to members of parliament, through petitions or demonstrations and through election campaigns, to new or revised demands.

The French political system

The French political system is a quasi-presidential regime, the Fifth Republic, which replaced a parliamentary regime (the Fourth Republic) in 1958. The Fourth Republic had been losing the confidence and support of the people for many years, because of the instability of governments and its inability to cope with problems such as Algerian independence and the economy. The Fifth Republic is based on a written constitution, parts of which have been amended since 1958, sometimes as a result of popular opinion expressed through referenda.

As in the UK, inputs are channelled through parties and pressure groups. But these are more numerous than in the UK, and their interrelationships more complex. On the left, the extreme left-wing Communist Party competes for support with a more moderate Socialist Party. On the right, the Republican

Party combines with some smaller centrist forces to compete with the Gaullist Rally for the Republic and the new National Front on the extreme right. The major pressure groups include separate christian, socialist and communist trade union organisations, a powerful set of agricultural pressure groups (such as the wine-growers), industrial and commercial organisations (of which perhaps the most powerful is the National Council of French Employers), and the Catholic church. One very significant channel of input to the authorities, involving the participation of national and local pressure groups, has been the national plan, which is prepared by the civil service in consultation with relevant interests, and which is then a framework for economic policy for the next five years.

The authorities in France depend for leadership and direction on the President. The President is elected directly by the people for a seven-year term, and is the effective head of the government as well as the head of state. He appoints a Prime Minister, but the Prime Minister is far less powerful politically than is, say, the Prime Minister of the UK or Italy. A government is then chosen by the Prime Minister to take charge of the various departments of state. Ministers may address the National Assembly and its committees, but must not be members of it. If they are appointed whilst they are members, they must resign from the legislature.

The National Assembly is elected for a five-year term (unless dissolved earlier). It debates laws and the budget, and may move a vote of no confidence in the government. But its powers have been restricted substantially by the constitution of the Fifth Republic so as to provide greater governmental stability than existed prior to 1958. Provided the government has a majority in the National Assembly, it need not fear defeat of its policies in the legislature.

France is governed through a system of regions and Departments, the responsible officers of which until 1982 were the Prefects, appointed by, and answerable to the government in Paris. There is also a system of local government, to run affairs of local importance.

The civil service is headed by a number of highly-qualified administrators, trained in the academies (Hautes Ecoles), and these may change with the political composition of the government. But each ministry has a small group of administrators appointed by the minister to act as his 'personal office', and these do change if the minister changes (though many come from, and return to other departmental positions within the ministries).

The outputs of the French authorities are communicated to the public through the broadcasting networks, and through the press. In general, political communication is more restricted and controlled than in the UK; de Gaulle, Pompidou and Giscard d'Estaing as Presidents all made blatant efforts to interfere with the mass media on occasion. But feedback does occur, and may result in, for example, the events of May 1968, the campaigns that defeated Giscard d'Estaing and placed Mitterrand in the presidency in 1981, in party manifestos, local inputs to the planning process, farmers' demonstrations, or other manifestations of popular opinion.

The West German political system

When the second world war came to an end, the territory of Germany was divided and occupied by four allied powers: the United Kingdom, France, Russia and the United States of America. Each had its own zone, and the city of Berlin, located in the Russian zone, was placed under four-power control and also divided into four zones. Although the original intention was to treat Germany as a single unit, quarrels between the western powers and the Russians led to a *de facto* division into four separately-governed zones. The three western zones were then linked in 1949 to form the new Federal German Republic. At the same time, the Russians took steps to transform their zone into the German Democratic Republic. Berlin remained under four-power control, excluded from these arrangements.

The new Federal Republic was formed on the basis of a democratic constitution drawn up by the Germans themselves and called the 'Basic Law'. It was regarded as a 'provisional' constitution, a substitute for a final version which would have to await the unification of the country. It reflected German and Allied concern that the new state should avoid the instabilities of the Weimar republic of 1919–33, Germany's only previous experience of a democratic regime, and the tyranny of the Third Reich. Democratic politics had been encouraged in the western zones before 1949 by the licensing of political parties and publications, by the introduction of local and provincial self-government, and by elections to local and provincial councils. The constitution of 1949 emphasises the rule of law, guarantees the rights of the citizen, and provides for the responsible role of parties and for stability of government.

Demands are processed by a variety of political parties and pressure groups. Four parties have representation in the national parliament: the left-wing Social Democratic Party, the liberal Free Democratic Party in the centre, the right-wing Christian Democratic Party (allied with a Bavarian sister-party, the Christian Social Union) and the ecology party, called the 'Green Party'. The Communists and right-wing extremists (the National Democratic Party) now share less than about one per cent of the vote between them. The major pressure groups are the German Federation of Trade Unions, to which most of the separate trade unions belong, the Catholic and evangelical churches, and the professional organisations representing lawyers, doctors, dentists, etc. A growing importance is assumed by local 'civic initiative' groups, which focus demands on local issues, such as public transport fares, housing schemes, motorway routes and the erection of nuclear power facilities.

The authorities consist of the government, headed by the Chancellor (who is elected by the Bundestag and can only be dismissed by means of the Bundestag electing a replacement), together with his cabinet (usually a coalition of two or more parties), and the two-chamber legislature: the Bundestag, elected by popular vote, and the Bundesrat, consisting of representatives of the provincial governments.[1] For the Federal Republic is a federation of ten different provinces (the *Länder*), which have major responsibilities for such matters as education, transport, the police and local government. They have their own governments and legislative institutions. Through the Bundesrat, they have the right to participate in decisions of the national authorities on matters which may affect them locally. Both the national and the provincial governments are assisted by administrators, most of whom are 'career' civil servants, though some of the top posts are occupied by political appointees, who change as the party composition of the government changes. Elections to the national and provincial assemblies occur normally every four years (except in two provinces, which have five-year terms). The head of state is the President of the Republic, elected for a five-year term by an electoral college, but who has very few political functions.

Feedback occurs through the mass media (including generous television and radio coverage of, for example, the budget debate in the legislature), of which the two television channels, the daily press, and weekly news journals such as *Der Spiegel* and *Die Zeit* are perhaps the most influential; and through political parties and pressure groups, who spend a lot of money on information services, educational courses and other means of communicating with their members and with the public.

Democracy as the resolution of conflict

Politics, in one sense, is the process of resolving conflicts within states or other associations on matters which affect the whole community. When politics breaks down, then violence replaces it, and the community itself dissolves into anarchy. But the political resolution of conflict does not necessarily imply that democratic procedures will be used. A variety of non-democratic forms of conflict resolution exists or has existed in the past: theocracies, such as Iran, or Tibet before the Chinese occupation, where religious authority is paramount; oligarchies, where the propertied classes and important landowners claim the right to make decisions; racial regimes, where one race or tribe is dominant and others subject to their decisions, as in South Africa; dictatorships of the military, as in some Latin American states, or of the party, as in Nazi Germany or the Soviet Union.

Democratic political systems differ from such non-democratic forms of political rule in two important ways:

1. In a democracy there is general popular acceptance of a set of political procedures to be used for making decisions and settling disputes; such acceptance usually depends on the public having the right from time to time to select the government and to change it through free elections;

2. Democratic political procedures are given a degree of permanence and legitimacy through their incorporation into a constitution; this limits the discretion of the authorities to do what they like, and enables appeals to be made to the courts in cases of

apparent breach of the constitution by the authorities (or by anyone else).

Written constitutions have developed as a political device since the eighteenth century, and the growth of constitutional government has been seen as inseparable from the process of democratisation of western society. They serve many purposes. They may include a manifesto of national aspirations and human rights (such as the French constitution of 1789, or the current Basic Law of the Federal Republic of Germany); they may list unchangeable features of the system (the federal and democratic nature of the West German state, for instance) as well as prescribe means of amending the constitution and adjudicating upon it.

Adjudication is necessary for two reasons:

– no attempt to set down rules in written form can hope to be completely unambiguous and to cover every conceivable future case; whether it be the rules of cricket or football, the constitution of a university student union or the Labour Party, the Basic Law of the German Federal Republic or the Treaty of Rome, some procedure is needed to settle disputes concerning what the wording of the constitutional rules actually means and how it is to be applied to a particular case;

– the parties to a dispute always have an interest in settling it in their own favour, hence the need for some kind of umpire or referee, whose independence of judgement and whose knowledge of the law are respected by the parties to the dispute and by the wider public.

In the German Federal Republic, the Constitutional Court fulfils these roles of interpreter and umpire. It has made several historic decisions, not all of which have met with the approval of the government of the day or with the general public, but which have met with acceptance because of respect for the Court. Extremist political parties have been banned on two occasions, because the constitution demands that parties be democratic. The Federal government was forbidden to set up a second television channel by the Court, because broadcasting was stated by the Basic Law to be solely a responsibility of the provincial authorities. Laws passed by the legislature have been declared invalid which dealt with methods of exemption for military service and with reform of the legal code on abortion, because they were held to conflict with the provisions of the Basic Law. Disputes between the federal and provincial governments on the treaties with east European states have been resolved by the Court by reference to the terms of the Basic Law. Judges are appointed by the legislature, but are only removable during their term of office for personal misdeeds, not for political reasons, and this preserves their independence from political pressure.

In France, the functions of the German Constitutional Court are divided between the Constitutional Council, which is concerned with the constitutional correctness of *procedure* in legislation, and the Council of State, which both advises on the constitutionality of the *content* of laws at the drafting stage, and later acts as a court of appeal which can declare laws to be invalid, as it did on several occasions during the de Gaulle presidency.

In the United Kingdom, there is no codified written constitution. Parliament is the supreme constitutional organ, and no authority may declare its decisions to be unlawful or unconstitutional. Of course, some laws and legal judgements, as well as documents of ancient importance such as *Magna Carta,* are assumed to be 'the British constitution'; but the precise definition of what is, or is not included in the constitution remains uncertain. Some commentators and political leaders have suggested that, far from being an advantage, the flexibility and ambiguity of an unwritten constitution could make it easier for democracy to be replaced by some authoritarian regime, and that the UK ought to produce for itself a written constitution, as it has helped many of its former dependencies to do.

Where there is no constitution, there is no problem of amendment. In France and West Germany, on the other hand, special procedures are required to amend provisions of the constitution. In France, Article 89 of the constitution prescribes the method of amendment as by a majority of both houses of parliament and subsequently, if the government so wishes, by popular referendum. However, de Gaulle was able, unconstitutionally, to amend the constitution in 1962 by proceeding directly to a referendum under Article 11. In West Germany, amendments require two-thirds majorities in both chambers of the legislature. Such special procedures make amendment an infrequent occurrence, requiring careful deliberation and broad-based consent. It is unlikely that any short-term single-party majority would be large enough to press through an amendment in either France or West Germany.

Besides constitutions, other constraints shape the pattern of procedures for democratic politics. Some of these are external to a country and may be binding on a government or reflect international agreement on principles which governments are expected to adhere to. The Treaty of Rome or the European Convention of Human Rights may restrict governmental discretion, and require that political disputes be settled in particular ways or resolved in particular arenas, such as via the institutions of the European Community or through the Court of Human Rights of the Council of Europe. Laws which are not themselves an integral part of the constitution may – as long as they remain in force – set conditions for the resolution of political conflicts: the Party Law in West Germany, the Representation of the People Acts in the UK, or laws regarding election campaigning in France, for instance.

But rules and constitutions, treaties and laws, are only the skeleton, as it were, of the democratic body politic. There is another extremely significant, factor which differentiates France from the UK, the German Federal Republic from Switzerland or Austria, and which 'fills out' the skeleton of the written procedures for democratic political life: the *political culture* of societies. One might even hazard a guess that, were Britain to have the very same written constitution and laws as France, political realities would still be very different, because of differences in political culture.

What is political culture? It consists of the knowledge about politics which a people possesses, combined with the attitudes and beliefs, prejudices and preferences, which they have in common and which result from a shared history and shared experiences.

It is, first of all, the product of growth over time. The political culture of the UK has developed over centuries; the French political culture, despite frequent changes of regime since the first French revolution, also has a recognisable continuity of development; the West German political culture, on the other hand, is a more recent and, still, a much more fragile development, which has had to replace in a short time (and in only part of the former territory of Germany) the discredited political culture of the Third Reich.

The political culture of the UK has been described as deferential: that is to say, the people accept the continued existence of the monarchy and the aristocracy, and, to a certain extent, are willing to vote for an educated and upper-class elite to represent them and act as the government. Well over one-third of all working-class voters vote Conservative. Even those who vote Labour usually elect middle-class representatives, led by politicians many of whom have public school and university education. But it is also a tolerant and a democratic political culture. Parties, pressure groups and associations of all kinds lay great emphasis on proper procedures, on secret ballots, on letting everyone 'have their say'. It is a secular political culture, more so than in France, West Germany or Italy, for example, and there is an underlying feeling that the churches should have no place in the political life of the nation. It has been a very homogeneous political culture, but in recent years stresses have appeared concerning racial divisions, concerning a perceptible 'north v. south' difference (as revealed, for example, by different patterns of voting behaviour), and by the growth of demands for separate political status in Wales and Scotland.

The French political culture is republican, and affected by the 'myth of the revolution': the idea that, if things go badly, the ultimate and legitimate recourse to revolution is available, as it has been in the past. It is a political culture which stresses the distinction between public and private life; many French people would be averse to disclosing their political sympathies to friends, let alone to strangers. It is a political culture marked by traditional loyalties, many of which go back to the nineteenth century: anti-clericalism, nationalism, radicalism, and, more recently, the membership of the wartime resistance. It is a unified and Paris-orientated political culture, though some regions such as Brittany, Corsica and Alsace are developing resistance to the domination of political life by Paris.

The new West German political culture has changed remarkably over the past twenty years. It began by being almost non-political; people voted, and reluctantly accepted the need for parties and politics, but were disinclined to join political organisations or otherwise participate in political life. 'Count me out', 'leave it all to the politicians' were common responses. Such an attitude to politics was a natural reaction to the extreme and total politicisation of life under Hitler. But, since the 1960s, this attitude has slowly changed. Germans now participate in politics in the same ways and to the same extent as, say, people in the United Kingdom or America. There is a growing degree of interest in politics, and a sense of pride in the achievements of the German system. It is a democratic culture, which rejects political extremism, but it does still retain a preference for settling disputes through the certainties of the legal process rather than by means of the more untidy procedures of political bargaining and persuasion. Though it is a unified political culture, it is still very much affected by the division of the German nation into two states, and by the attitude that nothing should be undertaken by politicians that would prevent eventual reunification.

In other countries, special features of political culture can be observed which influence the way political arrangements have developed. Belgium, for example, is deeply affected in its political life by the division of the country into two language areas, yet Switzerland seems relatively unaffected politically by the incorporation of four language areas within its boundaries. Italy, Spain and Eire are political cultures profoundly influenced by the position of the Roman Catholic church in the daily life of the nation. Finland's political culture is coloured by its proximity to the Soviet Union, and its conflict with Russia in the second world war.

Political systems are prisoners of their past. They are conditioned by the expectations and attitudes of their citizens, and these expectations and attitudes are the product of personal experience or the experience of past generations. In West Germany, memories of the hyper-inflation of 1923 when the value of money dropped day by day, of the Hitler period and the post-war occupation which followed it, of the Berlin Wall, and the student demonstrations of 1968, still colour political life and induce a special sensitivity toward inflation, political extremism and authoritarian decrees. In the UK, the general strike of 1926, the 'betrayal' of the Labour Party by Ramsay Macdonald when he joined the National Government in 1931, the abdication of King Edward VIII in 1936, the divisions in the Conservative Party over the Suez crisis in 1956 are still referred to in political debate because all still arouse powerful political memories and invoke prejudices or sympathies. In France, the 'Popular Front' government before the second world war, the division of France and the creation of the Vichy regime during the war, the de Gaulle take-over and the Algerian crisis in 1958 and the events of May 1968 play a similar role as symbols and references, positive and negative, for French politicians and for the French people.

Political culture, therefore, shapes and limits the way in which the political system can make decisions, resolve conflicts, produce laws and respond to demands. For a long time, no West German government could conceivably suggest bargaining with the East German authorities; it would have been electoral suicide for any party even to advocate such a step. Yet attitudes changed, and the negotiations and treaties of the Brandt–Scheel coalition between 1969 and 1974 did take place, and to the electoral benefit of the government involved. At present, no United Kingdom government could abdicate its responsibilities towards Northern Ireland by suggesting that it be united with the Irish Republic, yet attitudes may change eventually. In Italy, the idea of a 'historic compromise' resulting from a coalition of the Christian Democratic Party with the Communists is similarly regarded as out of the question, yet it would be rash to suggest that it will never happen. Political culture *can* change, though it usually changes only slowly. It provides a 'flavour' to democratic politics that is unique to each country.

Participation in politics

One of the most obvious and explicit demonstrations of differences in political culture is through political participation. The extent to which people participate in political life, what forms such participation takes, and why people participate, differ from country to country and, within a country, over time.

The simplest, most direct form of political participation is the act of voting. In few western European countries is voting compulsory (one example is Belgium). In the UK, France and West Germany it is voluntary, but the level of turn-out varies considerably across these three systems. In general elections, the turn-out in the United Kingdom in 1987 was 75 per cent; in the German Federal Republic in 1987 it was 84.4 per cent; in France in the presidential and legislative elections in 1988, turn-out varied between 82 and 66 per cent respectively. In local elections, turn-out in the UK is generally no higher than 30–40 per cent, while in France and in West German provincial elections it can reach well over 75 per cent.

But the act of voting is a very limited, and also very infrequent demonstration of political participation. Far fewer members of the public go beyond this, and involve themselves actively in electoral campaigning, by canvassing for votes, contributing money to a party, attending a political meeting, delivering leaflets or persuading acquaintances to vote in a particular way. In all three countries, it has been estimated that no more than ten per cent of the electorate engage in such forms of participation.

Party membership is a stronger commitment to participation. Discounting the members of the Labour Party in the UK who are 'passively' included by their affiliated trade union, the figures for France, the UK and West Germany are roughly similar, at about five per cent of the electorate, though left-wing parties tend to be more successful in recruiting and keeping members than liberal or right-wing parties. In West Germany, party membership, especially in parties to the right of the Social Democrats, was lower until the 1970s, partly because of a lingering distrust of such a personal commitment to political partisanship, partly because the Christian Democrats only began to recruit actively once they were in opposition in 1969. To the figures for party membership would have to be added those who join pressure groups, but often the same people are members of both types of organisation.

Being a nominal member of a party or pressure group is different from being an active member, especially to the extent of being a candidate for office, within the party or group, or on behalf of the party. Estimates based on surveys put the figure for this level of participation at about ten per cent of membership, or about one voter in every two hundred. Finally, the most intensive form of participation, that of being a professional politician (either in a parliamentary body or local council, or as a full-time staff member of a party) is limited to a very few people indeed.

So the slope of the pyramid of participation is steep. Yet democracy seems to make the assumption that the electorate will make use of their right to participate in 'government by the people'. What factors encourage or restrict participation?

1. Clearly, there are legal and administrative factors which

make a difference. The ease of obtaining a postal vote may affect turn-out. The process of electoral registration in the UK is much more cumbersome than that in West Germany, and much less accommodating to electors who change their residence from one constituency to another, for example. The fact that United Kingdom elections are always held on a weekday, those in France and Germany on a Sunday, may be regarded as part of the explanation for different levels of turn-out.

2. The electoral system may also play a role. In proportional representation systems, almost every vote 'counts' toward the election of members of one party or another; in safe seats in the UK, on the other hand, a vote for any candidate but that of the strongest party is almost certain to be 'wasted', as is that for small-party candidates in almost every seat.

3. Traditional attitudes play their part. In West Germany, it has been regarded as a civic obligation to turn out to vote, but in the UK social pressures are less strong. Similarly, only in the past twenty years has party membership and voluntary political activity again come to be regarded as 'respectable' in West Germany, whereas in the UK it has been considered acceptable for many years.

In each of the three countries, there has been an upsurge in recent years in willingness to join local and national campaigning organisations for special causes (see chapter 6) – for example, the anti-nuclear power campaigns or local civic initiative groups concerned with road safety or civic amenities. This, perhaps more than indicators of party membership, is a sign of the continued health of democracy in the UK, France and the German Federal Republic.

Notes

1. The German terms for the two chambers of the legislature are retained throughout; no suitable English translations exist.

3
POLITICAL ORIENTATIONS
IN WESTERN EUROPE

Introduction

In the two preceding chapters it has been noted that a competitive party system and periodic elections have been central features of the liberal democratic system of government. What, then, are the main differences in *political orientation* to be found among the parties competing for the support of the electorate in the states of western Europe? This chapter will seek to answer this question by examining a number of broad political tendencies which enjoy some degree of support within these states today – conservatism, liberalism, agrarianism, socialism, communism, christian democracy and the recent 'Green' (ecologist) movement, as well as the rather diverse category of regionalist and national minority movements.[1]

Generic terms of this kind, which are still in use as labels to characterise the general political orientations of different parties today, pose certain problems, however. Such terms were originally adopted to identify a series of new political forces, each of which arose in, and took its initial *raison d'être* from, a quite distinct historical context. However, differences between each country's social and economic class structure and the existence of other divisions along religious, ethnic or linguistic lines meant that, from the outset, there were considerable variations from one country to another among parties belonging to the same broad political 'family'.

Such differences in the social structure and the particular pattern of historical development of each country also meant that the whole range of political forces listed above were able to take root in very few countries. (Only the Scandanavian countries have agrarian parties, for example, and while both West Germany and Italy have major christian democratic parties but no non-denominational conservative party, the reverse is the case in the United Kingdom.) Subsequently, moreover, national parties belonging to each of these broad political families have adapted, in varying ways, to the particular terms of electoral and political competition operating in their own state. These issues – the impact of different kinds of *electoral system* and the number and range of parties to be found in each country (their *party systems*) – will be the subject of the following two chapters.

Here we are concerned rather with establishing general differences in political orientation among the political parties of western Europe. For this purpose it will be useful to adopt an historical approach, for it is in terms of their historical origins that the differences between these various political movements can be most firmly established. However, while it is not difficult to outline certain fundamental ways in which socialism and christian democracy, for example, differ from each other – in terms of the key issues and general ideological stances with which each has identified itself – the general proviso needs to be borne in mind that today the boundaries between many of these broad political tendencies are by no means clear cut.

In practice, there are substantial differences within some of these political 'families', between different national parties. This is the case with parties belonging to the liberal tradition, some of which can be described as left to centre (the Italian Radical Party, for example, and the Dutch Democrats '66) while others are distinctly conservative in outlook (the Liberty and Progress Party of Belgium, for example). Until the eighties there were marked contrasts within the socialist grouping between those parties committed to major programmes of economic reform (the French Socialist Party, for example, and PASOK in Greece) and other parties which sought to manage the existing social order with only quite limited perspectives of change (for example, the West German Social Democrats).

In addition, quite diverse political tendencies may co-exist, in an often uneasy alliance, within certain parties. This has been the case especially among parties belonging to the socialist and christian democratic movements. The Labour Party in the United Kingdom, for example, is currently beset by major political disputes, even after the departure of some on the right of the party to form the new Social Democratic Party. In somewhat similar fashion, there has often been considerable tension in both the

Italian Christian Democrat Party and the Belgian Social
Christians between the more socially progressive elements (close
to the christian democrat trade unions) and much more
conservative ones. The Belgian Christian Social Party, moreover,
is split along lines of regional and linguistic division, into two
distinct Flemish and Walloon parties (see chapter 5).

In the following two sections of this chapter the successive
emergence of major new political forces will be outlined, firstly in
the period up to the second world war, and then in the years since
1945. However, before examining these historical developments,
it will be useful to consider here a certain number of more general
points. In terms of their basic political orientations, there would
seem to be three distinct levels at which differences arise between
parties, these three levels being concerned firstly with *political
community*, secondly with *political regime*, and thirdly with
detailed issues of policy.

(a) The political community

At this first level there is the issue of identifying the political
community to which one belongs and deciding on the proper basis
for establishing separate states. On this issue most of the major
political families in western Europe have come to subscribe to the
ideal of 'the nation-state'. They thus share a similar general
orientation centring on a territorial definition of state
boundaries, which are deemed to correspond to distinct national
political communities. (Of course, from within this shared
orientation it is still possible to dispute the validity of existing
nation-state boundaries: to contest the current division of the
German people into two states, for example, or to argue for the
incorporation of Northern Ireland into an all-Ireland republic or
for the establishment of a separate state for the Basques.) Three
of the political families which we will be considering – socialism,
communism and christian democracy – have, however, associated
themselves with rather different stances on this issue.

The early socialist movement and, subsequently, the
communist movement both argued that fundamental divisions of
political interest operated *between classes*, rather than between
nations. Their outlook was therefore internationalist, looking
towards unity of action between working-class parties across

nation-state boundaries (and they therefore attached considerable importance to the establishment of international political organisations). Nevertheless, in varying ways which will be discussed in the following sections, parties belonging to both these movements in western Europe have come to marry some form of class analysis with acceptance of the nation-state unit.

A contrasting challenge to the nation-state ideal has come, primarily since 1945, from those who have argued that the peoples of western Europe together constitute a distinct political community, and that some form of supranational integration is required, with the creation of common state institutions for the whole area. This distinctive, 'Europeanist' political orientation has found support among certain elements within most of the major political families, but it has been christian democracy in western Europe which has most particularly identified itself with this perspective.

Finally, this initial issue of deciding who forms the political community – who should be included or excluded and why – also spills over into related issues, at the level of the political regime, regarding the eligibility of various sectors of the population (men with no property, women, young people between the ages of eighteen and twenty-one, immigrants, etc.) to participate in the institutions of the state.

(b) The political regime

At this second level there is the issue of deciding on the most appropriate form of political regime to adopt, that is, the procedures by which conflicts of interest within the political community should be resolved and laws, binding on all, be made.

Here a general contrast can be made between earlier historical periods when – as will be discussed more fully in the second section of this chapter – there was a range of attitudes towards the claims of liberal democracy, and the situation today, when most of the major political families operating in western Europe have come to share some degree of commitment to the liberal democratic system of government. However, the degree of consensus that exists today over liberal democracy can perhaps be exaggerated. Political forces of the extreme right, for example, still argue in favour of strongly authoritarian state institutions, but while these forces are not insignificant in countries like Spain, which only recently reverted to a liberal democratic constitution, Italy with the neo-fascist Italian Social Movement (MSI), and France with the National Front's recent growth, they have only a marginal presence in most other states. Moreover, even if all the major political forces, right across the rest of the spectrum from conservatism to Eurocommunism, are now committed to working within the institutions of liberal democracy, considerable differences of emphasis are to be found among them about how liberal democracy should work. And such debate about how best to achieve responsive and representative government in turn draws on different views about these national political communities, and about the conflicts of interest within them, and also feeds into debate about specific issues of policy.

Thus, for example, on the left both Eurocommunists and socialists – although with differing emphases – argue that political democracy by itself is inadequate and needs to be complemented by a substantial redistribution of wealth, an extension of public ownership and new forms of economic democracy. In recent years a variety of different political tendencies, most notably regionalists, ecologists, 'citizen-initiative' groups[2] and various elements on the radical left, have criticised the remoteness of government from the ordinary citizen and what they regard as the excessively centralised and secretive character of much policy-making, arguing that new methods are required for involving local communities, in particular, in the making of decisions that closely affect them.

(c) Detailed issues of policy

It is at this third level that the debate between parties is largely centred in western Europe today and it is in terms of their stances on a range of issues such as economic policy, the provision of social services and law and order that terms such as conservative, liberal, socialist and christian democrat are regarded as useful general labels for a range of parties in these countries.

However, a number of commentators have argued that some of these more general differences of policy between the major political families are now being superseded. It is suggested that, in an attempt to extend their electoral bases, parties have been increasingly concerned to devise more widely appealing programmes and electoral manifestos, discarding their earlier, more particularistic identities (for example, as parties of the Catholic community or of the working class).[3] Nevertheless, while some trends can be discerned along these lines since the late 1950s and early 1960s (in France and West Germany, in particular), the national party systems in western Europe are still remarkable for the persistence of patterns of division and indeed, in a number of cases, the trend has been towards increasing fragmentation (see chapter 5). Moreover, as was noted above, disputes between parties on specific policy issues are still interlinked with contrasting views which they hold, both about who should decide policy and how, and about what kind of shared interests hold members of these nation-states together, so that there is a potential for disputes about specific policies to develop into more serious conflicts about the issues of regime and political community.

Political forces in western Europe before the second world war

The modern conception of the nation-state came to prevail in Europe in the nineteenth century and by the close of the first world war state boundaries had been substantially redrawn. Greece won its independence from the Ottoman empire in 1827 and was closely followed by Belgium (in 1831) and Luxemburg (in 1839), both of which had been under the control of the Netherlands, while the process of national unification was finally completed in Italy and Germany in 1870 and 1871 respectively. In Scandinavia, Norway gained its independence from Sweden in 1905 and Finland emerged as an independent state in the wake of the Russian revolution in 1917. A year later the Republic of Austria was founded, following the collapse of the Austro-Hungarian empire. After this date, only Ireland, with the establishment of the Irish Free State in 1922 and then of the Republic of Eire in 1937, and Iceland, which did not become fully independent of Denmark until 1944, were able to press their claims for separate statehood successfully (and, in the case of Ireland, the full territorial claim has still not been met).

This was, therefore, a period in which nationalism was a powerful influence on the main political forces operating in western Europe, although in all the major countries national sentiment itself was inextricably linked with claims to imperialist leadership in other parts of the world, especially in Africa.

Conservatism, in the nineteenth century, embraced a range of political groupings sharing a common concern to preserve the privileges of a social elite that was, for the most part, based on land ownership and the principle of heredity. Yet there were substantial differences between them: in some countries they aligned themselves with absolutist states of the *ancien régime* type which persisted, in the case of Germany, until late in the nineteenth century; in others, for example, in Belgium, Denmark, the Netherlands, the United Kingdom and much of Scandinavia, they supported constitutional monarchies which allowed for some form of representative government; however, apart from Switzerland, almost everywhere where republics were established, however briefly, conservative forces opposed the republican principle.

The main opposition to these various conservative groupings came from liberalism, which drew much of its support from the bourgeoisie, an expanding class of industrial and commercial entrepreneurs, and from the professions. There were two distinctive strands to liberal thought: on the one hand political liberalism, which championed the principles of representative and responsible government, extended suffrage, freedom of speech and usually also a secular state; on the other hand, economic liberalism, with its defence of private property and pursuit of free trade policies. Liberal parties differed from one country to another according to the respective emphases which they placed on one or other of these two sets of principles.

The interplay between liberalism and conservatism was further complicated by different patterns of divisions between Catholic, Protestant and secular opinion in each country, with the issue of church–state relations giving rise to conflicts in many states, most acutely in France.[4] In Scandinavia a polarisation of interests developed between the towns and countryside which enabled a quite distinctive political force – agrarianism – to establish itself with a cross-class rural base.[5]

Faced with pressures for political change, conservative political forces displayed differing capacities for adaptation, the most successful being the Conservative Party in the United Kingdom. It was a Conservative government which conceded a substantial extension of the suffrage in 1867 and, to meet the new electoral challenge, Disraeli subsequently pioneered the development of a centralised national organisation and large-scale membership for the party, breaking with the loosely organised 'party of notables' format that was to remain characteristic of both conservative and liberal political forces in most of western Europe.

By the closing decades of the nineteenth century another major political force had emerged with the establishment of socialist parties seeking primarily to represent the new industrial working class. These parties, affiliated to the Second International which was established in 1889, had a distinctive stance on the issue of political community, being anti-capitalist and internationalist (see above pp. 40–41). Yet such positions of principle co-existed uneasily, until the first world war, with these parties' growing adaptation to the system of nation-states and with their concern to win parliamentary representation in order to secure such measures as the extension of political rights, social welfare provisions and the protection of trade union organisations.[6]

Even though some within the socialist parties continued to subscribe to the Marxist argument that those with economic power would continue to wield effective political power even under a fully liberal-democratic state, the idea gained ground that it would be possible for working-class parties in western Europe to win control over the state through the ballot box and then bring about a redistribution of economic wealth that would give a new reality to the workings of political democracy. However, at the outbreak of the first world war only a tiny minority were prepared to vote in their national parliaments against the financing of the war and in a number of countries socialists came into government for the first time as members of governments of 'national unity'.

The emergence of socialist parties served to polarise the political forces of liberalism, some seeking alliances to their left in order to extend and consolidate political democracy or to establish a secular state, others gravitating towards a more conservative stance in defence of the institution of private property.

After the first world war, the socialist parties split and their earlier stance of radical anti-capitalism and internationalism was taken up, in altered form, by communist parties affiliated to the Third International (Comintern).[7] These parties were convinced that a new kind of state (a 'dictatorship of the proletariat') was needed to dispossess the incumbent ruling classes of their political and economic power, and that such a state could only be achieved through revolution; they looked to the system of soviets established in Russia following the revolutions of February and October 1917 as their model. This new communist challenge to liberal democracy, however, became increasingly identified with support for the evolving practice of the Russian 'party-state', as the direct democracy of soviets was transformed by the exclusion of alternative parties and by the elimination of open debate between organised tendencies within what became a monolithic ruling party. Nevertheless, faced with the rise of fascism in Europe, the communist parties later sought to work within broad 'Popular Front' alliances to defend the institutions of liberal democracy, most dramatically in Spain, where they physically opposed other forces on the left that attempted to make a revolution.

By the mid-1930s, the most serious and immediate threat to liberal democratic states came, therefore, from fascist movements and from the success first of Mussolini in Italy and later of Hitler in Germany in establishing authoritarian, corporatist states in which, most notably, competitive elections were eliminated and the organised trade union movement crushed. Moreover, Nazism in Germany sought to redefine the political community in terms of claims about a shared (Aryan) racial inheritance. The expansionism of Hitler's Reich, associated with these claims, led directly to the second world war.

Political orientations in western Europe since the second world war

The rise of fascism in the inter-war period and, in a number of countries, the experience of German occupation during the war cast doubt on the commitment of some conservative political forces in western Europe to the institutions of liberal democracy and at the same time drew communist parties into the struggle to defend these institutions. However, this patterning of political forces, which was to be found, with variations, in the resistance movements and, subsequently, in a number of early post-war coalition governments, was very soon reshaped by the emergence of the cold war. Communist parties now became 'ghettoised' for the most part, while some conservative forces which had previously been discredited were re-integrated into the mainstream of political life.

Thus, what may be seen, retrospectively, as a new pattern of liberal democratic politics emerged. This identified competitive party systems and free elections as the hallmarks of liberal democracy (thus establishing a clear point of contrast with the one-party states of the Soviet bloc, to which the term 'totalitarian' was now commonly applied), while at the same time accepting the need to modify the economic environment in which liberal democratic institutions operated, through a commitment to full employment, welfare state provisions of various kinds, and some measure of public ownership. A broad consensus along these lines was to prove an enduring framework for the political process in most west European states until the mid-1970s, although it must be emphasised that there were considerable variations from one country to another, and there remained substantial differences of approach among the major political 'families'.

This conception of liberal democracy was, in part, geo-political and was associated with new definitions of political community, which came to the fore in this period. Political leaders in most of these countries came to identify the interests of their own nation-states with a wider Atlantic community (which took institutional form, from 1949, in the Atlantic Alliance).[8] A number of leading political figures also gave public support to the idea of building a supranational European political community, and this was to be closely linked to Atlanticism through the United States' backing for initiatives aimed at achieving economic and political integration in western Europe.

Christian democracy, which emerged as a major force in west European politics by the late 1940s, can be considered a distinctive product of this period, combining, as it did, a concern to distance itself from previous conservative forces (while taking over much of their previous electoral bases) with an unwavering adherence to both Atlanticism and the idea of an integrated Europe. These themes served to differentiate the christian democrat movement after 1945 from Catholic parties of the inter-war period, even where there was considerable organisational continuity (as in the case of the Belgian Social

Catholic Party and the Dutch Catholic People's Party). In the new republics established in Italy and West Germany, christian democrat parties quickly assumed a dominant position, while in France the new Popular Republican Movement also participated in almost every government until 1954.

These parties varied as to how far they professed a specific commitment to christian values in their programmes (and, indeed, as to whether they adopted a Catholic or christian reference in their party title), but they were united in affirming the possibility of 'a middle way': 'a combination of freedom and justice'.[9] While the first of these principles brought them close to more traditional strands of political conservatism, stressing the rights of the individual, the importance of the family, and individual property ownership, their commitment to extending social and economic welfare measures provided for some overlap with parties left of centre, but their concern to defend church schools, in particular, and to win state funding for them was distinctive (and a source of bitter division, in Belgium and France for example, with socialist parties committed to the principle of a secular state), as was their stance on industrial relations, where they sought to secure some 'share of control' with management for employees' representatives.

The success of christian democracy since 1945 has made it more difficult to map out the political forces of the centre and right-of-centre in western Europe. The most successful of these parties were able to win a broad cross-class electoral base, somewhat similar to that of the Conservative Party in the UK, with a bias towards rural support, but including a significant section of working-class votes. However, the christian democrat parties in Italy and Belgium, in particular, through their close links with major trade union federations (albeit of generally moderate outlook) have incorporated a wider political spread than, for example, the West German CDU–CSU, whose political stance has, therefore, been more nearly equivalent to that of the Conservative Party in the UK.

The appeal of christian democracy in many countries and the earlier establishment of agrarian centre parties in Scandinavia meant that political conservatism – whether in the form of parties calling themselves conservative (as in Denmark, Finland, Norway and Sweden) or of old-established liberal parties which had gravitated rightwards – has not succeeded in mobilising a substantial popular following in western Europe, outside the United Kingdom. Two other right-of-centre parties sharing a strongly nationalistic outlook have established a wider electoral appeal: Fianna Fail in Ireland and the Gaullist Party in France, under the Fifth Republic. It is perhaps worth noting that both these parties have adopted quite distinctive foreign policy stances (the official policy of the Republic of Ireland being neutralist, while France, during de Gaulle's presidency, left the integrated military command structure of NATO). The Gaullist Party was until the eighties, quite unique on the European right in its support for state intervention in the economy.[10]

The configuration of political forces operating on the west European left since 1945 has also been complex and, in recent years, has undergone a number of important modifications. In most of western Europe, the division that had developed earlier, after the first world war, between socialism and communism was re-established in heightened form after 1947. While the communist parties refused to accept that the Soviet bloc posed a military threat to the west, nearly all the socialist parties in the member states of NATO supported their countries' inclusion in the American-led alliance.[11] However, there were exceptions, notably the Italian and Icelandic socialist parties, and, as a result, in Italy the socialists were able to maintain their electoral alliances at the local and regional level throughout the 1950s with the larger Communist Party, while in Iceland a government coalition including the Communist Party was formed in 1956. (In addition, the Finnish Communist Party participated in government in the following decade.)

As was noted in the introduction to this chapter, the west European socialist parties have varied quite substantially in terms of the degree of social and economic change to which they have committed themselves in their party programmes and electoral manifestos. They have also varied considerably both in terms of how long they have spent in government in this period and in terms of the alliances they have been prepared to enter. The Swedish Social Democrat Party, for example, held office continuously for over forty years until 1976. Elsewhere in northern Europe, in Norway, Denmark, Iceland and the United Kingdom – and in Austria, too, from the late 1960s – socialist parties have totalled many years in government, either alone or in left-wing coalitions, while the West German Social Democrats held office with a liberal party (the Free Democrats) from the late 1960s until 1982. In contrast, the Belgian Socialist Party's considerable experience in national government since 1945 has chiefly been in Social Christian-led coalitions, and in Italy, too, where the Socialist Party participated in a number of Christian Democrat-led governments from 1963, before heading two coalitions from 1983 to 1987. Finally in France, where the socialists were excluded from government for over twenty years, the socialist-led governments from 1981 to 1984 included communist ministers.[12] Beyond these variations, however, governmental experience for most of the parties has led to internal conflicts over the kinds of reform which they should expect to achieve in office, and, in a number of cases, to the splitting away of either the more moderate or the more radical wings.

In this period the communist parties have also experienced considerable internal conflicts over their programmes and longer-term strategies, in part precipitated by the beginnings of the process of destalinisation in the Soviet Union in 1956 and by the Soviet Union's military intervention to crush the Hungarian uprising in the same year. By the mid-1970s a number of communist parties had followed the Italian and Spanish parties in adopting a range of positions which became known as 'Eurocommunism'. This involved a critical stance on the internal political system of the Soviet Union and its relations with other states in the Soviet bloc, with the Soviet model being held to be inapplicable to the advanced industrial societies of the West. Eurocommunists therefore advocated a firm commitment to political pluralism and parliamentary institutions as providing the appropriate framework for what would be a lengthy and gradual process of building a new social and economic order. Some parties, notably the Portuguese, and factions in a number of other parties resisted these doctrinal changes, while the French party's conversion has remained ambivalent. The alliance strategies adopted by the communist parties in the 1970s also varied; the Italians, for example, advocating a broad *compromesso storico* ('historic compromise') embracing all the major democratic political forces, including the Christian Democrats, while the French pursued a strategy of 'union of the left'.

These developments within both the socialist and communist strands of the left made room for a variety of other groupings on the radical, libertarian and, also, the extreme (Maoist and Trotskyist) left to win a modicum of support, for the most part among students and what are often called the 'new' (white collar) working class. However, in France in the events of May–June 1968 and in Italy in the 'hot autumn' of 1969, revolutionary politics on the left did seem to connect briefly with a wider surge of working-class militancy, which brought claims for 'workers' control' to the fore.

Some of the new parties established on the left in the 1960s, for example the renewed Italian Radical Party, the Dutch Democrats '66 and also the French Unified Socialist Party, are not easy to classify politically. These parties have more recently also taken up environmental concerns, as have certain older-established agrarian parties, and feminist issues. In seeking to account for these trends and for the more general rise of the Green (ecology) movement, some writers have referred to the spread of 'post-materialist values' in these countries as providing a new dimension in politics. Such values focus on issues concerning the quality of life rather than the distribution of wealth, and question the assumption, until recently shared by the major political families, that economic growth is desirable.[13]

Regionalist and national minority movements also developed a new militancy and experienced a growth in support in the 1960s and 1970s but they achieved national parliamentary representation only in Belgium, Spain and the United Kingdom and have entered government only in Belgium.

These movements have also acted on environmental issues and, in asserting the importance of local communities and of cultural ties, have taken up themes which are concerned, in a broad sense, with the issue of 'quality of life'. However, their primary purpose has been to shift the locus of decision-making from the central institutions of the state to the regions, and, in the case of some nationalist movements, like the Basque ETA and the Corsican separatists for example, to create independent new 'nation-states'.

Transnational party organisation in the European Community

The development of the European Communities has encouraged
parties in the member states belonging to the same broad political
families to organise links between themselves, in particular
through the establishment of transnational party groups in the
European parliament (see chapter 11). Subsequently,
preparations for the first direct elections to the parliament, held in
1979, stimulated parties in the nine states involved to develop
closer ties and this resulted in the establishment of six separate
groupings of parties, each producing an agreed platform for the
elections.[14]

The most cohesive of these groupings are those formed by the
christian democrats (the European People's Party, EPP, founded
in 1976) and the socialists (the Confederation of Socialist Parties
of the European Community, founded in 1974). The EPP was
initially comprised of twelve separate parties drawn from seven of
the nine member states (excluding Denmark and the United
Kingdom) while the Socialist Confederation included parties
from all nine states. However, even these two groups were
marked by internal divisions of some importance. In the case of
the Socialist Confederation, divisions centred not only on the
extent and pace of social and economic reforms to which the
member parties should commit themselves but also on differing
attitudes to the process of European integration itself. In the EPP,
although it was eventually agreed that there should be no christian
reference in the group's title, the West German Christian
Democrats, who favoured a larger grouping including
Conservatives from the UK and Denmark, failed to win support
for this. As a result these latter two parties joined together as the
European Democrats, while the French Gaullist Party and the
Irish Fianna Fail formed another group, entitled the European
Progressive Democrats (and the Scottish Nationalist Party's
single member in the European parliament subsequently
affiliated to the EPD parliamentary grouping).[15]

The Federation of Liberal and Democratic Parties of the
European Communities, formed in 1976 by fourteen parties in
eight of the member states, is a particularly heterogeneous
grouping of relatively small parties including, for example, not
only the Republican Party led by the then French president

Giscard d'Estaing, but also the left Radicals allied to the French Socialist Party.

Finally, a grouping of Communist and allies was formed which included an independent Danish party, the Socialist People's Party. However, differences in approach to the European Communities between the two major communist parties which are represented in the European parliament, the French and Italian parties, has led the Italian Communist Party to seek a closer working relationship with other parties in the community, notably with the French Socialist Party. The current distribution of seats among these transnational parties is shown on p. 250.

The complex pattern of political orientations in western Europe today, which has been outlined in the preceding two sections, is therefore, well illustrated by the lines of division which run both between and within these six federations of parties which have been established to cover the member-states of the European Communities.

Notes

1. In addition, reference is made in section 2 below to other political forces, such as fascism and anarchism, which have previously enjoyed varying degrees of support in a number of these countries.

For convenience, the term 'socialism' is used throughout this chapter to designate the parties belonging to the Socialist International (founded in 1951), although these parties have a variety of titles, notably Labour Party (as in Ireland, the Netherlands, Norway and the United Kingdom) and Social Democratic Party (as in Denmark, Sweden and West Germany) as well as Socialist Party (as in Austria, France and Italy).

2. On the *Bürgerinitiativen* in West Germany, and other similar groups, see chapter 6.

3. See, in particular, Otto Kirchheimer, 'The transformation of Western party systems' in J. La Palombara and M. Weiner (eds.) *Political Parties and Political Development* (New Jersey, Princeton University Press, 1966) pp. 177–200.

4. In the Netherlands, for example, the Calvinist Anti-Revolutionary Party (founded in 1879) was followed by a second, more conservative, protestant party, the Christian Historical Union (1908) and by the Roman Catholic State Party (1926, renamed the Catholic People's Party in 1946). These joined together in 1977 to form the Christian Democratic Appeal. Catholic parties were also formed, for example, in Italy (the Italian People's Party, 1919) in Germany (the Centre Party) and in Belgium (the Catholic Party, of 1884).

5. These parties in Norway, Sweden and Finland are now called Centre Parties, while the Netherlands retains a Farmers' Party and in Denmark what was originally established as a Farmer's Party subsequently designated itself as a liberal party, with the title *Venstre*.

6. On the political left, anarchists and syndicalist movements, opposed to working within the existing state institutions and seeing the general strike as the most effective weapon of the working class, also gained significant support in France, Italy and Spain.

7. The remaining socialist parties formed themselves into the Socialist and Labour International in 1921.

8. For details on membership of the North Atlantic Treaty Organisation, see p. 251.

9. R. E. M. Irving, *The Christian Democratic Parties of Western Europe* (London, Royal Institute of International Affairs, Allen & Unwin, 1979), p. 31.

10. However, the Gaullist Party's electoral base has narrowed considerably since the late 1960s while an alternative coalition of broadly conservative political forces, the Union for French Democracy, was established under President Giscard d'Estaing (see chapter 5).

11. Minorities in a number of parties were opposed to Atlanticism, while, in Italy, the minority opposed to maintaining an alliance with the Communist Party split to form the Social Democratic Party. The two parties subsequently reunited briefly in 1966 but split again in 1969.

12. Four from 1981 to 1983; two in the third Mauroy government formed in March 1983 which had only fifteen cabinet-ranking ministers.

13. See, in particular, R. Ingelhart, *The Silent Revolution: Changing Values and Political Styles among Western Publics* (New Jersey, Princeton University Press. 1977). For details on the ecology parties in nine west European states: Belgium, Denmark, France, Italy, the Netherlands, Norway, Sweden, the United Kingdom and West Germany, see F. Muller-Rommel, 'Ecology parties in western Europe', *West European Politics*, no. 1 (January 1982), pp. 68–74. Ecology parties gained seats in parliament in Belgium (from 1981) and West Germany (from 1983), as has the feminist party in Iceland (from 1983).

14. See G. and P. Pridham, 'Transnational parties in the European Community 1: the party groups in the European parliament; 2: the Development of European Party Federations', in S. Henig, (ed.) *Political Parties in the European Community* (London, Allen & Unwin/Policy Studies Institute, 1979), pp. 245–98.

15. However, a wider grouping of west European centre–right parties, the European Democratic Union, was founded in April 1978, linking together the UK and Scandinavian conservative parties, the Gaullists, and the West German CDU/CSU.

4
CHOOSING GOVERNMENTS: ELECTORAL SYSTEMS

What are elections?

Elections are a common feature of political systems all over the world, in liberal democracies, in socialist one-party states called 'people's democracies', in theocracies, such as Iran, and in Latin American dictatorships. The ancient Greeks and the Romans two thousand years ago used elections in their systems of government. The Pope is elected by the Cardinals of the Catholic church in a tradition extending back over many centuries. Local authorities, international organisations such as the United Nations and the European Community, trade unions and business corporations, and associations of many kinds, employ elections as a method of choice.

Elections are one way of selecting office-holders or representatives. There are other ways: the hereditary principle for deciding on monarchical succession; the random procedure of selection by lot, used to call citizens for jury service; or appointment by someone in authority, as ministers or ambassadors are appointed by the Prime Minister or President. But elections are used when there is competition for office, and where it is regarded as important that the electorate make a choice, rather than that an appointment should be made on the basis of qualifications or patronage. In democracies, such competition results from conflicts within society concerning political goals, and elections play a part in resolving such conflicts acceptably.

What do elections do?

In the political systems of western Europe, elections are used for three main purposes:

to select representatives of the electorate;
to confirm or change governments;
to give legitimacy to government.

As will be seen, these tasks are not always mutually compatible. Because some types of electoral system stress representation while others are primarily concerned with selecting governments and supporting them through stable majorities, the choice of electoral system itself is often the subject of contention, as will be further discussed below.

Elections to parliament or to a local council are primarily concerned with selecting representatives of the people, who will then debate and decide upon matters of political concern, on behalf of the people. In communist states, such as the USSR, elections are non-competitive: only one candidate is nominated, having been selected by the party, but the electoral process still goes ahead. Even in western Europe it is not unknown for a candidate to be elected unopposed (for example, in the UK and the Irish Republic it is usual for the Speaker of the parliament to be unopposed in his constituency). But in national elections, at least, it is normal for an election to be competitive, between candidates of different parties, though in local elections in some countries it is not uncommon for candidates to be unopposed because of the lesser importance of party affiliation and the greater significance of the candidate's personality and political record.

An important issue may be the number of levels of government in a society for which elected representation should be provided. All western democracies now have at least two levels – national and local – while federal systems have three (see chapter 10). However, the devolution debate in the UK, the introduction of elected regional councils in Italy and proposals for direct election to regional legislative bodies in France, demonstrate that this issue is not confined to federal states. Involved in this is the question of *what* should be represented through elections, particularly what level of sub-national community should have its own elected council, and what the constituency should be in terms of identity. The devolution debate in Britain, for example, raised the question of whether Scotland and Wales should have elected assemblies, and, if so, whether it was then proper or equitable to deny to the regions of England the same rights.

Although political parties in their modern form are not much more than a hundred years old, they are now an integral part of the electoral process. They select candidates and present the voters with programmes to guide them in their choice. They co-ordinate teams of successful candidates, as government or in opposition to government, once the election is over. A modern election is unthinkable without political parties; so much so, that party competition in free elections has become one of the properties which define liberal democracy.

So an election determines the party composition of the House of Commons, the French National Assembly, the West German Bundestag, as well as provincial legislatures in regions such as Bavaria and Sicily, and local councils such as the Surrey County Council. Each successful candidate owes his or her seat to the choices made by the voters.

Elections also confirm or change governments. Because governments consist of members of political parties, singly or in coalition, and depend on the support of party majorities in the legislature, the electorate, when it chooses representatives, simultaneously gives its verdict on a choice of government. It may decide to confirm a government in office, as it did in the German Federal Republic in 1987, or it may decide to put a new government in the place of the old, as it did in the UK in 1979, and in France in 1981 through the presidential and then the legislative elections. It may even leave the result of its choice apparently unclear, as in the UK in 1974 and in France in 1986. Election campaigns focus on this choice of governments, often minimising the role of the individual candidate in so doing. The voter is exhorted to vote primarily for a *party*, and the candidate will usually ask for votes on the basis of his party affiliation, rather than personal qualities. Indeed, some electoral systems confine the voter to a choice among pre-selected party lists, and the voter has little or no say in determining the personal composition of the legislature. Elections are thus a way of allowing the electorate to deliver a verdict on the policies of competing parties and on the past record of the government. There is a tendency for the successful party to claim that its victory provides it with a *mandate* – that is, it claims that the electorate, by its decision, has given the government a licence to proceed to implement the policy

proposals in its platform, based on its election manifesto. Mrs
Thatcher in 1987, Chancellor Kohl in 1987 and President
Mitterrand in 1988 all claimed after their victories that they could
now introduce (or continue) the policies and governmental
strategies that they had offered to the voters during the campaign.
(It must be noted that in France, with the notable exception of the
1986 legislative elections, the choice of government is made,
primarily, by the direct election of the President, who is the
effective leader of the government as well as the head of state.[1]
France is the only major European democracy to have a directly-
elected and politically powerful President.)

Governments do not only change as a result of elections. In the
case of coalition government, they may change because of
decisions made by parties within the coalition between elections,
as happened in the German Federal Republic in 1966 and 1982,
and as used to occur frequently in France in the Fourth Republic.
Table 1 gives the dates of elections in Britain, France and West
Germany, and the party composition of governments which
resulted.

Elections and governments in the United Kingdom, France and West Germany since 1945

Table 1   The United Kingdom

Year of election	Government
1945	Labour government formed
1950	Labour
1951	Conservative government formed
1955	Conservative
1959	Conservative
1964	Labour government formed
1966	Labour
1970	Conservative government formed
1974 (Feb.)	Labour minority government formed
1974 (Oct.)	Labour
1979	Conservative government formed
1983	Conservative
1987	**Conservative**

France

Table 2   Legislative elections under the Fourth Republic, 1946–58

Year of election	Government
1946	Communist, Socialist & Christian Democrat coalition (Tripartism) formed
1951	Radical, Conservative & Christian Democrat coalition
1956	Socialist, Left Radical & Progressive Gaullist coalition (Republic Front) formed

Table 3   Legislative elections under the Fifth Republic, 1958–81

Year of election	Government
1958	Gaullist
1962	Gaullist & Independent Republican coalition formed
1967	Gaullist & Independent Republican coalition
1968	Gaullist & Independent Republican coalition
1973	Gaullist, Independent Republican & Centre for Democracy and Progress [i] coalition
1978	Union for French Democracy [ii] & Gaullist coalition
1981	Socialist, Left Radical & Communist coalition
1986	Gaullist & Union for French Democracy coalition
1988	Socialist (Minority government)

(i)   Centre for Democracy and Progress, formed by pro-Fifth Republic elements of Christian Democratic tradition.

(ii)   Union for French Democracy: first ballot electoral alliance between Republican Party (formerly Independent Republicans), Radicals, Social and Democratic Centre (re-unified Christian Democratic Party) & Social Democrats.

Table 4   Direct presidential elections under the Fifth Republic

Year of election	President and new government
1965	de Gaulle: Gaullist & Independent Republican coalition
1969	Pompidou: Gaullist & Independent Republican (i) coalition
1974	Giscard d'Estaing: Gaullists, Independent Republicans, Radicals & Social and Democratic Centre
1981	Mitterrand: Socialist & Left Radical coalition
1988	Mitterrand: Socialist-led coalition

(i)   This government included some individuals from Radical and Christian Democratic traditions hitherto opposed to the Gaullist presidential majority.

Table 5   Federal Republic of Germany

Year of election	Government
1949	CDU/CSU & FDP coalition formed
1953	CDU/CSU & FDP coalition (FDP left coalition in 1956)
1957	CDU/CSU and minor parties coalition
1961	CDU/CSU & FDP coalition formed
1965	CDU/CSU & FDP coalition (FDP left coalition in 1966; CDU/CSU and SPD 'grand coalition' formed in place of former government)
1969	SPD & FDP coalition formed
1972	SPD & FDP coalition
1976	SPD & FDP coalition
1980	SPD & FDP coalition (1982 CDU/CSU & FDP coalition formed after the dissolution of the SDP & FDP coalition)
1983	CDU/CSU & FDP coalition
1987	CDU/CSU & FDP coalition

(note: minor parties in earlier coalitions are not specified)

Elections give legitimacy to government. They enable a government to claim to be 'government by the people', a claim that is essential if the political system purports to be democratic. This is why one-party communist states hold elections, even though the voter only has a choice between accepting or rejecting the single candidate nominated by the party. The 99.9 per cent which the candidate receives is regarded as indicative of popular support for the regime. In western democracies, emphasis on turning out to vote, even in 'safe' seats, is similarly to accentuate the legitimacy of the electoral process. (Figures for turn-out in the UK, France and West Germany are given in chapter 2.)

Types of electoral system

A wide variety of electoral systems can be found within western Europe. The first direct elections to the parliament of the European Community in June 1979 demonstrated just how varied electoral arrangements in the nine member-states were, as each member-state used its own system on that occasion. However, each national system is based either on the 'simple majority' principle, sometimes referred to as the 'first-past-the-post' system, or else on the principle of proportional representation (of which the single transferable vote system is a special case). There are also systems which include elements of both principles.

The United Kingdom and France use the simple majority system; the German Federal Republic uses a mixed system of simple majority election in constituencies and proportional representation based on party lists; Eire is one of the few states to use the single transferable vote (STV) system.

1. The United Kingdom

The electoral system of the United Kingdom has developed, without any major discontinuity, over many centuries. A degree of uniformity was first introduced by the Reform Acts of 1832, 1867, 1884 and 1885, which also extended the right to vote so that most of the male adult population possessed the franchise by the end of the century (the principle of universal male suffrage was adopted in 1918). The secret ballot, which did much to eliminate electoral corruption was introduced by the Ballot Act of 1872. Women received the right to vote in two stages, by legislation in 1918 and 1928, after the suffragette campaign had brought the matter forcibly to public attention before the first world war. The Representation of the People Act of 1948 abolished several remaining anomalies, such as the university seats in the House of Commons, which in effect gave graduates a second vote, and the remaining few double-member constituencies.

The voting system itself is very straightforward. Each of the 650 constituencies elects one member; the candidate who obtains the largest number of valid votes in that constituency is declared elected. There is no requirement that the winner should obtain an *absolute* majority of votes cast (i.e. over fifty per cent). With a few exceptions, all citizens over the age of eighteen who are on the electoral register may vote. Elections must be held on a working day, not at the weekend or on a bank holiday. A general election must take place not later than five years after the previous election; it usually occurs earlier, because the Prime Minister may select whatever date seems most opportune in the circumstances. If the government has only a small majority, an election may even take place within one or two years of the previous election (e.g. 1950 and 1951; 1964 and 1966; February 1974 and October 1974). Seats which become vacant between general elections are filled by holding by-elections. Candidates usually represent one of the political parties, but independents can and do present themselves for election. There are few restrictions on the right to stand for parliament, although members of the aristocracy may not be candidates. The nomination and subsequent election of Bobby Sands, who was on hunger strike in prison, for the Northern Ireland constituency of Fermanagh and South Tyrone in 1981 led parliament to pass legislation prohibiting prisoners serving sentences of one year or longer from becoming candidates.

2. *The French Fifth Republic*

In contrast to the uninterrupted development of the British electoral system, that of France has been revised radically on several occasions. In part, this has been a reflection of the changes of constitution which have occurred in France since the introduction of universal male suffrage in 1848. After the second world war the vote was extended to women and a party-list system of proportional representation, based on the provincial Departments, was tried, but was held to be partly responsible for the weaknesses of the political system of the Fourth Republic. When de Gaulle came to power in 1958 and founded the Fifth Republic, the voting system for the National Assembly elections reverted to the pre-war method of a two-ballot simple-majority system. This system (with slight variations) has also been used since 1962 for electing the President of the republic.

For legislative elections, with the sole exception of those held in 1986, the constituencies (now 577) each elect one member of the National Assembly.[2] The voting procedure is the same as in the UK (except that elections are held on a Sunday). However, to be elected on the first ballot, a candidate must receive an *absolute* majority of votes cast, i.e. more than all the votes given to his opponents together. Relatively few seats are filled in the first ballot. In seats where such an absolute majority is not attained, a second ballot takes place one week later. Only candidates who have received votes at least equal to 12½ per cent of the electorate on the first ballot can stand in the second round. In fact, as will be seen below, the introduction of the system of direct election for the presidency has encouraged the process of inter-party bargaining, so that in most constituencies in National Assembly elections also only two candidates contest the second round. The winner on the second round is the candidate with the highest vote, irrespective of whether this is an absolute majority or not.

Elections are held every five years, though the National Assembly may be dissolved earlier and new elections held (provided not less than twelve months has elapsed since the previous election) should the President so desire. This happened in 1981, following the election of President Mitterrand, a socialist, and again in 1988 following his re-election. Vacancies are filled by substitutes, elected at the same time as members of the National Assembly, but by by-elections if substitutes are not further available, or if, for example, a former minister who has passed on his seat to a substitute wishes to return to the National Assembly.

The President is elected every seven years (or earlier if a vacancy occurs). An absolute majority of votes is required for election. Should no candidate obtain this on the first ballot, the two candidates with the highest number of votes compete in a 'run-off' election two weeks later. The President is eligible for re-election once. The fact that only two candidates compete in the second round has encouraged the development of two party 'blocs' in the Fifth Republic: one on the right and one on the left. This system of direct election, introduced following a referendum in 1962, is still a matter of controversy in France, for it raises fundamental questions about the relationship between the executive and legislative branches of government, and the role of the National Assembly (see below, chapter 8).

3. The German Federal Republic

When the new German Federal Republic was founded in 1949, its choice of electoral system was influenced by the idea that proportional representation in the Weimar republic had contributed to the conditions that led to the downfall of democracy and its replacement by Nazism. The new state also had several years' experience of local and provincial elections in its zones of occupation to guide its choice. The system selected was one which combined the election of candidates in constituencies through the simple majority system with the use of party lists in such a way as to make the overall composition of the Bundestag proportional to the support given to parties by the electorate. After some amendments to the original scheme, the system adopted has remained in use ever since.

Each voter has two votes. With the first, the voter chooses a representative for the constituency, and the candidate with the highest number of votes is elected, as in the United Kingdom. Half the seats in the Bundestag are filled from the 248 constituencies in this manner. The other 248 seats are then allocated as a result of the second vote which each elector can use; this is a vote for party lists, and there is no requirement that this vote be given to the same party as that of the candidate which received the first vote. Cross-voting is indeed quite common. Each party receives list seats, so that the *total* number of seats a party obtains (taking constituency seats and list seats together) is proportional to the share of the second votes which the party has managed to win. One limitation is that a party must win *either* at least five per cent of the second votes *or* three constituencies in order to obtain a distribution of list seats at all. (Of course, if it wins less than three constituencies but does not get five per cent of the second votes, it keeps any constituency seats which it has obtained.) In the provincial elections in North Rhine Westphalia in 1980, for example, the Free Democratic Party received only 4.9 per cent of the vote, and, as it had not won any constituency seats, it lost its representation in the provincial parliament.[3] The result of the 1983 federal election (table 6) illustrates how this system operates.

Table 6   Federal election of January 1987

Party	% of 2nd votes	Total seats	Constituency seats won	List seats allocated
CDU	34.5	174	124	50
CSU	9.8	49	45	4
SPD	37.0	186	79	107
FDP	9.1	46	–	46
Greens	8.3	42	–	42

This shows:

(*a*) that the FDP and the Greens obtained all their seats from the list allocation (indeed, they were not even in second place in any constituency);

(*b*) that the Greens – the environmentalist party fighting the federal election for the third time – qualified for a list allocation;

(*c*) that the total number of seats for those parties represented in the Bundestag was very nearly proportional to their second-vote support.

Elections are held on a Sunday, every four years. Exceptionally, the President of the republic can give consent for an earlier election; this has happened only twice, in 1972, when elections were held a year ahead of time because the governing coalition had lost its majority, and in 1983 after the CDU/CSU–FDP coalition engineered its own defeat in a vote of confidence in the Bundestag in order to bring forward an election.[4] There are no by-elections; vacancies are filled between elections by the next available unelected candidate on the list of the party which held the seat when it became vacant. The number of seats held by each party thus remains unchanged between elections, unless elected members decide to change parties and 'cross the floor'.

4. Eire

Arthur Griffith, founder of the Sinn Fein party, called the single transferable vote system: 'the one just system of election in democratic governments'.[5] It is a system of election which produces more proportional representation of parties than do the UK and French systems, but its primary intention is not concerned with achieving a close correspondence between votes cast for each party and the proportion of seats that party wins, but rather with ensuring that each successful candidate in a constituency is, ultimately, preferred by a majority of the electorate to all the unsuccessful candidates.

The system as used in Eire is based upon multi-member constituencies, usually electing three or four members each (only two still elect five). The voter places candidates in order of preference, by putting '1' by the first choice, '2' by the second choice, and so on, using all or only some of the available preferences as the voter wishes. To be elected, a candidate must obtain a 'quota' of votes for that constituency. The quota is expressed by the formula:

$$Q = \frac{V}{(S + 1)} + 1$$

where Q is the quota, S the number of seats to be filled in the constituency, and V the number of valid votes cast. Thus, in a four-member constituency with 40,000 valid votes, the quota would be: 40,000 divided by five, plus one vote = 8,001 votes. Only four candidates can obtain 8,001 or more votes; five times the quota is 40,005, which is greater than the number of valid votes.

On the first count, any candidate with the quota is declared elected. If fewer candidates obtain the quota than there are seats to be filled, surplus votes of successful candidates are distributed to other candidates, in proportion to the second preferences on all the voting papers for that successful candidate. Unless that redistribution produces enough candidates to fill all the remaining seats, the next redistribution is carried out: the second preferences of the candidate with the least first preferences are allocated to other candidates. This process of re-allocation, using third and later preferences if necessary, is continued until all the seats are filled. Voters can, of course, disregard party loyalty in giving their preferences: they can vote for one party's candidate with their first preference, the candidate of another party with their second, an independent with their third preference, a candidate of the first-preference party with their fourth preference, and so on.

Elections are held on weekdays, and the period between elections may not exceed five years, though dissolution (as in the United Kingdom) may occur earlier at the desire of the Prime Minister. Vacancies between general elections are filled by by-elections, using the same election procedure as in a general election.

Rules of electoral systems

Although the method used to translate votes into seats is the most significant element of an electoral system, other factors contribute to the electoral process in the form of rules and laws.

There are normally rules relating to the matter of who can present themselves as candidates. Foreign nationals, citizens below a certain age, those in prison or whose civic rights have been withdrawn, civil servants, members of the aristocracy (in Britain) – these are examples of categories of persons disqualified from standing for election under various systems.

The rules concerning the right to vote are also a matter for legislation. The franchise, as this right to vote is called, has been extended during the nineteenth and twentieth centuries, as politics has become democratised. The franchise is now extended to all citizens who have come of age, irrespective of their wealth, religion, or social status, and includes women (though in Switzerland this was a change which only occurred following a referendum in 1971). The most recent major extension of the franchise was the reduction in voting age to eighteen in Britain (1969), France (1976), the German Federal Republic (1970) and Eire (following a referendum in 1972).

Two other important aspects of electoral rules concern expenditure and use of the media.

Normally, there are limits on the amount of money that can be spent, either by candidates individually or parties collectively, on the election campaign. In the German Federal Republic, though there may be inter-party agreement on limitation of expenditures (as there was in 1980), legal control extends only to the publication of accounts and sources of income. Indeed, German parties receive a sum of money from the state (currently 5 DM, equal to about £1.60) for each vote obtained, provided a minimum of one-half of one per cent of valid votes is won by the party. In the United Kingdom, the law limits the amount each candidate may spend on the campaign, based on the number of voters in the constituency.

Access to the media is sometimes regulated by law, or by inter-party agreement. This especially applies to broadcasting, since radio and television are usually controlled by the state, directly or indirectly. Agreements are reached about party political broadcasts, and allocations made in some proportion to party strength in the legislature before the election was called. French law prohibits the publication of opinion poll results relating to the election for a period of one week prior to polling day, because it is thought that such publication could influence voters unduly. Such a prohibition has been considered in the United Kingdom and West Germany, but not adopted.

Electoral reform

In few countries is there ever complete or lasting satisfaction with the electoral system in use. No system is ever perfect. The debate concerning the electoral system to be used for the future elections to the European parliament has given further stimulus to discussion about the different properties to be found in electoral systems, about what electoral systems should try to do and about how well they do it.

Although there are many controversial issues regarding details of electoral systems, the main debate concerning electoral reform is in relation to two questions:

What should be represented through the electoral process: local or regional constituencies? social categories, such as national or religious minorities? party preferences?

Should an electoral system give priority to the function of reasonably accurate representation of party preferences, or should it seek to translate votes into seats in such a way as to ensure support for a government which can have a stable legislative majority?

In countries where party preferences are not conveniently divided into two, and only two, alternatives, accurate representation of party preferences may prevent the formation of governments which can count on a safe majority of parliamentary seats sufficient to keep them in power until the next scheduled election.

The problem is related to the dominant role of parties in western democracies. Parties are the organisations which form governments. If parties are represented proportionally to their voting support, it is very likely that no party will secure a working majority by itself in the legislature, and hence any government will need to be a coalition. Coalitions are necessarily compromises, and are at the mercy of one partner or the other deciding to leave the government, or threatening to leave it as a means of forcing the other partner to concede more and more to it. This happened to the CDU–FDP coalition in West Germany in 1966, for instance, where the junior partner, the liberal Free Democratic Party, left the coalition because it couldn't get its own way on financial policy. A 'grand coalition' of the two major parties was formed. This Christian Democratic Party–Social Democratic Party government gave serious consideration to the possibility of changing the electoral system to that based on single-member constituencies with simple-majority election, as in the UK, in order to eliminate the FDP from the Bundestag and to guarantee single-party government in future. However, the Social Democratic Party estimated that such a change might condemn them to a permanent role as opposition party, since the Christian Democrats had an advantage in the constituencies. For this and other reasons, the matter was not pursued further during the lifetime of the grand coalition. In Eire, there have been two referenda to try to replace the single transferable vote system by the United Kingdom system, the most recent of which was in 1968. On both occasions, the electorate voted to retain STV. In France, on the other hand, the parties of the left, who felt unfairly disadvantaged by the two-ballot system, promised to introduce a

form of proportional representation, and did so for the 1986
legislative elections and for the first direct elections for the
regional councils held on the same day. The Chirac government,
however, re-introduced the previous elector system in September
1986.

It is in the United Kingdom, however, that electoral reform has
been thoroughly and frequently debated, even though no radical
change in the electoral system has ever been introduced. This is
because of the piecemeal development of the United Kingdom
electoral system, which pre-dates the invention of modern
political parties and which has never had to be redesigned after
some revolution or occupation by a foreign power, and where
therefore many anomalies and inequities have accumulated over
the decades. Alternative systems have been considered and
recommended. An all-party conference in 1917 unanimously
condemned the 'first-past-the-post' system, but its members
could not agree upon any one alternative to it. In 1929, the
Labour government actually succeeded in passing a bill through
the House of Commons to replace the simple-majority system by
a variation called the 'alternative vote', but failed to get the
measure through the House of Lords. The two general elections of
1974, with their inability to produce safe single-party majorities
and their gross inequity to the Liberal Party, revived the issue of
electoral reform. The Hansard Society produced an influential
report in 1976, analysing the faults of the system, and
recommending the adoption of either STV or a system very
similar to that of West Germany. The Social and Liberal Democrats and the SPD agree on the need for electoral reform as a
matter of urgency.

The United Kingdom system is defended because:

(*a*) it tends to produce safe majorities for one party, which can
then form a government, and provides a large number of seats for
a second party, which is then the officially-recognised opposition
and 'alternative government';

(*b*) it is simple to understand and to operate, compared to STV
or proportional representation systems: the voter makes one cross
opposite the name of the preferred candidate, and the candidate
with the most votes wins;

(*c*) it provides the possibility of personal identification between the member of parliament and the constituency.

It is criticised because:

(*a*) it greatly exaggerates relatively small changes in electoral opinion at elections, so that large differences in party strengths result;

(*b*) it is unfair to minor parties, unless, like the Scottish National Party, they have regionally-concentrated support;

(*c*) it leaves large regions of the country represented by only one party, despite strong support for other parties in those regions;

(*d*) it does not, in fact, *guarantee* either a working majority for one party or a fair result (in the sense that the party with the most votes does not always form the government, because another party has more seats);

(*e*) votes in some areas are worth more than votes in other areas, because of differences in the size of constituencies.

Consider the following facts:

(*a*) in 1974, the Liberals got 19.3 per cent of the vote in the February election, and 18.3 per cent in the October election, yet obtained only 2.2 and 2.1 per cent respectively of the seats in the House of Commons;

(*b*) since the second world war, no party has won fifty per cent of the vote, yet only one government out of thirteen has had less than fifty per cent of the seats in the Commons;

(*c*) in 1951 and in February 1974, the party which obtained the most votes did not obtain the most seats and did not form the government;

(*d*) in 1979, Newcastle upon Tyne Central constituency had 23,678 voters on the register, Manchester Central had 31,213 and Liverpool Scotland constituency 32,303; yet Buckingham constituency had 103,511 voters, Basildon 103,595 and Bromsgrove and Redditch constituency 104,375; in other words, the three small city constituencies had three MPs, yet together they had fewer electors than any one of the three rural or suburban constituencies! (This ignores other anomalies concerning Wales, Scotland and Northern Ireland which are the result of special legislation.) Periodic boundary changes are made by the Boundary Commissioners, who report to parliament, but these never remove such anomalies entirely, and have occurred too infrequently to keep pace with changes of population.[6]

(*e*) in 1983, the Conservative government was returned with an increased number of seats, yet it had received a smaller share of the vote than in 1979; the SDP-Liberal Alliance with 26 per cent of the vote (compared to Labour's 28.3 per cent) won only 3.5 per cent of the seats (while Labour won 37.8 per cent).

Certainly, were some form of proportional representation, or even STV, to be adopted for general elections in the UK, coalition government would be necessary. Experience in other European countries does not suggest that this need necessarily be weak government or unstable government. Neither the Labour nor the Conservative parties could expect to have an absolute majority of seats in the foreseeable future, which is one reason why both these parties are generally opposed to electoral reform.

Some commentators argue that the United Kingdom electoral system is not only unfair, it is also productive of inefficient government, for it encourages 'adversary politics', the idea that all issues have two, but only two, mutually incompatible solutions. It means, for instance, that the Labour government nationalises the steel industry, the Conservative government denationalises it, and the next Labour government renationalises it, and that similar violent swings of policy are found in the fields of industrial relations, education, housing and public finance. Such critics argue that a different electoral system would encourage compromise, as it does in other European countries, by producing coalition governments which would have to seek a consensus, and would have to try to win the 'middle ground' of politics if it were to hope for continuing electoral support. The system in the United Kingdom, on the other hand, seems to reward extremism in each of the two main parties. Politicians who embody the principles of the party most clearly get adopted for safe seats and climb highest in the party hierarchy, eventually becoming ministers in governments. Moderation is seen as a weakness. However, there is another side to the argument. In countries such as the German Federal Republic, voices are heard in criticism of the political compromises which proportional electoral systems produce. These critics maintain that the voter is not able to make a clear and decisive choice, and that negotiations which surround the process of government formation *after* an election pay little heed to the wishes of the electorate. Compromise, in other words, may be interpreted as misrepresentation of the voters' decision in the election.

Finally, it should be noted that some political systems incorporate another method of allowing the people directly to affect policy through their vote, by referenda and plebiscites. France, Austria, Italy, Switzerland and Eire, for example, all have such devices and have made use of them. In France, President de Gaulle made use of referenda on the Algerian issue and on the mode of election of the President; in Switzerland, referenda have been held on votes for women and the status of foreign workers; in Italy, they have been employed to decide on the matter of divorce law; in Eire, referenda were held on membership of the European Community and reform of the electoral system. In the UK, the referendum is a novel institution, not laid down in any general law. Instead, it has twice been employed on an *ad hoc* basis: once to consult the electorate on the matter of the United Kingdom's membership of the European Community (1975), and – for the electorates of Wales and Scotland – on the question of devolution (1979). As with arguments about electoral reform, so similarly the desirability of the referendum as an institution has its critics and its proponents. On the one hand, it has been termed the **'Pontius Pilate' of politics,**[7] since it enables a political party to 'wash its hands' of an issue (such as membership of the European Community) by declining to take a decisive stance; it passes the responsibility to the voter – and can be condemned for diluting responsible government. On the other hand, especially on issues which divide the country deeply, such as divorce in Italy, and on matters which do not relate very directly to the fundamental differences between parties, it can be regarded as a useful supplement to the democratic process, which 'trusts the people'. The debate continues, but what seems clear is that the introduction of the referendum as an institution will not leave electoral systems, parties or the role of governments unaffected.

Notes

1. In March 1986 the election of a right-wing majority, albeit a narrow one, in the French National Assembly forced the incumbent president of the left into a period of "cohabitation" with a coalition government of the right led by J. Chirac.

2. Prior to 1986 there were only 491 constituencies. For the 1986 elections a system of proportional representation like that of the Fourth Republic was introduced and the number of seats in the Assembly was increased to 577.

3. Provincial electoral systems differ only in detail from that used in federal elections.

4. Because of the change in government in October 1982, a general election was held in March 1983, eighteen months ahead of schedule.

5. Quoted by Cornelius O'Leary, 'Ireland: the North and South', in Finer, (ed.), *Adversary Politics and Electoral Reform* (Anthony Wigram, 1975), p. 155.

6. The 1983 election was fought on the basis of constituencies revised only a few months earlier by the Boundary Commissioners. Although the most glaring discrepancies were removed some substantial differences remained; for example, among English constituencies Isle of Wight had 94,226 electors, while Hammersmith had 46,178.

7. S. E. Finer, '*Introduction*', *op. cit.*, p. 18.

5
LINKAGE ORGANISATIONS: POLITICAL PARTIES

Party-systems and democracy

In chapter 2 the role of political parties and their competition with each other through elections were claimed to be essential features of modern liberal democracies. All western European states that are classed as democracies have competitive party-systems, and it is hard to imagine how a democracy would function effectively without parties. A party-system – the term used to denote the several parties within a political system and their interrelationships – structures political competition through elections, so that voters can make clear and meaningful choices when they cast their ballots. It allows all the significant groupings in society, such as social classes, regions, linguistic groups, as well as those social and economic 'interests' which are thought to be politically important, to participate in politics in a coherent manner. It provides competing 'teams' which can act as the government, or become challengers to the governing parties. It transmits the demands of the citizen to the governing authorities: to ministers, local councils, parliaments, presidents – and informs the citizen of what those authorities have done. In relation to the diagram of the political system used in chapter 2, parties are 'linkage organisations', intermediaries between the people and the powers that be, between 'us' and 'them'.

This function of acting as a two-way linkage organisation is what all competitive party-systems have in common. Where only one party is permitted to exist, as happened in Nazi Germany, or as is the case in Cuba or the Soviet Union, the single party tends to identify with the government, with the state authorities, with a single, overriding ideology, and is not able or willing to concern itself with the wishes of all the people and of all types of social group. The challenge of Solidarity in Poland to the ruling Communist Party there is a recent indication of the failure of a one-party system to transmit popular demands effectively to the authorities.

But, although all competitive party-systems share, by and large, the same functions, great differences obviously emerge when the composition of national party-systems is more closely examined. Even in the same country, changes of circumstances, a new constitution or electoral-system, or social and economic developments can result in a changed party-system. The party-systems of Germany before the first world war, in the Weimar republic, in the early years of the post-war West German state and today, have all been markedly different in terms of the number of parties, the types of parties and the ideological positions adopted by those parties. The French party-system today is very different from that of the Fourth Republic in the early 1950s. The formation of the Social Democratic Party in the UK and its close association with the Liberal Party promised to change the British party-system more radically than has anything since the rise to prominence of the Labour Party after the first world war.

Another type of party-system difference is the efficacy with which parties fulfil their 'linkage' functions. Parties may become too similar to provide the voter with a clear choice. They may be too involved with the system of government, with all its privileges and powers, to transmit effectively the demands of the voting public, and too bureaucratic and complex in organisation to communicate readily with the public. In West Germany, for example, critics of the party-system claim that the 'establishment' parties in Bonn have many of these failings, and that fresh parties must be formed to revivify the party-system. The Social Democratic–Liberal alliance in the UK claimed success because it was trying to change established patterns in the UK party-system.

Four major features (or dimensions) of party-systems can be distinguished.

1. Most obviously, the *number* of parties which exist, or which present candidates at elections, can vary. Some countries have a two-party system (Malta, for instance); others have three significant parties, such as Ireland; yet others have numerous parties, such as Italy or Belgium. Much depends on what one is

counting: the parties which are successful in winning seats in the legislature, those with a certain significant percentage of the vote, those which can realistically hope to form, or participate in a government, or all parties which possess an identifiable label, present candidates at elections, and have some form of party organisation which persists over time.

2. Even where the number of parties is the same, the *relative size* of parties may differ from country to country. Take the UK in 1979, and West Germany in 1980, for example; both had three significant national parties winning seats. But in the UK, the Conservatives got 44 per cent, Labour 37 per cent and the Liberals 14 per cent of the vote, while in West Germany the Christian Democrats got 44½ per cent, the Social Democrats 43 per cent, and the Free Democrats 10½ per cent. In the UK the Conservatives obtained 53 per cent of the seats (an absolute majority), Labour 42 per cent, the Liberals only about two per cent. In West Germany, their proportional electoral system gave the Christian Democrats 45½ per cent, the Social Democrats 44 per cent, but the Free Democrats 10½ per cent – five times the share of the British Liberals, who had obtained a larger share of the vote!

3. The *cleavages* which form the foundation of party conflict may vary. In the UK, broadly, social class, in association with an urban–rural division, forms the basis of differences among the parties. In Belgium, alongside regional identity and class, language plays an important role. In Italy, Spain and, to a lesser extent, West Germany and France, religion is a factor as well as social class. Regional parties exist in the UK, Spain and Italy. Agrarian parties break into the pattern of class conflict in the party systems of Scandinavia and Holland. Now ecological parties have appeared in France, the UK, West Germany and the Netherlands, with varying degrees of electoral success. Thus the 'menu' of parties offered to the voter is different in each country, and changes in each country over time.

4. Party-systems vary in terms of the *ideological distance* between different parties. In some cases, such as West Germany, all the principal parties are quite close to each other in ideological terms. No extremist party has more than a minute membership or

gathers even one per cent of the vote at general elections – and parties which reject the democratic order altogether can be banned by the Constitutional Court. In Italy, on the other hand, the Communists and Christian Democrats, the two largest parties, are at extremes from each other ideologically, as are many of the Ulster parties, which have totally opposed views on the relationship which Ulster should have to the United Kingdom and to Eire. Two indicators of ideological distance are:

(*a*) whether parties, at least in principle, are able to contemplate forming coalitions with each other, should that be necessary to obtain a legislative majority; those which cannot form coalitions with some other party presumably have incompatible ideological positions with reference to the other party;

(*b*) whether some parties are 'anti-system': that is, do they profess to seek to overthrow the existing regime, whether by peaceful or violent means.

Of course, it must be recognised that there can be considerable ideological distance between sections of the same party: the West German Social Democrats, the Labour and Conservative parties in the UK, the Italian Christian Democrats, for instance, all contain within one party groups or 'wings' which may differentiate themselves from other groups very distinctively, on principles as well as on particular policies. When the question of coalition arises, it may be that sections of parties may join with other parties, even if the party to which they belong cannot.

Having established that party-systems vary, and the ways that they can vary one from another, there remains the question of *why* they vary.

Obviously, the party-system in a society reflects its history and signifies its degree of homogeneity. If a nation is deeply divided – by class, by race, by religion or language – its parties will probably reflect those divisions. Historical experiences, such as occupation by an enemy in wartime, resistance to such occupation (France, Italy), civil war (Spain, Eire), religious divisions and anti-clericalism (France), or the overthrow of a dictatorship (Portugal), can be reflected in party distinctions. The law may impose limitations on the type of party that may exist, as in the German Federal Republic. Or the electoral system may make it difficult for small parties to survive or new parties to establish themselves: the United Kingdom's 'winner-take-all' constituency-based system which discriminates against smaller parties (such as the Liberals), and the restricted proportional representation systems of West Germany and Sweden which deny representation to parties which obtain less than some stated percentage of the vote, are examples.

Party systems of western Europe

By describing briefly the party systems of seven western European countries, the variations in the number of parties, their ideological basis, and their ideological distance from each other, can all be illustrated.

(a) the United Kingdom

Sometimes misleadingly characterised as the most typical of the two-party systems, the United Kingdom party-system has never had fewer than three of its parties represented in the House of Commons (though it is true to say that since the end of the second world war, only two parties have formed governments, alternating with each other). The Conservative Party is mainly a middle-class party, strongest in the south and the rural areas of England, and primarily concerned with preserving a free-market economy alongside a limited welfare-state provision of social services. The Labour Party, with a socialist programme, draws its support from working-class voters, more especially in the north of England, south Wales and the urban areas of Scotland. It has close links with the trade unions, many of which are affiliated to the party. The Liberal Democrats are strongest in the south west and in Scotland, but have strength in a variety of areas, such as Liverpool and some of the London suburban districts. Its supporters are mainly middle class and tend to be younger than those of other parties, on average. Its policies are generally mid-way between those of the Conservative and Labour parties, between free enterprise and collectivism. The Scottish and Welsh Nationalist parties, and the Unionist and nationalist parties of Ulster, have limited regional strength. The new Social Democratic Party, founded initially by four former leading members of the Labour Party, made rapid strides since its 'launch' in March 1981 as an alternative to an increasingly left-wing Labour Party, since the Labour Party annual conference set about changing its constitution in favour of the conference and the National Executive Committee at the expense of the powers and discretion of the parliamentary Labour Party. The Social Democratic Party then attracted many Labour members of the House of Commons, as well as one Conservative, to its parliamentary ranks, quickly won a considerable paid-up membership and high levels of support in opinion polls, local council elections and by-elections, and produced an electoral sensation when Shirley Williams, one of its founders, won a by-election in November 1981 in the hitherto 'safe' Conservative seat of Crosby.

The Social and Liberal Democrats would not object to coalitions with other parties (the Liberals having agreed to a Liberal–Labour 'pact' in the House of Commons in 1978), and a Liberal–SPD Alliance fought the 1983 and 1987 elections. It is less clear that the Conservatives or the Labour Party – which still has bitter memories of Ramsay MacDonald's coalition with the Conservatives in 1931 – would ever agree to involve themselves in coalition arrangements, although it is possible that individuals, or even groups, from those parties might have some sympathy for a coalition, should it appear necessary.

Extremist parties sometimes receive publicity, but appear to have very little popular support at times of an election. The electoral system operates against smaller parties unless these are regionally concentrated, as with the Scottish Nationalists, for instance.

Table 7   The general election of 11 June 1987

	Votes (%)	Seats (no.)	Seats (%)
Conservatives	42.3	375	57.7
Labour	30.8	229	35.2
Alliance	22.6	22	3.4
Scottish Nationalists	1.3	3	0.5
Welsh Nationalists	0.4	3	0.5

(In addition there were 17 seats in N. Ireland)

(b) France

France now has a five-party system. This situation has developed out of the multi-party system of the Fourth Republic and early years of the Fifth-Republic, partly as a consequence of the overwhelming support given to the Gaullist Party until de Gaulle's resignation in 1969, which also encouraged opposition to de Gaulle to coalesce on the left of the party spectrum, and partly due to the influence of the presidential elections on the creation of party alliances.

The five major parties are:

1. the Gaullists, a right-wing and conservative party with special strength in middle-class urban and some rural areas;

2. the Union for French Democracy, a confederation of parties (see above, p. 59) within which the dominant element to date has been the Republican Party, the party of the former President, Giscard d'Estaing, which, although conservative, has been more pragmatic in its approach to economic and social issues than the Gaullists; it attracts many votes from liberals and uncommitted voters of the centre;

3. the Socialist Party of President Mitterrand, which now has a moderate programme and includes in its voting support members of all social classes, though it relies predominantly upon white-collar and manual-worker votes:

4. the Communist Party, which draws its sharply declining support primarily from traditional working-class urban areas, and which has, in the past at least, closely followed the Moscow line.

5. the National Front, led by Le Pen, which campaigns on a racist and populist 'law-and-order' platform.

The two parties on the right have been able to form coalitions or 'working arrangements' to some degree, and, though they have varied in relative size from election to election, the Republicans became the senior partner at government level after the election of Giscard d'Estaing to the presidency in 1974, though the Gaullists were still the largest party in terms of parliamentary seats. The two parties on the left had an agreed 'common programme' in 1972 and joined together on the second ballot at parliamentary and presidential elections (to make optimal use of the two-ballot electoral system) until the Communists left government in 1984. The success of the Socialists in the presidential and legislative elections of both 1981 and 1988 confirmed them not only as the dominant party of the left, but as the largest party in the state.

The basis of the divisions within the French party-system is social class, complicated by regional affiliations, attitudes to the church, and historical traditions reaching back to the first French revolution.

Table 8   The national elections of 1988

	Presidential elections			Legislative elections		
	1st ballot (%)	2nd ballot (%)		Votes (%)*	Seats (no.)	(%)
Socialists	34.1	54.02	—	37.5	276	48
Gaullists	19.8	45.97	—	40.4	128	21
Republicans	16.5	—	—		130	23
Communists	6.8		—	11.3	27	5
National Front	14.4			9.8	1	0.2

1. includes notes for non-affiliated candidates of right, 13 of whom were elected.

(c) the Federal Republic of Germany

When the Bonn Republic was established in 1949 and the first post-war national elections were held, it was feared that the multi-party system of the inter-war period would re-establish itself. Nine parties obtained seats in the first Bundestag. By 1961, however, in part because of the electoral system, in part also because of the rejection of minor and extremist parties by the electorate, only three parties still had parliamentary representation: the Christian Democrats,[1] a right-wing, conservative party based on identification with the teachings of the Christian churches; the Social Democrats, who had broadened their electoral appeal by abandoning Marxism and adopting a more pragmatic platform, the Godesberg Programme, in 1959; and the liberal Free Democrats, a party which espoused the free market economy and which was the most nationalistic of the three parties.

The Christian Democrats have formed coalitions with the Free

Democrats on seven occasions since 1949. In 1966 the two largest parties, the Christian Democrats and the Social Democrats, formed a 'Grand Coalition' to cope with West Germany's first serious economic recession since 1949. When that alliance came to an end at the 1969 general election, a coalition of the SPD and Free Democrats was formed, which lasted until quarrels over the budget brought it to an end in October 1982, when a Christian Democrat–Free Democrat coalition replaced it.

Because the two largest parties are each unable at present to win an absolute majority of votes (normally essential, under the West German electoral system, if they are to secure a majority of seats) they are forced to ally with the much smaller Free Democrats in order to form a government. In the *Länder* parliaments (the provincial legislatures) sometimes one party has an absolute majority, but here, too, such coalitions with the Free Democrats by one of the larger parties have been usual, though the recent decline of the FDP and the electoral successes of the Green Party have complicated the situation in Berlin, Hamburg and Hesse.

Table 9   The federal election of January 1987

	Votes (%)*	Seats (no.)	Seats (%)
Christian Democrats	44.3	223	44.9
Social Democrats	37.0	186	37.4
Free Democrats	9.1	46	9.3
Green Party	8.3	42	8.4

(*based on second votes: i.e. votes for party lists)

Although one extreme right-wing party, the National Democrats, had a brief success in local and provincial elections in the period 1966–9, it failed to get the necessary five per cent of votes to qualify for seats at the 1969 general election, and its support has since dwindled to less than one per cent of the electorate. The Basic Law erects constitutional prohibitions against parties which are opposed to the democratic order embodied in the constitution, and two parties (in 1952 a right-wing extremist party and in 1956 the Communist Party) have been banned by the Constitutional Court, though a new

Communist Party formed in 1969 and has survived unchallenged in the Court. More recently, the ecological movement has formed its own party, the 'Greens', and they have won representation in eight *Länder* parliaments, Bavaria, Bremen, Baden-Württemburg, Berlin, Lower Saxony, Hamburg, Hesse, and Rhineland-Pfalz, and in the 1983 election won representation in the Bundestag.

(d) the Irish Republic

The Irish party-system is composed chiefly of two opposed Republican parties, Fianna Fail and Fine Gael, whose differences have their origins in the period when Eire was winning its independence from Britain. Fine Gael was the 'pro-treaty' party, which supported the negotiated settlement with Britain that partitioned Ireland, whilst Fianna Fail took a more uncompromising line. The class-based parties to be found in the UK, France, Italy, the Scandinavian countries and West Germany are not to be found in the Irish party-system except for the small Labour Party. Fianna Fail and Fine Gael possess areas of local and regional strength, and the electoral system of the single transferable vote reinforces the importance of personal, rather than ideological difference at elections, since voters need not vote exclusively for one party or another. Fine Gael and the Labour Party have formed coalitions, but Fianna Fail may perhaps also be ready to consider coalition in order to form a government in the future, given the small differences in electoral support for the two main parties. The Irish party-system is thus without parallel in western Europe, being a system dominated by two parties, but lacking any explicit social, linguistic, religious or ideological cleavage which corresponds to the historic distinction between the two parties.

Table 10   The general election of February 1987

	Votes (%)*	Seats (no.)	Seats (%)
Fianna Fail	44	81	49
Fine Gael	27	50	30
Progressive Democrats	12	14	9
Labour	6	12	7
Others	11	8	5

(* = first preference votes)

(e) Italy

The post-war republic, created in 1948 to replace the monarchy, developed a system of parties based on cleavages of social class and religion. Some of the parties in Italy trace their roots to the turbulent inter-war period: the Socialists, Communists, Christian Democrats, and the small neo-fascist parties of the extreme right. Others have formed to fill small gaps in the centre of the party spectrum, or have split away from other parties.

The present system of parties in Italy is dominated by the Christian Democrats on the right (though this party is broad enough to include a wide variety of ideological groups within it), bound closely to the Catholic church, strongest in small towns and rural areas, and always in government since the war, whilst on the left the Communists, always in opposition but comfortably the second largest party in Italian politics, is very dependent upon northern and urban support. Between these two, there exists a collection of liberal, republican and socialist parties which have been collectively crucial to the formation of Christian Democratic-led coalitions, the socialists finally winning the premiership from 1983 to 1987. As well as small extreme right-wing parties, such as the MSI (Italian Social Movement), there

Table 11   *The general election of June 1987*

	Votes (%)	Seats (no.)
Christian Democrats	34.3	234
Communists	26.6	177
Socialists	14.3	94
MSI	5.9	35
Republicans	3.7	21
Social Democrats	3.0	17
Radicals	2.6	13
Greens	2.5	13
Liberals	2.1	11
Proletarian Democracy	1.7	8

(Other parties obtained 7 seats)

are small regional parties, such as the South Tyrolean People's Party, which seeks autonomy for their region.

A central question about the Italian party-system has been whether, or when, a 'historic compromise' will occur, with the Christian Democrats agreeing to share power with the Communists.[2] The bitter rivalry between these two 'ideological' parties, sharply and amusingly depicted at local level in the *Don Camillo* novels of Guareschi, has been moderated somewhat by the more liberal 'Eurocommunist' stance of Communist leaders in Italy, by the violence of political extremists which all orthodox parties (including the Communists) abhor, and by the reduction in the coalition options open to the Christian Democrats as their support, and that of their small allies, fluctuates and declines.

(f) Sweden

Sweden, Norway and Denmark share rather similar party-systems, since each possesses several class-based parties, with dominant social democratic parties and small communist parties.

The Swedish party-system consists of a large Social Democratic Party, often supported by over half the voters, and which had ruled almost continuously, alone or in coalition, until 1976; this party is in competition with a conservative party (the Moderates), a liberal party and an agrarian party (the Centre Party), as well as with the Communists.

Social Democratic coalitions have been formed with the Centre Party (regarded to some degree as a kind of rural working-class party) or they have governed with Communist support. From 1976 to 1982, alternative governments, coalitions of

Table 12   The general election of September 1985

	Votes (%)	Seats (no.)	Seats (%)
Social Democrats	44.7	159	45.6
Communists Left	5.4	19	5.4
Moderates	21.3	76	21.8
Centre Party	12.4	44	12.6
People's Party	14.2	51	14.6

Conservatives and Liberals with the Centre Party, consigned the Social Democrats to opposition until they returned as a minority government in September 1982.

The Swedish party-system well-illustrates how some countries enjoy a lack of substantial ideological cleavages or anti-system parties, and how a multi-party system can operate without governmental instability or difficulty in putting together coalitions.

(g) Belgium

The Belgian party system reflects the superimposition of the division of the country into French-speaking and Flemish-speaking areas onto the more usual social-class divisions which are found elsewhere in Western Europe.

The largest parties are the Social Christians (a Catholic and predominantly middle-class party), the Socialists and the Liberals. The high salience of linguistic and regional issues in recent years has resulted in these three, and also the ecologists, being separately organised in Flanders and Wallonia. In addition, three linguistic parties, two Flemish and one French-speaking have gained representation in parliament, while the small Communist Party lost its remaining seats in the last elections.

Table 13   The general election of December 1987

	Votes (%)	Seats (no.)	Seats (%)
Flemish Social Christians	19.5	43	20.3
Francophone Socialists	15.7	40	18.9
Flemish Socialists	14.9	32	15.1
Flemish Liberals	11.5	25	11.2
Francophone Liberals	9.4	23	10.9
Francophone Social Christians	8.0	19	9.0
Volksunie	8.0	16	7.6
Flemish Ecologists	4.5	6	3.0
Francophone Ecologists	2.6	3	1.5
Vlaams Blok	1.9	2	1.0
Francophone Democratic Front	1.2	3	1.5
Others	2.8	0	

The inability of any one party to secure a majority of legislative seats by itself means that Belgium cannot escape having coalition governments – usually from some combination of the three largest parties, though a linguistic party has been included more recently. The need for multi-party coalitions where religious, as well as other cleavages may complicate policy-making has led to a tendency toward unstable government in the past few years.

The functions of political parties

For as long as modern political parties have existed, critics have accused them of being detrimental to the political health of the nation, of encouraging selfish and partisan interests, rather than the 'good of all', of being divisive, demagogic and even anti-democratic. But, whatever truth may lurk in these criticisms, any attempt to operate a democratic form of political life in the complex and economically advanced states of today, in which political parties played *no* part, would surely fail. It is interesting to note that the only serious efforts in the twentieth century in western Europe to create a political regime without party competition were all associated with dictatorship or one-party tyranny. The 'rule of the colonels' in Greece between April 1967 and June 1974 involved the prohibition of parties, but, in effect, the prohibition of democratic politics as well. The dictatorships of Hitler and Mussolini, of Franco in Spain and of Salazar in Portugal, were all based on 'movements' or parties that were closely identified with the state and which were, by law, the only parties permitted to exist in those years of authoritarian rule.

Parties, for all their faults, perform several extremely necessary functions which enable democratic societies to maintain and develop democratic politics. In some cases, it might be possible to imagine alternative methods of fulfilling those functions. In other cases, it would be difficult to find satisfactory substitutes for parties. Parties carry out a *combination* of necessary functions, and do so more effectively than could any alternative institutions.

There are five essential functions which parties perform in democracies, each of which is an important contribution to democratic politics:

1. Most obviously, parties *represent* different interests or social groups within the political arena: at elections, in parliament, in

local government, in the European Community and in other institutions. They voice the demands or criticisms of their 'clientele': the working class, in the case of the United Kingdom Labour Party or the Italian Communist Party; the farmers, in the case of Scandinavian agrarian parties; the middle-class and business interests, in the case of conservative parties; special causes, in the case of ecology parties or nationalist parties. Parties will speak for these groups and interests through their elected members, by means of delegations to ministers, in the context of election campaigns, and so forth. Without parties, such groups and interests would be confined to sporadic pressure group activity, their interests would be represented less coherently and less effectively.

2. Most parties endeavour to obtain enough support at elections to enable them to *form the government*, or to participate in a coalition with other parties. Those that fail have the opportunity to act as opposition to the government: criticising it, challenging its decisions, and trying to demonstrate that they could do the job better – given the opportunity! Of course, some small parties may never have any realistic chance of being included in a government, particularly if they are extremist parties, and hence difficult for other, more moderate, parties to ally with, or if they are concerned with some single overriding issue, such as nuclear energy, withdrawal from the Common Market or regional autonomy, but even small parties may hope to influence the government by their criticism or their representation in the legislature. The wooing of small parties by the Labour government of the UK in 1979, after it had lost its majority and the pact with the Liberals had been terminated, showed how, in some circumstances, even very small parties can obtain important concessions or patronage from the government. The West German liberal party, the Free Democrats, has been a member of governing coalitions in Bonn for more years since 1949 than either of the two larger parties, because its share of seats in the Bundestag has been necessary to construct a governing majority. Yet the FDP has fluctuated between only five and thirteen per cent of the vote. Parties want to be in power, or to influence those who are in power, in order to realise their policies. Governmental office is the prize in the political game because parties represent

their supporters' wishes, and seek to translate those wishes into governmental programmes.

3. Parties act as *channels of recruitment* of political leaders. In liberal democracies, based on governments responsible to parliaments, it is rare indeed for the head of the government or for other ministers not to be long-serving members of political parties. Exceptionally, political leaders can be brought in from 'outside': Ernest Bevin in the wartime coalition headed by Churchill was a trade-union leader rather than a parliamentarian (though of course he was a long-standing member of the Labour Party); Ludwig Erhard, the Minister of Economics in Adenauer's early governments, only joined the Christian Democrats a few months before becoming minister; in France, where such exceptions are not quite as rare, Raymond Barre, Prime Minister under Giscard d'Estaing, was appointed to that office before joining Giscard's party.[3] But the overwhelming majority of mayors, Chancellors, Prime Ministers, leaders of local councils and members of cabinets reach such positions of public importance only after many years' service in their party. First there is the hard work within the party organisation, and perhaps election to party offices; then comes the struggle to enter the legislature, followed by a period on the back benches, making speeches, serving on committees, nursing a constituency; this is followed by the slow climb up the ladder of promotion until appointment as a minister, and, eventually perhaps, election as party leader. Even the step from party leader to leader of the government can take a long time: Willy Brandt and François Mitterrand both lost several general elections before they were eventually successful.

4. Parties offer the most important (though not the only) channel of *political participation* for the public. Members of the public who bother to join a political party have opportunities open to them to select candidates who will represent the party – which, in a safe seat, may be equivalent to nominating them as a member of the National Assembly, the Bundestag or the House of Commons. Party members can influence the programme which a party finally offers to the electorate as a whole, and which, if the party is successful at an election, may pass through the legislature as government policy. Party members can serve as delegates to party conferences, hold local or national offices within the party

organisation, and even hope for selection themselves as candidates on behalf of the party for some public office. The fact that so few members of the public *do* join parties (see above, chapter 2) increases the relative influence of those who are members. By offering people such opportunities for democratic participation, parties contribute to the reinforcement and spread of democratic ideas in the political system.[4]

5. Finally, parties provide two-way *channels of political communication* between the public and the government. They transmit the demands and opinions of the public (especially, of course, their own members and supporters) to ministers or to the legislature. In return, they justify or criticise – and thus clarify the complexities of – government policy for the ordinary citizen, at elections, most obviously and intensely, but also through the mass media (in the UK, through party political broadcasts, for example), at public meetings or party events, or, very simply and directly, in conversations with constituents, such as the 'surgeries' which many members of parliament in the UK hold regularly at weekends in their constituencies.

The organisation of parties

Political parties manage to perform such a range of functions by efficient organisation and through appropriate structures. Nearly all parties of any significance in the various party systems of western Europe possess similar structures, which have developed in similar ways. This is not surprising; the development of party structures has often occurred in response to changes in the organisation of politics, and the politics of states such as the UK, Germany, France and the Scandinavian states have, through the years, though not always simultaneously of course, undergone similar stages of democratisation, increases in the scope and complexity of government, and increases in the expectations which the public have of government. And parties, like other organisations, learn from each other about structural and organisational improvement. One example of this is the attention given by the West German liberal party (the Free Democrats) to the successes of the United Kingdom Liberal Party in Liverpool. The Germans were so impressed that they devoted a major brochure to the story of the Liverpool Liberals' victories in council elections, which they distributed to local branches of the FDP. Cross-national party links, such as the Liberal and Socialist Internationals and the European organisations of parties in the parliament of the European Community, also act as opportunities for spreading ideas about party organisation.

Three distinct levels of party organisation can be distinguished.

1. The earliest in the history of party development is *parliamentary organisation*. (Although, once a party-system in the legislature was established, later parties – such as the Labour Party in the UK, or the 'Greens' in West Germany – were founded on the basis of extra-parliamentary initiative and organisation.) Parties first developed in many countries from the tendency for members of a parliament who shared similar ideas or principles to associate together, to discuss problems and co-ordinate legislative strategies. This happened with the Whigs and the Tories (forerunners of the Liberals and Conservatives) in England at the beginning of the eighteenth century; it happened in France with the groups of the National Assembly in the French revolution; it happened in Germany with the various liberal and radical groupings of the 1848 Frankfurt parliament. Today, the parliamentary party exists to co-ordinate support for the government or criticism of it. It often has – provided it is large enough – its own structure of committees dealing with specialised sectors of policy, its own chairman and other officers, and, in some cases, such as the Conservative Party in the UK, it elects the party leader. An important official of the parliamentary party is the 'Whip' or business manager, who is responsible for communication between the party leadership and the backbenchers, for ensuring party unity in crucial legislative votes, and for arranging speakers for parliamentary debates.

2. Since members of parliamentary parties wished to secure their own re-election, they fostered the growth of party organisation at the level of the *constituency*. This is the 'grass-roots' level of party organisation, where local party members come into direct contact with the voter, especially at election time. Indeed, in the nineteenth century (with the exception of some working-class parties, such as the German Social Democrats) many local parties existed almost exclusively

as organisations to contest elections, and went into hibernation at other times. Today, local parties are not only organisations concerned with election campaigns; they are also involved in fund-raising, membership recruitment, acting as communication channels between the electorate and the authorities, selecting candidates for public and party office, discussing policy ideas and perhaps preparing motions for party conference, and numerous other tasks.

3. Local party groups came together to form *national party organisations.* These usually consist of a headquarters, generally with professional staff and secretarial help, perhaps also including sections for research and the production of party publications. Authority is exercised by an elected national executive committee, which takes day-to-day decisions and implements the resolutions of the national party conference, which is usually the 'sovereign' body in a political party. The extent of the authority of the national party organisation will vary from one party to another, and may often be a matter of controversy within a party. In France, for instance, the power of local 'notables' who jealously preserve their independence of party headquarters is one cause of the relative weakness of the national party organisation of some parties of the right and centre. The national party also acts as a link between local party organisations and the parliamentary party, and – as in the Labour Party – may arbitrate in disputes between local parties and the parliamentary party. In many parties, the leader is elected by the conference, or by some associated 'electoral college' arrangement (for example, the principle West German parties, the French parties, and the Labour and Liberal parties in the UK). Especially in federal states, such as Austria, Switzerland and West Germany, there may also be a regional or provincial level of party organisation. In 'unitary' states, such as the UK, this intermediary level may be entirely an administrative convenience (except for the separate Scottish and Welsh levels of party organisation), but in West Germany, for example, it is of great political importance because it parallels the regional level of government and of elections to *Länder* parliaments, so is responsible for campaigning for those elections, holding regional party congresses and so on.

The most recent level of party organisation to be created is that of the European Community. At this level, cross-national parties have been formed, from groups of similar parties represented, or seeking representation, in the parliament of the Community. The first direct election to that parliament in 1979 gave considerable organisational impetus to these transnational parties.

Many parties have auxiliary organisations which may officially be part of the structure of the party or which may be, at least nominally, independently organised. Most parties, for example, have a youth organisation. These often act as special links to younger citizens, particularly those just coming up to voting age or at university, and are usually a potent and radical influence on party policy. They may also act as 'nurseries' from which future leadership talent can be obtained. Some parties have separate women's organisations, although such separate organisation is coming to be regarded as patronising and redundant. Various interest-groups may have formal organisational links to parties. The trade unions in the UK which are affiliated to the Labour Party (to which party, indeed, they gave birth in the early years of this century) is the most obvious example, but farmers, Catholics, members of professions such as doctors and lawyers, are all examples of other groups with close links with continental parties.

In an ideal situation, a united party uses its organisation to perform its various functions, to win elections and defeat its opponents, to refine its policies and ensure a steady supply of leadership talent. But parties not only engage in national and local politics: they also have their own internal political differences. The recent conflicts in the British Labour Party demonstrate how organisation becomes a prize in the struggle between factions in a party. The issues of how the leader (and thus potential Prime Minister) was to be elected in the party, who was to draft the electoral manifesto, and whether Labour members of parliament were to be subject to reselection procedures, were conflicts about the distribution of power in the party between the moderate and pragmatic wing, based on the parliamentary party, and the more radical and ideological national party organisation. Most parties experience factional disputes from time to time. In some parties, it may be almost a permanent condition. The French Socialists have an influential left-wing and intellectual faction, as does the West German Social Democratic Party. Many West European communist parties have been torn by struggles between more moderate 'Eurocommunists' and more doctrinaire pro-Moscow factions. In some cases, factional dispute may lead a group to try to form a 'splinter' party. This may be successful (the Independent Socialists, who later became the Communists, in Germany in the first world war and Weimar republic periods, or the Social Democratic Party in the UK more recently, for instance) but most such breakaways fail after, at most, a few years.

The life and death of parties

No party-system is ever completely static for very long. New parties are organised, perhaps from factions which split away from existing parties, perhaps to represent some new or hitherto neglected cause, and old parties disappear, especially if they are unsuccessful.

In the United Kingdom, the Labour Party was a good example of a new party, which was in part a breakaway from the Liberals, but more importantly an attempt to represent directly the interests of the newly enfranchised working class in parliament. The Social Democrats appeared to be the most important new party to come into existence since then, though the Ulster Unionists, Scottish and Welsh Nationalists, Social Democratic and Labour Party of Northern Ireland and the National Front can all claim some degree of political significance since the end of the second world war.

In France, the Gaullists were a new party at the start of the Fifth Republic (indeed, in their political style, their 'personality cult', and the breadth of their political appeal, were something of a political innovation altogether). The National Front and the Ecology Party are other French examples of new parties, each based on a rather narrow cause, while the Poujadists, a middle-class anti-tax party in the fifties, can be classified among the unsuccessful parties which have since died out.

In West Germany there are many examples of new parties, and parties which have not survived, since the end of the second world war. Of course, most of the post-war parties were new creations: only the Social Democrats and the Communists, along with the remnants of the Centre Party (now practically extinct), were direct continuations of Weimar republic parties. Many parties on the extreme right have been formed, sometimes have amalgamated or split away from each other, and have sunk into insignificance. Only the National Democratic Party, which just failed to gain entry into the Bundestag, made any real impact, and that party has now less than one per cent of the vote at a general election. On the other hand, the Green Party (the West German ecological party) has won seats in provincial parliaments, local councils, and now in the Bundestag.

New issues come into prominence, old causes become irrelevant, social and political conditions change, and voters come to perceive new matters as politically important. So parties, and the party-system itself, have to adapt, and parties which are not adaptable are destined to divide or disappear.

Notes

1. The Christian Democrats (CDU) have operated, at electoral level and in parliament, in close alliance with the Christian Social Union (CSU), their Bavarian sister-party. The CDU does not present candidates in Bavaria, and the CSU does not offer candidates outside Bavaria. They form a joint parliamentary group in the *Bundestag*. References in this chapter to the Christian Democrats include the CSU.

2. The term 'historic compromise' originates from the ideological vocabulary of the Italian Communist Party, which laid great emphasis on achieving a coalition with the Christian Democrats in order to obtain governmental power in the 1970s.

3. France, in fact, is something of an exception concerning the importance of a party career to political advancement.

4. For illustrative data concerning participation, see above, chapter 2, pp. 35–7.

6
LINKAGE ORGANISATIONS: PRESSURE GROUPS

Introduction

Besides political parties there exists another set of linkage organisations, which are often less visible than the parties in their political activities and their exercise of influence, but which are more varied, much more numerous, and, sometimes, as influential in affecting the options and outputs of government: *pressure groups.*

Because of their variety, and because of their differences in size, resources, scope and political activities, it is difficult to define pressure groups very concisely. Pressure groups are organisations, some part of whose purposes and activities are concerned with the exercise of influence on government, either to produce changes desired by the group, or to prevent changes which would be undesirable to the group. Such groups range from the trade union confederation, with millions of members, to a local citizens action group of a dozen people, determined to prevent a local authority from locating a crematorium in their neighbourhood. The chief dimensions along which such groups can vary are listed and elaborated below. However, it is useful at this point to emphasise a definitional distinction: pressure groups are distinguished from political parties by three major differences:

(*a*) pressure groups seek to *influence* the exercise of power, whereas political parties seek to *participate* in the exercise of power;

(*b*) pressure groups, therefore, only exceptionally nominate candidates at elections, and then mainly for purposes of publicity, in contrast to parties, which exist in order to contest elections for public offices;

(*c*) pressure groups usually confine themselves to specific issues or sectors of public policy; parties generally offer proposals relevant to the whole spectrum of public policy.

'In essence, democracy in modern society may be viewed as involving the conflict of organised groups competing for support', wrote Lipset,[1] and more recently many commentators have confirmed that liberal democracy depends upon the free competition of groups – pressure groups as well as parties – for the exercise of political power or for influence upon those who do exercise it. Pressure groups reflect the *interests* of the public: economic interests, with which trade unions or professional bodies may be concerned; political interests, such as those of the Electoral Reform Society in the UK, or the West German associations of local authorities; social and cultural interests, such as those represented by the motoring organisations or sports councils; religious interests, mainly represented by the spokesmen of the various churches; or any of a variety of interests of other kinds, banning the bomb, for example.

The very diversity and multiplicity of such groups and their interests provide the *pluralism* that presents an obstacle to the accumulation of too much power by the state and its organs. Conversely, in autocracies, such as Franco's Spain, and Greece during the period of military rule 1967–74, and even more so in one-party dictatorships such as Nazi Germany or the USSR, such groups are prohibited, or remain subject to strict state control of their organisation, resources and activities. The recent crisis in Poland resulted from the attempt by 'Solidarity' to maintain a trade union organisation which was independent both of the Communist Party and of the state which that party controlled. Such a search for independence threatened the totalitarian claims of the state, and hence had to be opposed. Liberal democracies, on the other hand, not only permit but *require* the articulation of interests so that government can respond to the needs of its citizens. Parties play an important role in the representation and transmission of demands from the public to the authorities, but pressure groups also have a significant contribution to make.

Pressure groups in western Europe

Because the states of western Europe can all be categorised as liberal democracies, it follows that each will possess a range of pressure groups which seek to influence governmental outputs. It follows also that the political activity of such groups, when they seek to exercise political pressure, will normally be regarded as legitimate. Furthermore, because of the similarities of economic systems and social structures in most west European states, the basic constellation of pressure groups in such states will also be very similar. It will not be surprising to find that a trade union movement exists in each state, as well as some kind of employers' organisation. In some states, one or several religious denominations will, from time to time, become involved in the political process. The farming community will be politically important in every state, though in different ways and perhaps in different circumstances, reflecting the differences in agrarian structure in various countries. Few west European states now lack a well-organised and well-publicised ecological movement. Most have at least one motoring organisation, a consumer movement, professional associations, some kind of feminist movement, and so on.

The national differences in the patterns of pressure groups are, in many ways, less interesting than differences between groups, and between types of groups, *within* one country. So this section will first investigate the more significant dimensions along which pressure groups in all west European states can be differentiated and distinguished, and will then focus upon the national patterns of groups in four countries, by way of illustration: in the United Kingdom, France, West Germany and Italy. Reference will also be made to the development of pressure groups on a cross-national level in the European Community.

1. The first dimension along which pressure groups can be usefully distinguished is their *degree of politicisation*. Some, like the Anti-Corn Law League or the Chartist movement in the nineteenth century, or the peace movement or the Electoral Reform Society today, are highly politicised, in the sense that the main purpose and the great majority of activities of the group are directly related to securing some political goal. The most highly-politicised groups are often those formed explicitly to produce political effects: the *Bürgerinitiativen* (civic initiative groups) in West Germany, for instance (see below); or the movements to secure political autonomy in the Basque and

Catalan regions of Spain. Other organisations: the churches, trade unions, farmers' associations and charitable institutions, for example, are mainly concerned on a day-to-day basis with non-political activities, and may only rarely seek to intervene in politics – though such intervention when it does occur may be highly publicised; for the purposes of this analysis, however, they too can be termed 'pressure groups'.

2. Pressure groups differ in terms of their *organisational characteristics*. They may be organisations which are national in scope, such as professional associations; they may be regional, confined to Scotland or Bavaria or Corsica; or they can be localised, based on a village about to be affected by some proposed new construction scheme. They will vary according to their financial resources, their membership levels, the percentage of the potential membership which actually joins the group (trade unions in the UK vary, for example, from one hundred per cent membership in 'closed shop' industries, such as coal mining and the railways, to only about thirty or even twenty per cent membership in some service industries or white-collar occupations, though membership of unions in the UK is relatively high, compared to some other west European countries). Some groups will have a democratic form of organisation; others will be run by a self-perpetuating elite, not elected by, or answerable to the membership. Some will have a professional staff and a complex communications network at their disposal, while others will have little more than an office address and a few part-time honorary officers. Such characteristics will affect the influence which groups may exercise on the political process, the targets and channels of access which they select for influence, the methods they choose to press their claims on the public and the politicians and, of course, may also affect how far the issues which they pursue do in fact represent the true interests of their members.

3. The *range of issues* over which a pressure group claims to seek to exert influence differs from group to group. A federation of trade unions may find almost every policy sector relevant at some time or other to the interests of its members. On the other hand, a pressure group to prevent the construction of an additional runway at Frankfurt airport because of the ecological damage it would cause, or a local parent–teacher association in

Liverpool seeking to prevent the closure of a neighbourhood school, focuses on a single issue. This aspect also draws attention to the distinction between those organisations that have a continuous existence (for example, the Consumers' Association in the UK, or the Catholic church in Italy and Spain), and those groups formed for a particular purpose which, once that purpose has been achieved – or once its achievement has, for the time being, become improbable – disband: the Anti-Corn Law League, after the Corn Laws had been abolished, or the groups formed to promote and to oppose the introduction of commercial television in Britain in the 1950s, are examples.[2]

4. Finally, some groups tend to be *defensive*, whilst others are *promotional*: that is, a group may seek to defend its interests against a proposed change in the law, whilst others seek to bring about such a change. Of course, many groups, especially 'permanent groups', may be both defensive and promotional simultaneously, if the range of issues relevant to their interests is wide enough. A trade association, for instance, may seek to liberalise tariffs on items it imports for the manufacture of its products, yet seek to maintain quotas on the importation of competing products. But, especially for 'temporary groups', it is surprising how frequently, on any one issue, some groups are defending the status quo, whilst other groups seek to change it: membership of the Common Market, the 'closed shop' in industrial relations, regional legislatures for Scotland and Wales have all been issues in United Kingdom politics which have attracted group support on both sides of the question. Similar examples from other European countries could be listed. This balancing of groups raises important issues concerning the democratic role of pressure groups, discussed at the conclusion of this chapter.

The United Kingdom

Rudimentary forms of pressure group activity can be identified in United Kingdom politics as long ago as the eighteenth century. But it was the processes of industrialisation in the nineteenth, and of democratisation in the twentieth, centuries that particularly stimulated pressure group activity. Today, the political process of governments responding (or, at least, claiming to respond!) to the wishes of the electorate not only tolerates, but even encourages the participation of pressure groups. For example, the government of the day encouraged the formation of the Confederation of British Industry by amalgamation of existing industrial federations, in order to be able to consult with a single, authoritative spokesman for industry. In 1982, groups were invited by the Department of the Environment to submit proposals for reform of the system of local government rates to the Department, to assist it in the process of preparing legislation.

The most publicised, and perhaps also the most influential, groups in United Kingdom politics are those concerned principally with economic policy: especially the trade unions and the business associations. Many trade unions are affiliated to the Trades Union Congress (TUC), which claims to represent a membership of about nine million employees. Equally important is the affiliation of many trade unions, representing both 'blue-collar' and 'white-collar' unions, to the Labour Party. The close political relationship between the government and major industries owned, wholly or partly, by the state – such as coal mining and electricity supply – as well as the large numbers of employees in state-run services and central and local government, necessarily directly involves relevant unions in consultation, negotiation and conflict with governments. The interests of business are represented by a variety of trade associations, many of which are linked through the Confederation of British Industry (CBI), as well as through the Institute of Directors and the chambers of commerce. These groups have strong influence, particularly on Conservative governments, from time to time. Organisations representing the professions can be influential in politics, particularly on matters directly affecting their interests; the influence of the British Medical Association on the legislation creating the National Health Service,[3] as well as on its later development, is a good example.

The churches have not been particularly prominent in politics in the UK for many years, except in the case of Northern Ireland, even though the United Kingdom is unusual in having an established church that is directly represented in the House of Lords. However, on issues which usually fall outside the realm of party conflict, such as divorce reform, abortion legislation or Sunday observance legislation, churches and church-related groups have made themselves heard, and can sway some votes in parliament.

Otherwise, the spectrum of pressure groups in the UK can be divided into two categories: first, those organisations which have a permanent existence, but which are not very frequently involved in political matters, though when something directly affecting their interests emerges they can be vocal and, sometimes, influential: the National Farmers' Union and the Royal Society for the Prevention of Cruelty to Animals are examples; and, second, those groups which are formed for a specific political purpose, and which can be 'temporary', depending on whether they are successful or not. Many groups in this second category are local or regional: groups opposed to the location of a third London airport, for instance. Others are national in scope: groups formed to bring about the United Kingdom's withdrawal from the Common Market at the time of the referendum, for example.

France

During the Fourth Republic, pressure groups flourished in France in part because the fragmented nature of the party system encouraged each party to develop close working relations with organisations representing important sections of its own electoral base. Given the lack of a coherent majority in the legislature, moreover, the parliamentary spokesmen of organised interests were well-placed to win piecemeal concessions from successive short-term governments. However, the procedures established to elaborate five-year National Plans after 1945 fostered a rather different pattern of pressure group participation. This institutionalised consensus-building at the national level (which the French call '*concertation*') was subsequently extended in the Fifth Republic to the regional level.

The major interests within French society have continued to sustain vocal and active pressure groups in the Fifth Republic, even though the parties have taken on a more responsible role than they had under the Fourth Republic. The state-sponsored drive towards economic modernisation – summed up in the image of the 'technocratic' planner – has had an unsettling impact, entailing rising prosperity in some regions and decline in others, and has generated resistance, in particular, from small-scale business, commercial and farming interests. These issues have been further complicated by membership of the European Community and by the exclusion of the parties of the left from government for a period of twenty-three years. The continuing role of the church in social affairs and in education contributes a further mode of pressure group activity.

As a result, even though the most significant groups, as in the United Kingdom, are those concerned with the economy, they are fragmented along political and, in some cases, religious lines. This is most marked in the case of the trade union movement, where there are four major confederations, all independent of party affiliation (unlike the United Kingdom) but, nevertheless, closely aligned with differing party tendencies. The largest union, claiming under one million members is the Confédération Générale du Travail (CGT), whose leadership is predominantly drawn from members of the Communist Party, followed by the Confédération Française Démocratique du Travail (CFDT) which broke away from the Catholic Confédération Française des Travailleurs Chrétiens (CFTC) in 1964 and is now close to the Socialist Party. The third main confederation, Force Ouvrière (FO) was formed by an anti-communist minority split from the CGT in 1948, while the CFTC itself now has perhaps only a quarter of a million members. This situation is further complicated by the existence of an anti-strike employer-dominated union, the Confédération Française des Travailleurs, with some strength in the private sector of the car industry, while most French teachers belong to an independent union, the Fédération de l'Education Nationale (FEN), and a separate organisation, the Confédération Générale des Cadres (CGC) recruits among managerial and executive staff.

Agricultural interests are similarly fragmented along political lines: the main organisation, the Fédération Nationale des Syndicats d'Exploitants Agricoles (FNSEA), to which half the farmers belong, being challenged by an organisation on its right and three others on its left, as well as by its own young farmers' wing which has been influenced by progressive Catholic thinking and has espoused greater state intervention to achieve an efficient, modernised agrarian sector.

Most large French employers in the private sector are organised, along with the leaders of public sector enterprises, in the Confédération National du Patronat Français (CNPF), while a separate organisation, the Confédération Générale des Petites et Moyennes Entreprises (CGPME) caters for medium- and small-sized firms. Here, too, progressive Catholicism has had its impact, in the young businessmen's organisation, the Centre des Jeunes Dirigeants d'Entreprise (CJD), while the Comité d'Information et de Défense–Union Nationale des Artisans et Travailleurs Indépendants (CID–UNATI) organises small shopkeepers seeking to resist modernisation, whether in the form of competition from hypermarkets or more efficient tax-collection methods.

Such organisational fragmentation has undermined the effectiveness of French pressure groups and has contributed to the widespread resort to direct action. The revolutionary tradition seems to legitimise and encourage such direct action by pressure groups. Demonstrations in the streets, civil disobedience campaigns, barricades – whether by students, steel-workers or farmers – are regarded as acceptable in France, whereas in the UK or West Germany they would be considered exotic and unusual. The 'events of May' in 1968, when student unrest precipitated a spontaneous general strike movement, is the most spectacular recent example of such direct action; for a time, it seemed to endanger the de Gaulle presidency and even the Fifth Republic itself.

The church is still a powerful 'interest' in French politics, especially on social and cultural matters, such as education, family-related policies and social services. However, secularisation of political life has tended in France, as in other countries, to dilute the importance of the church and church-related groups at the national level, even though locally they may still be important.

West Germany

The development of pressure groups after the war was affected by the occupation of Germany and the need to ensure that Nazism, which had utilised and then absorbed organisations such as trade unions and industrial associations in the Third Reich, would not be able to do so again. Organisations could only be formed after the war with the permission of the Allies, until the foundation of the Federal Republic in 1949, but, by then, trade unions and other associations had been organised on a democratic basis, and of course groups such as the churches were able to exert political influence on developments because many of their post-war leaders could claim clear dissociation from Nazism, and some had suffered persecution in the Third Reich for their beliefs.

The influence of the Allies on the revival of democratic institutions in West Germany is nowhere more clearly demonstrated than in the 'rationalised' pattern of trade union organisation developed after the war. Each union is based upon a complete industry or sector of industry: the chemical industry, engineering and metal industries, mining and extractive industries, and so on. The sixteen major trade unions thus formed are linked in a single confederation: the Deutscher Gewerkschaftsbund (DGB). Though not directly affiliated to the Social Democratic Party (such affiliation of groups to political parties is prohibited in West Germany), the unions are generally closely associated with the SPD, while the Communist Party has little influence compared to, say, France or Italy – though it does secure some representation on union committees and on plant-level supervisory boards elected by the employees. There is also a small christian trade union organisation, and organisations representing business executives and higher civil servants.

The interests of the owners of business enterprises are represented by the Bundesverband der deutscher Industrie (BDI), as well as by an association of employers and local and national chambers of commerce. These groups exercise much influence on economic and industrial legislation and, like the unions, are frequently invited by the government to comment upon new proposals before the bills go forward to the legislature. At the legislative stage, these organisations have the opportunity also to present their case to the relevant committees of the lower house, the Bundestag. Similar opportunities exist in provincial legislatures.

As in France, a range of agrarian groups in West Germany (sometimes called the 'Green Front') represent the interests of farmers, and are especially vocal in discussions concerning price subsidies for their products. So successful have these groups been that now few farmers have to pay income tax, despite, in many cases, very high gross incomes, and a wide programme of generous subsidies for such items as diesel fuel, as well as special social payments, exist for their benefit – though at an ever-increasing cost to the taxpayer.

The civil service – including local and provincial public employees – must also be mentioned as a major interest in West Germany which, like the farmers, has succeeded in developing and defending a large programme of special benefits for its members. Together with the unions, business enterprises and the agrarian interest, the civil service has developed a considerable defensive 'bloc' of legislators in the Bundestag who ensure that changes unfavourable to these groups are not allowed to become law. In contrast to the UK, in West Germany it is very easy and not at all unusual for civil servants to be elected to the legislature. They also have the advantage that they can return to their administrative careers at any time, without loss of promotion, should they tire of their legislative activities.

Both the Catholic and the Protestant churches have traditionally played an important role in German politics, and this continues today. The issue of abortion reform in the late 1970s was just one instance of their involvement in politics. The churches obtain financial aid from the state, in the form of a proportion of income tax from all those who have not taken the step of 'contracting out', and successfully defend the continuance of this against periodic criticism. The Catholic church, especially, has close links with the Christian Democratic parties (CDU and CSU), and has been criticised recently for too blatantly using its position in election campaigns to influence voters in their choice of party.

Recently, the emergence of locally and regionally based citizen initiative groups has been a notable development, especially in the field of nuclear energy policy, but also in matters concerning other forms of environmental protection, public transport, housing and town planning. One section of this 'movement' contributed to the formation of an ecological party (the Green party) which has gained representation in the national and provincial legislatures (see chapter 5).

Italy

In Italy, as in France, important pressure groups exist which possess close links with either the Communist Party or with the Catholic church, and hence with the Christian Democratic Party. The dominance of the Christian Democrats in government since the last war has encouraged a particular type of relationship between certain pressure groups (particularly those to do with the economy) and ministerial departments; this relationship has been termed *clientelism*. It exists where a pressure group dominates some activity or policy area with which the ministry is concerned, such as energy supply or banking. The ministry depends on the pressure group for information and technical advice; in return, the group gains enhanced access to, and influence upon the ministry.

The trade union movement is divided among three main 'conglomerates': the Communist and Socialist Confederazione Generale Italiana dei Lavoratori (CGIL), the smaller Republican and Social Democrat-linked Unione Italiani del Lavore (UIL), and the Catholic Confederazione Italiana Sindicati Lavoratori (CISL). About half of all employed workers belong to either the CGIL or the CISL. The unions exercise influence through sympathetic members of the legislature and through their respective political party patrons. Even though all governments since the war have been dominated by the Christian Democratic Party, the unions have been consulted systematically on relevant bills before they have been passed into law, and they are often also involved in implementing legislation to do with the economy, the workplace or social policy. However, attempts in the 1960s to develop tripartite discussions on the economy among government, trade unions and business representatives (similar to the National Economic Development Council in the UK or the West German 'concerted action' discussions) were not a success, and the unions have now come to distrust such tripartism.

As in France, business-enterprise relations with government have been affected by the rapid growth of 'state entrepreneurship' and by the growing polarisation of interests between large-scale enterprises (both publicly and privately owned) and the many smaller businesses, which are often dependent upon the large-scale enterprise for custom. Such divergences of interest have led to an increasing dependence of the business sector on the Christian Democratic Party for any influence which they hope to be able to exert over policy outcomes, rather than reliance on any representative organisation for business interests.

Though agriculture is still an important employer and source of foreign exchange in Italy, its location principally in the less-developed southern regions and its fragmented structure have robbed it of the status *vis-à-vis* government possessed by the unions or industry. Its representative organisations have been less successful than their counterparts in France or Germany in obtaining benefits from the state or in securing advantages from the institutions of the European Community, as the 'wine war' with France demonstrated.

The Catholic church remains a powerful pressure group in Italian politics, as illustrated by its – unsuccessful – efforts to defeat the reform of the divorce laws by forcing a referendum on the issue in 1974. Its influence on policy relies particularly on its links with the Christian Democratic Party, at national and also at regional and local levels.

The factionalism which exists in the Italian party system and within the Christian Democratic Party especially, is echoed in the structure of pressure groups in Italian politics and in their relations to parties and government. Groups tend to be defensive in purpose, trying to protect their status and privileges against erosion through the competition of other groups, political adjustments, economic modernisation and social changes. Their inability to prevent such erosion accounts for much of the tensions and instability observable in contemporary Italian politics.

The European Economic Community

Pressure group activity at the cross-national level of the European Community is still relatively underdeveloped; this is in contrast to the extent to which some groups are organised across national boundaries in Europe: the Catholic church, for instance, business enterprises and trade associations, such as the railway authorities, or cultural organisations.

Pressure-group organisation within the context of Community institutions is also less developed than the cross-national party organisations which have formed in the European parliament. Groups have a voice in the proceedings of the Economic and Social Committee (see chapter 11), but exercise influence most effectively through persuasion of *national* governments, whose representatives at the Council of Ministers then determine the policies of the Common Market. The annual agricultural price review is the most notorious example, where farmers press their national governments (especially successfully in France, West Germany and Eire) to obtain the highest levels of price support for their products, but other recent examples of group pressure have been by the steel-workers, fishermen, and the dairy industry in the UK concerning retention of doorstep deliveries for milk. Presumably, the organisation of effective Community-wide groups (of trade unions, businesses, occupational groups, consumers, or even of taxpayers) will only really gain impetus when a much higher degree of political unity for the European Community has been attained, in which case Community institutions such as the Commission and the parliament will become targets for persuasion, rather than, or in addition to, national governments.

Pressure groups and the political process

Whatever the pattern of groups in any specific political system, in their efforts to procure or obstruct political change, and in their struggle for patronage, resources, and the status of being legitimate and respected participants in the political process, they contribute to the accumulation, clarification and transmission of the political demands of the public.

Nevertheless, in this task groups will be faced with a range of options concerning how best to press their demands on the governmental authorities. Some options will offer easier access to political 'targets', will require fewer resources, will perhaps promise a swifter response than others. Unfortunately, the most accessible 'targets' for pressure group influence are not always the most important or the most powerful elements in the political system. Much will depend on the nature of the regime, on the rules of the political game, and on the customs and conventions that hold within the system at any given period (for example, the contrasts between the French Fourth and Fifth Republics, or the Weimar and the Bonn republics in Germany). In federal systems, such as Switzerland or West Germany, there will be the complication of an additional 'layer' of government to be taken into consideration, which may be a constraint or an opportunity. Evidence seems to show that it is more difficult in federal systems to persuade governments to 'initiate' new programmes or policies, and thus that federal systems favour 'defensive' groups.

The most apparently accessible, fundamentally most powerful yet most diffuse target is *public opinion*. Many pressure group

campaigns have been aimed at persuading the general public of
the merits of a particular case: banning the bomb; the British
Police Federation's plea for the reintroduction of capital
punishment, anti-nuclear power campaigns in West Germany.
Even if a group concentrates its efforts on more specialised
targets, it will often include a 'public relations' campaign as a
supplement: for instance, trade unions' attempts to modify
industrial relations legislation, or the efforts of French
businessmen to avoid nationalisation under the new Mitterrand
presidency. The problem is that the general public is politically
very restricted in its power – limited in effect to voting for a
government every four or five years, and rarely moved to
intervene in politics to the extent of contacting its representatives
on the local council or in the legislature, let alone writing to
government departments directly. The general public is also not
easily persuaded by the efforts of any one single group or cause to
take action about anything political. At best, it can switch or
withhold its votes at an election, but loyal Conservative voters in
the UK or lifelong Communist supporters in France are unlikely
to change parties at an election on the basis of *one* issue, however
strongly they feel about it. Only if there is a referendum can a
group be optimistic about using public opinion as a major target in
its campaign.

A group may seek to influence a *party*, or its *candidates*, at an
election. It is usually the case that a candidate will receive a large
mailbag of leaflets and letters urging him or her to support
particular issues, and inviting a written response 'for the record'.
Candidates, however, are usually too canny to commit themselves
to any cause that they do not already favour anyway, for to do so
could lay themselves open to embarrassment in the future if the
issue comes before the legislature and their commitment is
publicised as a way of persuading them to vote in favour.
Candidates, especially successful candidates, are usually party
nominees (and, in some cases, will be selected by the party for a
'list') and are loyal to the platform of party positions and
principles which, by their acceptance of nomination, they are
pledged to support. So pressure groups may hope to influence
political parties, as a way of influencing candidates. If the party
then enters government, the group will hope for favourable action
by the government. Once again, there are flaws in this strategy.

Parties draw up their programmes and manifestos with an eye to three main considerations:

what is in accord with party principles? (a socialist party can hardly be in favour of denationalisation, nor a Catholic party support abortion on demand);

what is likely to be electorally popular?

what is going to be practical to implement?

Many pressure group demands fail one, or several of these tests, and hence fail to be adopted by political parties.

To influence the *legislature* is an obvious ambition of any pressure group. If successful, it would mean victory for its cause. Because legislatures in western Europe are subject to more-or-less tight party discipline (unlike the US Congress, for example) this strategy is successful only when a non-party issue is under debate: ethical issues, such as capital punishment or divorce reform, or issues upon which the parties are uncommitted or internally divided, such as membership of the Common Market in the UK, or support for Scottish devolution, for example. Nevertheless, modification of legislative proposals is sometimes achieved by pressure groups, especially in the legislatures of countries such as Sweden or West Germany where the committee work of the legislature is important, and where groups are encouraged to present a case to the specialised committees which deal with legislation. This especially applies to 'technical' policy sectors, such as energy, transport and scientific research.

The principal target of pressure group activity must be the *government*, of course. If the government can be persuaded of the merits of a case, *and* if it can be convinced of the need to give it priority, then it can use its legislative majority to introduce a law, or its executive authority to implement some administrative action. As with the parties which form governments, however, constraints of political calculation and administrative feasibility will apply. In particular, it is increasingly obvious in recent years that certain groups will enjoy access to government, will possess, if not always the trust, at least the respect of government, and will acquire the status of accepted participants in the political process. This applies to most trade unions, employers' associations, professional organisations, industrial groups, churches and major charitable institutions. Other groups, because they are newly-constituted, because of their novel or radical strategies, or because of the unpopularity of their demands, fail to acquire such acceptability. Some groups, 'accepted' or not by the government, possess sanctions which they can use to exert pressure on a reluctant government. Unions may call 'political' strikes (as they have done in the UK over legislation introduced to impose restrictions on trade union privileges); business may withhold investment or close down factories, especially if they are foreign-owned firms; groups of all types may withdraw co-operation upon which the government may have come to rely. Such tactics, whether considered legitimate or not, are part of the bargaining process which constitutes the context of political action.

The tendency for governments not just to *permit* groups to contribute to the policy-making process, but to *rely* on them to do so by offering detailed advice, technical data and even political support (the United Kingdom Labour Party and the TUC, the Italian Christian Democratic Party and the Catholic church, are two of the most obvious examples), has led commentators to ask two questions about the role of pressure groups in the democratic political process.

First, the close relationship which the government has with trade unions and organisations representing industry, commerce and agriculture (and sometimes the churches) has increased to such an extent that such groups have almost acquired a claim to veto unfavourable legislation, and can demand to be heard in legislative discussions on relevant bills. Other groups, representing other interests, such as consumers or independent producers, are in consequence practically excluded. This tendency has come to be termed *neo-corporatism* in some studies of pressure group–state relations, pointing to institutionalised consultations, mutual patronage, group representation on quasi-governmental organisations (called 'quangos' in the UK), and the transfer of elites between government and pressure groups as manifestations of this trend.

Second, observers have increasingly called into question the assumption that pressure groups, as set out in the beginning of this chapter, invariably contribute to, and serve to protect democracy. Not only the scandals and charges of corruption that emerge from

time to time (the Poulson case in the UK; the Lockheed affair that
affected politicians in West Germany, Italy and the Netherlands;
the problems that clouded the administration of Giscard
d'Estaing in France) raise questions about pressure group activity.
The quite legal, but certainly undesirable power of some groups at
the expense of others; the failure to produce the 'balance' of
groups on issues which a democratic political process would seem
to require; the suffocation of the opinions of unorganised
interests; the close links between some groups and political
parties (including the election of group spokesmen to legislatures,
sometimes as sponsored representatives); the trend to
neo-corporatism; these and associated aspects of pressure groups
have led to demands for greater regulation of their organisation
and greater 'openness' of their political activities.

'Most theorists now consider that the representative system of
government would neither be efficient nor really democratic
without interest groups' wrote Professor Blondel in the 1960s.[4]
While agreeing with that claim, one can very properly be sensitive
about the dangers to democracy that pressure-group activity can
involve. Representative democracy, which benefits from the
linkages between the public and government which parties and
pressure groups create, can only be harmed by unrepresentative
expression of group interests and opinion.

Notes

1. Seymour Martin Lipset, 'Introduction', in Robert Michels, *Political
Parties* (New York, Free Press, 2nd edn., 1968), p. 36.

2. The campaign for commercial television is the subject of a case study
by H. H. Wilson, *Pressure Group* (London, Secker & Warburg, 1961).

3. See H. Eckstein, *Pressure Group Politics* (Allen & Unwin, 1960).

4. *Voters, Parties and Leaders* (Harmondsworth, Penguin, 1966),
p. 159.

7

PARLIAMENTARY POLITICS

The importance of parliamentary institutions within the west European liberal democracies has lain historically in their embodiment of the principle of electoral representation. As we saw in chapter 2, electoral representation has been seen as the primary means of ensuring that those who govern will be responsive to the interests and wishes of the members of each national political community. Members of parliament, as the elected representatives of the nation, have traditionally been held to undertake two major functions. They are members of the *legislature*, and this term itself designates their original function: *to make the laws*. They are also empowered to exercise a variety of *controls over the political executive*. In addition, commentators in recent times have emphasised a third broad function of parliamentary bodies: they act as a *means of channelling communications* between the electorate and those most closely involved in the policy-making process. In this way political parties, organised interests and government are linked together through parliament, which thus serves both to express and to mould public opinion.

The three functions of parliaments

While it will be useful for the purposes of this chapter to separate these three functions in order to provide a clear picture of how different parliaments work, it must be remembered that what we are dealing with here are various aspects of a single process: the process whereby *demands* and *supports* from within the political system and from its environment are *converted* through the institutions of the state into *binding policies* (see chapter 2).

Through the functions that they perform, parliaments intervene in a number of ways at different stages of the policy-making process. A consideration of figure 2, which offers a simplified breakdown of the different phases involved in making policy, will help to make this point clearer.

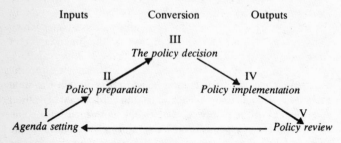

Figure 2　The five stages of policy-making

(*a*) In as far as policies can only become binding laws by vote of parliament in the countries of western Europe, then these parliaments' first function is associated centrally with the third phase of the policy-making process, the *policy decision* itself (III). However, this legislative function also contributes, through private members' bills and through the parliamentary debates and committees which consider and amend draft legislative proposals to the second stage, that of *preparing policy* (II).

(*b*) The second function of these parliaments, that of controlling the executive, extends their influence into the second and fourth stages of the policy-making process, *preparing and implementing policy* (II and IV). The principles of governmental responsibility and accountability require that parliament be kept informed of the actions of the executive, especially as regards new policy proposals being discussed and prepared by ministers and the ways in which existing legislation is being implemented. In particular, written and oral questions and the investigations of select committees enable parliaments to scrutinise the activities of the executive.

(*c*) Such action is primarily concerned with obtaining information and making it public and therefore contributes also towards their third function, as 'a nodal point of communications, the meeting place of a number of routes to and from the electorate'.[1] This third function, however, is particularly focused on the first and last stages of the policy process, *agenda setting* and *policy review* (I and V).

'Agenda setting' is the term applied to the processes by which members of parliament and the government of the day come to accept that particular demands and interests raise issues which require the creation of new legislation or the amendment of existing legislation. This is an important stage of policy-making. We need to understand how and why some issues get on to the political agenda, while other issues fail to secure attention in spite of their inclusion in party manifestos or the existence of organised campaigns promoting them. Examples of issues which did become part of the political agenda in most west European countries in the last two decades include divorce law reform, regional reform and devolution, and measures for protecting the environment. The lobbying of parliament by organised interests, parliamentary questions to ministers, select committee reports and private members' bills all play a part in this process of agenda setting. These same activities also feed into discussion, debate and fact-finding about the consequences of existing legislation, that is, into the phase of *policy review*. In terms of parliamentary activities, these first and last stages of the policy-making process will in many cases be closely linked to each other.

While all the parliaments in western Europe are similar in that they do, to some extent, carry out each of these functions, there are important differences between them. Such differences can be explained in part by reference to the formal rules regulating their activities. In terms of these rules, some parliaments can be said to be strong, while others, notably the French parliament, are weak. This issue of the relative strength or weakness of parliamentary bodies can best be understood by examining some of the ways in which the formal rules regulating the three main parliamentary functions may vary.

(a) Law-making

A strong parliament is one that enjoys a range of positive rights in the making of laws, including:

the right of individual members of parliament to initiate legislation;

the right of parliament to vote on the annual budget;

a special role for parliament in amending the constitution (that is, altering the rules which regulate the ways in which laws can be made);

in the case of legislation initiated by the government (and the bulk of legislation today is sponsored by government in all these countries), the full house will debate not the government's original draft, but its legislative proposals as subsequently amended by the appropriate parliamentary committee.

The first three of these rights are enjoyed by most of the west European parliaments, although there is no provision for private members' bills in Austria, Norway and Switzerland and in France, under the Fifth Republic, it has proved possible, in practice, to bypass parliament in amending the constitution. In respect of legislation initiated by government, the parliament of the Fourth French Republic provided the one outstanding example in western Europe of a committee system enjoying very substantial powers of amendment. Elsewhere, in practice, the work of the committees is concerned with matters of detail, rather than with challenging the main principles of government-initiated legislation.

However, even where parliaments do enjoy the first three powers enumerated above, their role in the legislative process may nevertheless be circumscribed. For example, in France under the Fifth Republic only certain areas of policy are deemed to fall within 'the sphere of law'; in other policy areas the government is able to promulgate decrees without requiring parliament's approval (see chapter 8). In most countries legislation that has been voted by parliament may subsequently be delayed, or even vetoed, because there is a requirement that a further authority – such as a constitutional court (see below, p. 126) or even an elected head of state (as in Finland and post-1958 France) – consent to its promulgation.

In addition policy may, in some circumstances, be decided not by parliament but by referendum, that is by consulting the full electorate directly on a specific issue (as happened, for example, in Switzerland in 1971 on female suffrage, in Italy in 1974 on the issue of divorce law reform, and in the United Kingdom in 1975 on the issue of continuing its membership of the EEC). It is also common for parliaments to be able to delegate their legislative powers to government, in which case there will usually be limits on how often or for what length of time a government can assume such delegated powers. Finally, there may be provision for parliament's legislative role to be suspended by the proclamation of a state of emergency as under the Fifth French Republic and in the new Republic of Greece.

(b) Controls over the executive

There are two distinct aspects to this parliamentary function. Firstly, and common to all parliaments, is the principle of *governmental accountability* to parliament. Here a strong parliament will enjoy a wide remit of powers, being able to secure and scrutinise information about the action of the whole executive branch: not only the political executive (comprised of head of state, head of government and ministers) but also the state bureaucracy organised in the various ministries and departments of government. However, the range of procedures available vary considerably, from general debates through written and oral questions, to specialised permanent committees, committees of inquiry and a parliamentary ombudsman. Their effectiveness also varies.

As regards the issue of governmental accountability, certain areas of policy, such as public expenditure and foreign and defence policy are of particular interest for assessing the relative strength or weakness of different parliaments. Public expenditure has traditionally been the subject of special procedures, whether these involve a specialised body reporting to parliament (as with the Court of Accounts in France or the Comptroller and Auditor General in the United Kingdom) or not (as in West Germany, where the government submits all its accounts to a sub-committee of the Bundestag budget committee). In the fields of foreign and defence policy, the formal rules in most countries allow the executive to act with greater independence. The scope for parliamentary action, whether it be in the form of prior consultation or subsequent scrutiny, is limited although parliament's authorisation will normally be required for the ratification of treaties. Matters have been further complicated in those countries which are now members of the European Community because of the difficulties which members of parliament face in disentangling the role of their own governmental representatives from the extremely complex and extensive bargaining that surrounds policy-making in the EEC (see chapter 11).

The second aspect of parliamentary control over the executive that needs to be considered concerns the principle of *governmental responsibility* to parliament. As will be discussed below (see pp. 122–3), there is a fundamental distinction between presidential and parliamentary democracies in respect of parliament's powers to appoint and dismiss members of the executive. Here we will confine our remarks to parliamentary democracies since most of the west European states fall into this category. In this type of regime the relative strength or weakness of parliament can be assessed by considering whether the offices of head of state, head of government and other ministerial posts are all filled by decision of parliament; whether, in addition, an incoming government must submit a statement of its intended programme of legislation for parliament's approval; and, finally, whether parliament can dismiss the government by passing a motion of censure or by a vote of no confidence. In these three respects there are considerable variations in the powers of the parliaments of western Europe. Moreover, in most of these countries the powers of parliament are counterbalanced by the right of the prime minister or the head of state to dissolve parliament before its mandate expires, although there are exceptions to this pattern. For example, in Norway parliament cannot be dissolved and in the German Federal Republic this can happen only under very limited circumstances (see chapter 8).

With regard to the functions of legislating and controlling the executive a further type of limitation on a parliament's capacity to act may arise from the rules regulating parliament's *internal organisation*. Considerations such as the number of days on which parliament is allowed to sit each year (a maximum of five months in each year under the Fifth French Republic, compared to the absence of any constitutional limits on the duration of any session in West Germany, Denmark and the Netherlands) and whether parliament itself or government controls the use of parliamentary time, are obviously important. So, too, are the arrangements for parliamentary question times: for example, whether supplementary oral questions can be put to the head of government and other ministers. Of particular significance is the committee system of parliament – the number and size of committees, and whether they are permanent committees with members specialising in a particular policy area which corresponds to one of the government ministries, or are organised *ad hoc* to deal with a specific piece of legislation.

(c) A forum of communications

The organisation of parliamentary time, arrangements for oral and written questions, and the question of whether a parliament allows broadcasting of its own sessions – particularly question time and major policy debates – are also of especial importance to parliament's third function as a forum of communications, affecting the extent to which its proceedings directly influence public opinion. Also of significance is the nature of the committee system, whether committees are permanent or not and whether they have powers to question ministers, civil servants, outside experts and the spokesmen of organised interests. Issues such as these will, moreover, affect the extent to which organised interests find it useful to lobby individual members and the specialist policy committees of the parliamentary parties, or even to retain, on a paid basis, the services of individual parliamentarians (relations of this kind being recorded, in the United Kingdom for example, in an annual register of members' interests).

Variations in the constitutional status of parliament

While all the countries dealt with in this book are now regarded as liberal democracies,[2] there are significant variations in their political systems which have important implications for the formal structures and powers of their parliamentary institutions. For example, nearly all of these countries have *bicameral* parliaments, with an upper and a lower chamber. (Exceptions to this are the Danish Folketing and the Swedish Riksdag, which have been unicameral, that is single chamber, parliaments since 1953 and 1970 respectively.) Yet the historical bases for the existence of two separate houses of parliament, the different forms of

representation embodied in each house and the division of powers
between them vary considerably from one country to another.

In order to understand the reasons for the main variations in the
constitutional status of these parliaments, three features of their
political systems will need to be considered here. Firstly, there is
the type of *political regime* in force, whether presidential or
parliamentary (or, as we shall see in the case of France under the
Fifth Republic, a hybrid of the two); and within the second
category, parliamentary regimes, there is a further subdivision
between parliamentary republics and constitutional monarchies.
Secondly, there is the *structure of the state*, whether it is unitary or
federal. And thirdly, there is the particular pattern of *checks and
balances* which each constitution provides for between the main
branches of government.

(a) Parliamentary and presidential democracies

It is in the operation of parliamentary control over the
executive, the second of parliament's functions discussed above,
that the major contrast between these two types of regime lies. *In
a parliamentary democracy popular sovereignty is directly and
exclusively vested in the parliament.* The main political offices of
the state – head of state, head of government and other ministers –
will therefore be filled either by decision of parliament, or subject
to its approval.

This is clearest in the case of parliamentary republics, like those
of West Germany, Italy and pre-1958 France. For example, under
the French Fourth Republic (from 1946 to 1958) the head of state
(the president) and the head of government were both elected
into office by parliament, the former by the two houses of
parliament meeting jointly, and the latter by a majority of the
lower house (the Assemblée Nationale).[3] In other parliamentary
regimes which are constitutional monarchies (like those of
Belgium, Denmark, the Netherlands, Norway, Spain – since 1975
– and the United Kingdom), the prime minister and his
government may only come into office and stay in office with the
support of parliament. The position of head of state, however, is
filled by heredity and the monarch retains certain powers in the
appointment of the government. These are largely formal powers
today and parliamentary supremacy is the rule.[4] Nevertheless, the
monarchy enjoys a separate basis of legitimacy from that of

parliament and it is possible, therefore, that the powers of the monarch might, in conditions of political crisis, come to be used in opposition to democratic procedures.

In contrast, in a presidential democracy the offices of head of state and head of government are combined in the presidency which is *not* an emanation of parliament, *the president being directly elected and enjoying a popular, representative legitimacy equal to that of parliament.* In such a regime, neither the president nor the members of his government are formally responsible to parliament. None of the west European states are presidential regimes in this sense. A number of them, however, have incorporated one feature of presidential regimes – the direct election of the head of state – while retaining a separate office of head of government, with responsibility to parliament. In Austria, France (since 1962), Iceland, Ireland and Portugal (since 1976), the head of state is directly elected by universal suffrage, while in Finland there is a more restricted, but nevertheless popularly constituted electoral college for presidential elections. The result in some cases (such as France, Finland and Portugal) is a hybrid regime, the head of state exercising greater powers in respect of the appointment of the head of government, the composition of the government and its duration in office, than is normal under a parliamentary regime, and also having specific powers in the making of laws.[5]

(b) Unitary and federal states

The major distinctions between unitary and federal states will be outlined in chapter 10. Here we are concerned only with the implications which these different kinds of state structure have for the role of parliament.

In federal states, such as Austria and West Germany, the functions of parliament are shared between a bicameral federal parliament and a number of unicameral parliaments, one in each of the constituent states. Thus in West Germany there is the Bundesparlament in Bonn (composed of the Bundestag and the Bundesrat) and a Landtag in each of the *Länder*. In contrast, unitary states will normally only have one set of central parliamentary institutions. However, there are certain exceptions to this in that limited legislative powers may be devolved to elected regional assemblies. (This was the case, in the United

Kingdom, of the Northern Ireland parliament at Stormont until 1972, and there are directly elected regional assemblies in Italy, while France introduced direct elections in 1986 for the hitherto indirectly elected regional councils set up in 1972, but their legislative functions remain quite restricted.)

In a federal state, the upper chamber of the central parliament undertakes a quite distinct function, that of representing and safeguarding the interests of the constituent states of the federation. It is for this reason that the upper chamber (the Bundesrat in West Germany, for example) enjoys special powers, firstly, to delay or veto legislation and, secondly, in respect of amendments to the constitution. There is thus a distinctive rationale for the existence of a second chamber in the parliament of a federal state, because the political community needs to be represented in two separate ways at the federal level. The electorate are, on the one hand, members of the federal state and as such they directly elect representatives to the lower house. On the other hand, the electorate are also members of the separate states of the federation and as such they are represented in the upper house.

(c) Checks and balances

The federal system of sharing powers, on a territorial basis, between two sets of authorities and the powers of the upper chamber of the federal parliament to act as a check on the popularly elected lower house afford particular examples of a more general pattern of checks and balances that is common to all the west European liberal democracies. As was noted in chapter 2, a fundamental feature of this type of political system has been its concern to limit the exercise of power. By establishing a system of checks and balances between the main institutions of government, the necessity for consultation and compromise are built into the policy-making process. This in turn may serve to promote the creation of a wider consensus in society.

Such checks and balances, operating between the legislative, the executive and the judiciary and between the two houses of bicameral parliaments, affect parliament's role both in the making of laws and in its control of the executive. The marked *separation of powers* characteristic of presidential regimes offers one important way of establishing a system of checks and balances. In a presidential democracy with full separation of powers the head of state is not elected by parliament and cannot be dismissed by parliament (except in cases of treason or incapacity). The president appoints and dismisses the members of government who are normally drawn from outside parliament. However, parliament cannot be dissolved by the head of state or the government of the day. Thus legislative and executive are established as separate authorities, neither of which can coerce the other; both must work together if the business of governing is to proceed. Moreover, under a system of separation of powers there will be a third independent authority, the judiciary. The highest judicial body will be designated to act as the guardian of the constitution and will have the power to review the legislative acts of parliament, and adjudicate on their conformity to the constitution.

In contrast, some *fusion of powers* is generally associated with parliamentary regimes. In such regimes, the head of government and his ministers are normally drawn from the membership of parliament, and the government can only come into office and remain there if it enjoys the confidence of parliament. This fusion of powers will be further strengthened if the highest court of appeal of the judicial system is constituted by a body that is not independent of parliament and if its role is limited to interpreting the intentions of parliament, without any remit to judge the constitutionality of laws passed by parliament. (This is the case, in the United Kingdom, of the Law Lords who sit in the House of Lords.)

Nevertheless, the constitutional provisions regulating the main institutions of the state in the parliamentary regimes of Western Europe do introduce certain kinds of checks and balances. This is true even where parliament is supreme, that is, where the extent of fusion of powers is considerable, as in the United Kingdom. As has been noted, the prime minister can normally, in conjunction with the head of state, dissolve the lower chamber of parliament and call early general elections. In addition, the upper chamber may serve as a check on the lower chamber of bicameral parliaments: designated on a separate basis from the lower chamber, it is usually able to delay, if not veto, legislation passed by the lower chamber. Where opposition parties, as in the United Kingdom, have the right to control some part of parliament's time, this offers an additional check on the role of the parliamentary majority.

Moreover, some parliamentary regimes have incorporated a degree of separation of powers by making provision for a special constitutional court, as is the case in Italy, Switzerland and West Germany. In these countries parliament is not supreme, since its actions are subject to the court's powers of judicial review. (A number of other countries, including Denmark, the Netherlands, Norway and Sweden, have advisory bodies which review legislation.)

A noteworthy, contrasting example, where the checks and balances characteristic of west European liberal democracies are present only in a quite weakened form, is provided by the Fifth French Republic. Here the introduction of some features of a presidential regime (such as direct elections for the presidency and, in practice, the right of the president to dismiss the government without reference to parliament) have combined with the retention of certain features of a parliamentary regime (such as the right of the executive to dissolve the lower chamber) and the absence of a full constitutional court to make for an unusually powerful presidency.

The decline of parliament

In the last two decades politicians and analysts alike have charted a decline in the capacity of parliamentary institutions in western Europe, and elsewhere, to carry out these three functions. The impression gained is that all parliaments have declined, even where the kind of formal arrangements that have been discussed in the first section above provide for a relatively strong parliamentary institution. Beyond these formal rules, a combination of other factors have contributed to this situation. Some of these factors are worth noting here.

Firstly, the scope of government intervention in society and the economy has been extended enormously in this century, and this has resulted in an increase in the volume and the complexity of the policy issues needing to be processed through the political system. Moreover, alongside the large corporations that have emerged in the public sector, the pattern of ownership and control within the private sector has not only become highly concentrated but has also assumed new forms, with the rise of multi-national firms. Until the mid-1970s, the commitment to full employment since the second world war in many of these countries also gave the trade union movement greater bargaining power.

These developments, it can be argued, have provided a changed context for the policy-making process, and for the role of parliament within this process. In so far as major economic forces have on occasion been able to challenge or evade governmental policies which have been legitimised and sanctioned by parliament, then this has affected the credibility of parliament. At the same time policy-making has become increasingly focused on close consultative relations between government and civil servants on the one hand, and organised interests, on the other. Organised interests which provide 'a second pillar of representation' have thus tended to supplant, rather than merely to supplement, the 'first pillar' of electoral representation. In the stages of agenda setting and policy preparation, in particular, the best organised interest groups are more concerned with building up contacts in the upper levels of the civil service and with ministers, than with individual members of parliament, parliamentary party groups or parliamentary committees. Indeed, draft legislation prepared by the government of the day may be such a tightly organised package of agreements reached between civil servants, ministers and contending interest groups that there is little scope for significant amendment by parliament.

The nature of the party systems which have developed in western Europe provides a second factor of major importance. For example, when a highly disciplined parliamentary party can effectively assure the government of a loyal majority in parliament – as has been the case in Britain for nearly all the post-war period and in France for much of the Fifth Republic – then the formal powers accorded to parliament may not be fully utilised. In contrast, a party system which results in shifting and fragmented governmental coalitions – as has been the case in Belgium in recent years, and also in Italy – may allow small parliamentary factions and cliques to exercise a disproportionate influence over policy outcomes and over the government's ability to continue in office. This may in turn lead to a loss of public esteem for the institution of parliament itself. More generally, whatever the particular character of the individual national party systems, the advent of modern political parties has transformed the working of parliamentary representation.

Parliamentary democracy has thus increasingly come to be identified as party democracy. Where there is cause for dissatisfaction with the claims of the parties in parliament to be representative, then this will serve to undermine parliament's own legitimacy as the body representing the interests and needs of the nation as a whole. Such questioning of the effectiveness of parliament as a representative body has also been reinforced by public awareness that the membership of the parliaments of these countries does not reflect the sexual, class and ethnic composition of their populations. Most obviously, women, skilled and unskilled workers, ethnic minorities and, indeed, voters under the age of forty are in this sense 'underrepresented' in these parliaments, which are overwhelmingly composed of older, professional and middle-class men.

Notes

1. Quoted from Gordon Smith, *Politics in Western Europe: a Comparative Analysis* (3rd edn., Heinemann, 1980), p. 172.

2. Liberal democratic principles of government have only recently been re-established in three countries, Greece, Spain and Portugal and, in the case of Portugal, only partially so. See chapter 8, pp. 142–5.

3. The West German electoral arrangements for the presidency are more complex, since it is a federal state (see chapter 8), while Italy includes a limited number of regional representatives along with the members of both houses of parliament in its presidential electoral college.

4. Only Sweden has, however, reduced the role of its monarchy to purely ceremonial functions, its previous role in government formation having been assigned, in 1975, to the elected president of the single-chamber parliament. In addition, in Belgium and the Netherlands the monarch appoints a leading parliamentarian as 'informateur', to sound out the party leaders and recommend to the monarch whom to designate as candidate prime minister ('formateur').

5. For details on the powers of the French and Portuguese heads of state, see chapter 8. In Finland, it is the president who appoints the prime minister and members of government (no vote of confidence being needed from parliament) and who has right to dissolve parliament. The president also has the power to initiate and veto legislation (parliament only being

able to override this veto if, after dissolution, the same bill is repassed by the new legislature).

6. Apart from Denmark and Sweden and the recently established parliaments in Greece and Portugal (see chapter 8, pp. 142–4), which have only one chamber, the second chambers of the Finnish, Icelandic and Norwegian parliaments are all, effectively, committees of the lower house, with members drawn from the elected membership of the lower house. In addition, in Belgium, Italy, the Netherlands and Spain an incoming government requires a double investiture, from both houses of parliament.

8

THE NATIONAL PARLIAMENTS OF
SELECTED WEST EUROPEAN STATES

The first three sections of this chapter will examine in some detail the ways in which the main parliamentary functions outlined in chapter 7 – those of making laws, controlling the executive and channeling communications – operate today in three countries, France, West Germany and the United Kingdom. The *formal* powers of these parliaments range from a case of distinctive strength (that of the United Kingdom, with its claim to 'parliamentary supremacy') to one of decided weakness (that of the demoted parliament of the Fifth French Republic). The constitutional arrangements of these countries also diverge in other respects, France and the United Kingdom being unitary states – the former a republic, the latter a constitutional monarchy – while West Germany is a federal republic.

These three case studies will, therefore, illustrate the ways in which such varying constitutional arrangements interact with differing party systems. The final section of the chapter will then outline the patterns of parliamentary institutions that have been established in the three southern European countries where authoritarian regimes (Portugal and Spain) and a military dictatorship (Greece) have recently been dismantled.

Parliament under a constitutional monarchy: the case of the United Kingdom

The parliament of the United Kingdom is a composite body, being formally comprised of the House of Lords and the monarch as well as the House of Commons. The lower house is made up of 650 MPs, elected for a maximum term of five years, each representing a single-member constituency. The House of Lords includes over one thousand members of the nobility (very few of whom play an active role), representatives of the established (Anglican) church, and the highest members of the judiciary (the Law Lords), as well as three hundred and sixty-five life peers and peeresses created since 1958.

A number of different forms of representation are thus combined in its composition, reflecting the unusual pattern of piecemeal constitutional developments in the United Kingdom. The adequacy of parliament as a representative institution has, however, been questioned in recent years, two major issues being the continuing existence of a non-elected second chamber and the desirability of devolving some legislative and scrutiny functions to regional, elected assemblies in Wales, Scotland and also Northern Ireland. The lower house, in practice, is composed disproportionately of older men, active in the professions and in business (and, in the parliament elected in 1987 there were only 41 women MPs).

The United Kingdom's lack of a codified constitution sets it apart from its neighbours. Moreover, many of the more important aspects of parliament's role are regulated by conventions, that is by unwritten rules of practice. Examples are the requirement for parliament to meet annually, the collective responsibility of ministers to parliament, the need for a government which loses a vote of confidence to either resign or advise the monarch to dissolve parliament, and the special status of the opposition in the Commons.

While in terms of its formal powers the UK parliament provides the outstanding example of *parliamentary sovereignty*, the party and electoral systems have together profoundly modified the strength of the lower house. In formal terms, parliament's supremacy is clearest in respect of its legislative role, for no court or other authority within the state can set aside or override a statute that has been duly passed by a majority in both houses and which has received the assent of the monarch. Moreover, most existing constitutional arrangements could be altered by the simple procedure of a majority vote in both houses, and there is no bar on laws that act retrospectively. Today it is the elected lower house which undertakes the major functions of parliament: the monarch's powers are formal, and not effective ones while the House of Lords' role is limited, as regards legislation, to delaying bills passed by the Commons for one year. (This, however, can pose real problems for a Labour government, given the upper house's built-in Conservative majority.)

In practice, however, the lower house's exercise of many of its formal powers of legislation and executive control is often nominal. Since the war, with the exception of the 1974–79 period, one of the two major parties has won a clear overall majority of seats in the Commons at each election. Parliament has therefore sustained single-party governments. Within the lower house, the loyalty and discipline of the two major parliamentary parties, with their system of Whips, general meetings and specialist policy committees, have helped to shift effective power to the executive. At the same time, since there is a considerable breadth of opinion represented in both major parties in parliament, and since governments do need to maintain the support of their backbenchers, some legislative and control functions are in effect carried out by party organisations (chiefly those of the parliamentary party of the party in government) rather than by parliament itself.

The Commons' *legislative function* is, in practice, heavily circumscribed. The government itself controls the House's timetable and initiates all major legislation, and bills are submitted for detailed discussion in committee only after they have been approved in principle by the full house. The government is normally able to rely on party discipline both in votes in the full house and in the committee stages (the committees being established *ad hoc* with non-specialist members drawn proportionate to party strengths in the House). As a result, the legislative impact of the House is not great; it is particularly marginal on taxation and expenditure. Nevertheless, governments may concede amendments to their own backbenchers and, on occasion, a government has decided to withdraw controversial draft legislation (for example, the Labour government's industrial relations White Paper, *In Place of Strife*, in 1969).

As regards parliament's control over *the formation and duration of governments*, the Commons is limited to voting on the incoming government's proposed legislative programme (the Queen's Speech). It does not directly vote on the composition of government, the choice of Prime Minister being effectively made by the electorate in conjunction with the main parties' internal procedures for electing their own leaders, while the Prime Minister designates his or her own cabinet, taking into account the different political tendencies within his or her parliamentary party. Ministers are by custom expected to be members of one of the two Houses and they are, of course, collectively responsible for government policy to the House and individually responsible for the conduct of their own departments. However, the strength of party discipline has ensured that only a minority government (Labour in 1979, on the issue of devolution reform) has been voted out of office since the war. The resignation of individual ministers in the face of parliamentary criticisms (for example, those of three ministers of the Foreign Office in April 1982) is also extremely rare.

The operation of party discipline also affects the House of Commons' role in *scrutinising the actions of the executive*. A considerable range of procedures is available, including the Prime Minister's twice-weekly question time, daily question times with other ministers, select committees, the opposition's right to force a debate on issues of current urgency, and, since 1967, the appointment of a parliamentary commissioner (ombudsman). In recent years concern at parliament's ineffectiveness has focused on the traditional select committee system, leading to its reform in 1979 with the establishment of twelve specialist, departmentally-based committees with wider powers to investigate the preparation and implementation of policy and departmental expenditure estimates. Although their powers to obtain information from ministers and civil servants are still not extensive and they have very limited resources, their proceedings are normally public and are reported in the press.

Parliament has nevertheless sustained its importance as a *forum of communications*: it is to parliament that key statements of government policy are made and time can be made available for the full house to debate major policy issues of current concern. There is, however, only limited radio coverage of its proceedings and as yet only proceedings in the House of Lords are televised. Whilst the focus of much interest group activity has shifted to the executive branch, there is still considerable lobbying of MPs, particularly the members of party policy committees and parliamentary select committees. Above all, the United Kingdom parliament serves to sustain the focus of political activity around government and opposition – that is, around what has been termed an 'adversary mode of politics'.[1]

Parliament in a federal republic: the case of West Germany

In the West German federal republic the lower chamber, the Bundestag, is elected for four years and has 496 full members (plus twenty-two non-voting members from West Berlin), elected by a mixture of single-member constituencies and party lists for each *Land*. The Bundestag is unusual in having a predominance of civil servants and permanent officials of parties and interest groups in its membership: together they comprise some sixty per cent.[2] Women are significantly underrepresented with only fifteen per cent of the membership, but from 1976 to 1980 the elected president (Speaker) of the lower house was a woman.

The upper chamber, the Bundesrat, is not an elected body, its forty-one members being delegates from each *Land* government. (The distribution of these delegates, with a minimum of three and a maximum of five per *Land* according to population, gives a disproportionate weight to the smaller states.) The composition of the Bundesrat means that the parliamentary opposition in each of the states is not represented; moreover, for most of the upper chamber's business, the *Land* governments send leading civil servants rather than ministers to represent them, and this has in the past given it a distinctly administrative outlook, eclipsing party politics. However party political concerns were influential from 1972 when the CDU/CSU opposition in the Bundestag used its majority in the upper house to oppose the SDP–FDP majority in the lower house.

In West Germany, the special role of the second chamber in protecting the interests of the *Länder* is largely confined to parliament's legislative function. It plays no role in the designation or removal of the chancellor and his government, nor in the election of the federal president. The electoral college for the federal presidency is comprised of the members of the Bundestag and an equal number of deputies drawn in proportion to party strengths from the *Länder* parliaments. The Bundesrat's approval is necessary for all legislation affecting the *Länder*'s direct responsibilities (such as education, *Land* and local government etc.) and for constitutional amendments; in these matters it enjoys an absolute veto. In other matters, rejection by the Bundesrat can be overridden by a further vote in the Bundestag. There is also provision for a joint conference committee to resolve differences between the two houses and this is usually successful.

The constitution of the West German federal republic does not confer legislative supremacy on the federal parliament, since the Basic Law established a Federal Constitutional Court with the power of judicial review. Its sixteen members are designated half by the Bundestag and half by the Bundesrat and it can adjudicate on the constitutionality of legislation. Thus legislation duly passed by the two houses can be invalidated by this court, as happened in 1975 with the government's abortion law reform.

In assessing the operation of the lower house's legislative and control functions, the nature of the parliamentary party groups (called *Fraktionen*) is again a factor of importance. These have been characterised by strong organisation and a high degree of party discipline. This may seem surprising, given that the Bundestag has had to sustain coalition governments ever since the foundation of the republic (even though one party – the CDU/CSU – did control an overall majority of seats for the period 1957–61). However, while coalition-building in multi-party systems often serves to exacerbate ideological divisions both **within and between parties, West Germany's four-party system** now restricts the coalition options available to the two main parties and their overriding concern has been to remain, or to become, a party of coalition government. One result has been for the main opposition party in parliament to play a lower-key and more 'constructive' role than would be regarded as appropriate for its counterpart in the United Kingdom. Indeed a large majority of government bills are not contested by the opposition at their final reading. However, the CDU/CSU's frustration at remaining in opposition between 1969 and 1982, the FDP's 1982 decision to leave the coalition with the SPD, the advent of the Greens and the growing policy debate within the SDP have combined to produce a more assertive role for the Bundestag.

The Bundestag's *legislative role* is important, even though the government initiates nearly all the legislation that is passed and is normally assured of majority support in the lower house. The parties in parliament do stress their role, and their competence, as legislators and this is reflected in the importance assigned to the committee stage of the legislative process when it is common for constructive amendments to be proposed. The committees, of which there are some twenty, are permanent and specialised, their members, however, being drawn in proportion to party strengths in the chamber. They mirror the division of departmental responsibilities among ministries and are able to call before them not only ministers and civil servants but also representatives of interest groups, other specialists and also members of the Bundesrat. Moreover, a body elected from within the Bundestag (the Council of Elders) has responsibility for allocating the use of the house's time.

The Bundestag exercises its control over *the formation and duration of governments* through its control over the chancellorship. After legislative elections a Chancellor can only come into office, after nomination by the Federal President, by securing the support of a majority of the Bundestag's members. The vote takes place without debate (although the Chancellor indicates the composition of his proposed cabinet) and is a vote for the Chancellor and not for the government's programme. To date, this procedure has been a formality, since coalition negotiations and the electorate's choice have effectively settled the issue in advance. Between elections the Chancellor can only be removed by parliament through what is termed 'a constructive vote of no confidence'; that is, an alternative Chancellor-candidate must be proposed and must win a majority. Such a vote has only taken place twice. In 1972 the CDU/CSU opposition narrowly failed to remove Brandt but in October 1982 Chancellor Schmidt was removed from office, following the FDP's decision to change coalition partners, and was replaced by the CDU leader Helmut Kohl.

The Chancellor himself can only request the President to dissolve parliament if he fails to win a vote of confidence. Loss of a vote of confidence had to be engineered by Brandt in 1972 and by Kohl in December 1982, in order to seek an increased majority through early elections. (With these exceptions, therefore, each parliament has served its full term of four years.) However parliamentary party pressures played a part in the early resignations of three Chancellors from office (Adenauer in 1963, Erhard in 1966 and Brandt in 1974).

In the *scrutiny of executive actions*, the same permanent committees which consider legislation again play a role of importance. The committees meet in private and are concerned more with eliciting information than with developing public debates over policy. Increasing use has, however, been made of the question hour in the house and of the provision of a 'current affairs period' when ministers can be questioned about a specific policy issue at the request of a group of deputies. In contrast, provision for establishing special parliamentary investigating committees has been little used. One unusual control exercised by the Bundestag since 1956 is its designation of a defence commissioner to investigate grievances and complaints concerning the armed forces.

Finally, in terms of parliament's third function *as a forum of communications*, the upper chamber clearly provides an essential linkage between those active in the policy-making process at *Länder* and federal levels. In the lower chamber, the committees offer a meeting place for parties, organised interests and the government whose usefulness (to the participants involved) may well be enhanced by the fact that they take place in private and attract no media coverage. The large amount of time given over to committee work, however, correspondingly limits the Bundestag's effectiveness in providing a linkage with the electorate although there is now television coverage of important debates in the Bundestag.

Parliament under a hybrid, 'presidentialist' regime: the case of France

In France, the constitution of 1958 retained the basic principle of governmental responsibility to parliament, but it effectively circumscribed parliament's powers to legislate and to control the executive. At the same time the role of the presidency, with its seven year term of office, was strengthened substantially at the expense of parliament. For example, it is by decision of the President that the Prime Minister and his government come into office, and no vote of confidence, either in the Prime Minister or in his government programme, is required from parliament. The right to dissolve parliament is also vested in the President as is the right to declare an emergency. In the field of legislation, he can refer back a bill that has been duly passed by parliament for reconsideration and on his decision a policy issue can be decided by referendum, bypassing parliament.

The parliamentary component of this mixed parliamentary–presidential constitution was further eroded in 1962 when the constitution was modified by referendum to introduce direct universal suffrage for elections to the presidency. The monopoly over the direct electoral representation of the French people which the lower house of parliament had traditionally enjoyed was thus broken.[3] Direct presidential elections have transformed the French party system and resulted in the development of stable majority coalitions in parliament organised in support of the four successive incumbents of the presidency to date. (Indeed the Gaullist party in 1968 and the Socialists in 1981 both won an overall majority of seats in the house but still organised a parliamentary alliance corresponding to their presidents' wider electoral bases.) These majority parliamentary alliances have been notable for their high level of discipline, with the partial exception of the Giscardian–Gaullist alliance from 1976 to 1981. The subservience of the parliamentary parties of the majority to the incumbent President has itself been a reflection of their sense of dependence on him for their own level of electoral success, and this has served to demote parliament further. The term *presidentialism* has as a result been used to characterise this hybrid regime, in order to differentiate it from a normal presidential system's pattern of separation of powers, while at the same time signalling the predominant political weight of the presidency.

The bicameral parliament of the Fifth French Republic is comprised of a directly elected lower chamber (the Assemblée Nationale) and an indirectly elected upper chamber (the Sénat) with subordinate legislative powers. The 577 members of the lower house are elected for a maximum term of five years, each deputy representing a single-member constituency. The 304 senators representing France's ninety-five departments are elected by an electoral college made up of some 100,000 local and departmental councillors together with the deputies.[4] The senators sit for nine years, one-third of the membership being renewed every three years.

Under the Fifth Republic, with a majority of seats held in the lower house by parties of the right and centre until 1981, there was a marked over-representation of members of the liberal professions, businessmen and higher civil servants.[5] With the Socialist Party's victory in the legislative elections of June 1981, members of the teaching profession acquired a sudden predominance (with 159 out of that party's 265 deputies). The house has always had remarkably few women members (currently there are 25). The existence of a second chamber whose method of election has resulted, since the beginning of the Third Republic, in the overrepresentation of rural France at the expense of urban areas, has not gone without challenge. The most recent attempt, by President de Gaulle, to reform the senate's composition by referendum in 1969 failed, however, and resulted in the President resigning from office.

In the field of legislation, the French parliament had enjoyed extensive powers under the Third and Fourth Republics but parliament's supremacy was removed under the 1958 constitution, which established a new constitutional council to police the boundaries of parliament's sphere of legislative competence. The constitution introduced a restrictive definition of 'the domain of law', listing those policy areas (such as public liberties, criminal law and taxation) in which parliament has the right to vote on detailed texts, and others (such as education, local government and the organisation of defence) in which parliament may determine the fundamental principles only. All other matters were deemed to fall within the government's rule-making powers and are dealt with by governmental decrees. At the same time the Assembly lost its control over its own agenda to the government, while its legislative role was further undermined by the Assembly's shortage of time and by the establishment of only six permanent committees (replacing the system of specialist committees corresponding to ministerial divisions of responsibility used in the previous republic). Again, in contrast to the Fourth Republic, it is now the government's original draft that is considered by the full house.[6]

In addition, the government has been given a number of procedural mechanisms to help secure the passage of its own legislation. For example, it is able to insist on a single vote on the whole or part of a piece of legislation (the 'package vote') avoiding clause by clause amendments. It also has the right to make a bill an issue of confidence which means that unless a censure vote is called within twenty-four hours and is carried, the bill is not voted on by the Assembly but is deemed to have been approved by it. In somewhat similar vein the budget may be put into effect by governmental decrees if the Assembly has failed to reach a decision within seventy days. In these ways the constitution-makers sought to bolster the coherence of governmental legislative programmes, in the face of the expected wrecking tactics of a faction-ridden Assembly. In practice, although governments since 1962 have enjoyed the support of a majority in the house, they have also made liberal use of both 'package' votes and the question of confidence. Governments have, however, on occasion modified draft legislation to satisfy criticism from their own parliamentary supporters (as happened, following the events of May 1968, to the draft university reform judged by Gaullists in parliament as too liberal, and to Giscard d'Estaing's capital gains tax proposals which were substantially modified by the Gaullists in parliament in 1976).

As regards parliamentary control over *the composition and duration of government*, the new constitution introduced limited features of separation of powers. The government not only comes into office on the President's authority, as previously noted, but its members are barred from holding a seat in parliament.[7] However, the office of Prime Minister, distinct from that of head of state, was retained. So too, was the provision for the government to resign following a vote of censure in the Assembly (although to be successful a censure motion needs to win an absolute majority of the votes of all deputies; that is, those absent or abstaining are counted as having voted for the government), and for an incoming government to seek, at its own discretion, a vote of confidence on its programme.

In practice, the *presidentialist* character of the regime has been consolidated since 1962 at the expense of parliamentary control. Prime Ministers unsure of their majority (for example, Pompidou in 1967 and Barre in 1976) have not sought a vote of confidence on their legislative programme. Governments, and their parliamentary supporters, have accepted that the principle of governmental responsibility to the President in effect takes precedence over their responsibility to parliament, giving the President the right to dismiss a government by obtaining a letter of resignation from the Prime Minister (most notably in the case of Prime Minister Chaban-Delmas, in July 1972, who had just previously received an overwhelming vote of confidence from the Assembly). The provision for incompatibility of office between government and the legislature has enabled Presidents to make key ministerial appointments from outside of parliament, including the appointments as Prime Minister of Pompidou by President de Gaulle in 1962 and of Barre by President Giscard d'Estaing in 1976.

Above all, *the real power-house of policy-making – the presidency – is not answerable to parliament.* This was demonstrated most clearly when President de Gaulle proposed to amend the constitution (to introduce direct elections for the presidency) by referendum in 1962. This procedure was unconstitutional, since the 1958 text specifically required parliamentary approval of constitutional amendments but the Assembly could only censure the government, not the President. This was the only occasion on which the Assembly has forced the resignation of the government under the Fifth Republic and the Assembly, in turn, found itself dissolved by the President.

Parliamentary scrutiny of the actions of the executive branch has also in practice been very much weakened under the Fifth Republic. The weekly 'question time' in the house, in particular, has proved an ineffective forum for eliciting information, although the number of questions asked in recent years has risen quite considerably. Limited reforms introduced during Giscard d'Estaing's presidency, enabling parliament to establish special committees of investigation, for example, and enabling a group of fifty parliamentarians to challenge the constitutionality of government bills before the constitutional council, have not significantly altered this situation.

Finally, *as a forum for both mobilising and reflecting public opinion* the parliament has been quite weak, even though debates are televised. Major policy proposals are announced and explained, not in parliament, but at presidential and prime ministerial press conferences and in broadcasts to the nation. Interest group leaders have redirected their energies to the state administration and to the personal staffs of the ministers, in particular, while public opinion has been unimpressed by the role of the French parliament, even though turnout for legislative elections remains high. When legislative elections did, in 1986, result in a government politically independent of the President being appointed, parliament's powers did not acquire any new significance.

Parliament and the renewal of liberal democracy in Greece, Portugal and Spain

In April 1974 a revolution led by a section of the military in Portugal and, in the following year, the death of General Franco in Spain, brought to an end the authoritarian autocracies that had been in place in these two countries for nearly forty years. In 1974 the Greek military junta that had seized power in 1967 also collapsed. In each of these countries a notable feature of the ensuing process of political change has been the re-establishment of representative, elected parliamentary institutions and of the principle of executive responsibility to parliament. Their current parliaments, however, vary considerably in their structures and powers, operating, in the case of Greece, within the framework of a parliamentary regime with some presidentialist features; in Spain, under the aegis of a constitutional monarch of some political weight; and in Portugal, within a peculiarly hybrid regime, in which both the president and the military encroach upon the normal prerogatives of parliament. The process of renewing parliamentary democracy has not proved to be entirely straightforward, or uncontested, in any of these countries.[8]

(a) Greece

Here the changeover to a representative democracy was set under way very rapidly, with elections for a constituent assembly to draw up a new constitution held in November 1974. A month later, the Greek people, consulted by referendum, decided by a clear majority (69 per cent of those voting, with a 75 per cent turnout) to establish a republic and not to restore the monarchy. Under its new constitution, approved in 1975, Greece has become one of the few west European states with a single-chamber parliament. This has three hundred members, elected for a maximum term of four years by a form of weighted proportional representation. The Prime Minister and government are responsible to parliament and parliament also elects the head of state. The support of a two-thirds majority of the members of parliament is required for election to the presidency, and its term of office is five years.

Alongside such provisions which are typical of a parliamentary regime, however, there are other elements which gave the new republic some potential for developing into a hybrid regime on the lines of the Fifth French Republic, with a politically dominant president. The power to dissolve parliament lies with the President, for example, and his decision does not require the assent of the Prime Minister who is responsible to parliament. Equally the President can bypass parliament on major issues of national policy by calling a referendum, and the President has the power, at his own discretion, to proclaim martial law. These 'presidentialist' provisions were opposed in 1975 by the major party of opposition, the Greek Socialist Party (PASOK). However, following its clear victory in the 1981 elections, PASOK in government has not sought to amend the constitution. Indeed, the position of personal dominance which Papandreou has achieved within PASOK appears to have led, instead, to a concentration of power in the office which he now holds, that of Prime Minister.

(b) Portugal

In Portugal, the rupture with the old regime took a more dramatic form with the revolution of April 1974 in which a leading role was played by military personnel, organised in the *Armed Forces Movement*, the MFA. (This movement was initially organised in opposition to the continuing wars by which Salazar's successor, Dr Caetano, sought to maintain control over Portugal's colonies in Africa, but subsequently developed a radical stance on Portugal's domestic political situation.) A constituent assembly was elected a year later but its role was limited to ratifying the constitutional pact negotiated between the MFA and the major political parties. This new constitution set Portugal apart from the other liberal democracies of western Europe by committing the new republic, in its first article, to 'the attainment of a classless society', and guaranteeing the nationalisations and land collectivisation, which took place in 1975, as irreversible.

The constitution, in its initial form, also afforded a major political role in the new republic to both the president and the military, circumscribing the legislative powers of the parliament and the principle of governmental responsibility to parliament. However, these provisions were the subject of growing tensions from 1979 between centre-right governments, on the one hand, and both President Eanes and elements of the armed forces on the other. In August 1982 the necessary two-thirds majority was obtained in parliament to vote in a substantial revision of the constitution. These amendments were intended to enhance the control of the single-chamber parliament (the *Assembly of the Republic* with 250 members elected for a maximum of four years) over government, since Prime Ministers, once nominated by the President, no longer need to submit their proposed list of ministers to the President for approval before seeking a vote of confidence from the Assembly on their governmental programme, and governments can now only be dismissed by a vote of no confidence in the Assembly (and not, as previously, by the President as well). The President, who is directly elected for a term of five years by universal suffrage – presidential candidates being expected to be members of the armed forces – has retained the right to dissolve parliament but has lost his previous exclusive powers over military appointments. In the legislative sphere the Supreme Council of the Revolution, the SRC, composed of the President and military representatives of the chiefs of staff and the MFA, which enjoyed a suspensive veto on most issues (which could only be overridden by a two-thirds majority in the Assembly) and an absolute veto on military matters, has been abolished. Legislation passed by the Assembly will now be subject to judicial review by a constitutional court.

(c) Spain

In Spain, in contrast, a clear rupture with the old regime was avoided. Prior to his death in November 1975, General Franco had arranged for the state to revert to a monarchy, and had designated Juan Carlos to accede to the throne. As a result new parliamentary institutions were established in Spain under the aegis of a politically powerful monarch and the armed forces continued to be directly represented in successive governments until 1981. The election of a constituent assembly did not take place until June 1977. The constitution which it drafted was submitted to a national referendum in December 1978, winning the support of 87 per cent of those who voted (although 32 per cent of the electorate abstained). However, the principles of parliamentary democracy continued to be contested by political parties of the right while elements within the military have been embroiled in a number of abortive plots against parliament, notably in February 1981 (see chapter 1) and immediately prior to the elections of October 1982.

The new Spanish constitution provides for a bicameral parliament (the Cortes). The lower house (Congress of Deputies) has 350 members elected on a regional basis by a system of proportional representation, while the upper house (Senate) is quite unusual in including forty-one members appointed by the monarch alongside 208 elected by the majority system. The constitution also made provision for regional self-government, subject to majority votes being obtained in referenda organised in each region (see chapter 10).

In the field of legislation the Spanish upper chamber enjoys considerable powers, although in the case of a dispute between the two chambers, it may be overriden by an absolute majority in the Congress of Deputies. The constitution itself cannot be amended unless an absolute majority of the members of both chambers vote for the amendment which must then be submitted for popular approval in a national referendum. The government, however, is responsible to the Congress of Deputies alone. Governments may be removed from office either if they fail to win a simple majority on a vote of confidence or if the Congress endorses a motion of censure, naming an alternative Prime Minister, by an absolute majority.

With the establishment of freely elected parliaments and of the principle of governmental responsibility to parliament in these countries, there are now no major exceptions to the liberal-democratic pattern of government in western Europe. However, as was seen in the case studies of the French, West German and United Kingdom parliaments, there is a contrast between the continuing importance of parliaments in legitimising the governmental process within these liberal democracies and the relatively limited ways in which they now carry out their three main functions.

Notes

1. On this term, see in particular, S. E. Finer (ed.), *Adversary Politics and Electoral Reform* (Anthony Wigram, 1975).

2. On the right of civil servants to stand as parliamentary candidates, see below, ch. 9, pp. 167–8.

3. Originally the constitution provided for an electoral college composed of members of both houses of parliament together with some eighty thousand elected representatives drawn from municipal and departmental councils. This was used only once, in November 1958.

4. In addition the Senate includes representatives of overseas territories and of French citizens living abroad.

5. See note 2 above.

6. See chapter 7, p. 118.

7. On the system of parliamentary substitutes, see above chapter 4, p. 63. In practice all ministers, even when they have been recruited to office from outside parliament, have, since 1967, been expected to stand for parliament at subsequent legislative elections.

8. A useful account of these developments is provided in B. Kohler, *Political forces in Spain, Greece and Portugal*, Butterworth, London, 1982.

9

EXECUTIVE GOVERNMENT

In the political systems of the west European states the *executive branch* is comprised of two different and, in principle, quite distinct sets of personnel at the national level. First there is what can be termed the *political executive*: the relatively small number of national political leaders who together form the *government* of the day and who come into office and are subject to periodic change or confirmation through the electoral process. In addition, operating under the responsibility of these members of the government, there is the permanent civil service, a vast and extremely diverse body of people staffing the many separate departments and specialised agencies of the *state administration*.

The term 'executive', however, may be misleading if it is taken to signify that the primary function of these two sets of personnel is the execution of decisions taken elsewhere. Quite clearly neither the government nor the state administration has ever been limited to *policy implementation*, stage IV of the policy process outlined in figure 2 in chapter 7.

In part, the dominant position achieved by the executive branch today is the obverse of parliament's decline, and the reasons for that decline – such as the increased responsibilities of the state, the complexity and technicality of much legislation, the impact of modern parties and the rise of organised interest groups, as well as more specifically constitutional factors – are also important here. The executive branch has thus expanded its role in the other stages of the policy process – *agenda setting* (I), the *preparation of policy* (II), the effective *taking of policy decisions* (III) and *policy review* (V) – at the expense of parliament.

Within the executive branch the role of higher civil service personnel is not purely technical. At the very least there is considerable room for them to *exercise discretion* when advising ministers in the preparation of draft policies, supervising the implementation of existing legislation, or preparing the data on which policy reviews will be based. However, the exercise of discretion ultimately involves political choices as to the order of priorities for allocating limited resources.[1] In this sense, higher civil servants may be regarded as contributing certain *inputs* of their own to the conversion process of the political system.

Moreover, the case studies of chapter 8 suggested that effective public scrutiny by parliament of the actions of the executive branch as a whole is limited. It remains true that in all of the countries of western Europe the governments are formally responsible to parliament and are also, although to varying degrees, dependent on parliament and parliamentary elections for their claims to be representative of the community and responsive to the wishes and interests of their people. Nevertheless, a common feature of these states is the *relative autonomy* which the executive branch enjoys *vis-à-vis* parliament.

In order to assess the main processes which serve to shape policy outcomes at governmental level, three sets of relationships will require examination here: firstly, *relations between governments and the electorate*, as mediated by different party systems and electoral systems; secondly, *relations within the government itself*, especially between the head of government and other ministers; and thirdly *relations between governments and the state administration*. These correspond to three major issues on which debate about trends in the governments of western Europe has been most closely focused:

1. The question of how a 'government of the majority' can be sustained in societies in which there are considerable divisions of interest (of a socio-economic, religious or regional nature) and in which competitive party systems give organised expression to such divisions. The result may be alternating one-party government (as in the United Kingdom) or some type of coalition government (as in nearly all the other west European states); stable governments (as in the United Kingdom, West Germany and France under the Fifth Republic, for example) or patterns of persistent governmental instability (as in Italy, Belgium, and France under the Fourth Republic).

2. The question of the balance of power *within* the political

executive itself. There is now growing concern about the concentration, and indeed personalisation, of power in the position of head of government.

3. The question of the relationship between the more or less temporary personnel of the political executive and the permanent personnel of the state administration. In addition, there is a broader issue concerning the growing interplay between governments, higher civil servants and the leaders of the major organised interests, which is often referred to as 'neo-corporatism'. This has already been discussed in chapter 6 (see p. 113 above).

The political executive

In all the west European countries the government is formally headed by a Prime Minister and composed of a number of senior ministers (each in charge of a separate department of government) and junior ministers (who usually have responsibility for a special policy area within a major ministry). The number of ministerial posts varies considerably. The second Kohl government, formed in March 1983 in West Germany, had as few as seventeen, the second Mauroy government in France, appointed in June 1981, had forty-three, while Mrs Thatcher in May 1979 made ninety-four ministerial appointments and the government formed by A. Fanfani in Italy in October 1982 had eighty-five.[2] However, the *cabinet*, which is the governmental forum for collective decision-making, does not include all ministerial personnel in countries like France, Italy and the United Kingdom (M. Mauroy's cabinet numbering thirty-four, A. Fanfani's twenty-eight and Mrs Thatcher's twenty-one).

In the case of the Fifth French Republic, (see pp. 137–8 & 140–41) the effective head of government is not the Prime Minister but the President, and it is the President who chairs the weekly cabinet meeting. In most other west European republics elected heads of state participate to a limited extent in the work of government, most especially in the fields of foreign policy and defence where they are normally accorded a special status under the constitution. In contrast, most monarchs do not intervene formally in the work of government.

(a) The recruitment of political leaders

As has been noted previously, parties and parliament provide important channels of recruitment for governmental office in western Europe. The major exception to this pattern is the Fifth French Republic, where about a quarter of all government ministers have been appointed without any previous parliamentary experience and, indeed, without necessarily being members of any political party. Notable examples include both Georges Pompidou and Raymond Barre when appointed as Prime Minister, as well as several ministers of such important departments as foreign affairs, finance and defence. Indeed, under the Fifth Republic, an initial career as a higher civil servant, followed by experience in the personal office ('cabinet') of a minister, has become the most common pathway to high political office.

Caretaker governments of 'technicians' have also been appointed in the two other states – Finland and Portugal – which share with the Fifth French Republic certain features of 'presidentialism'. Indeed, the current Social Democrat President of Finland, Dr Koivisto, elected in January 1982, started his career as a technician minister (having moved from the banking sector to the finance ministry in 1966) and was Governor of the Central Bank from 1970 to 1979, between serving as Prime Minister from 1968 to 1970 and 1979 to 1981.

Elsewhere it is normal for ministers to have had several years' experience in party politics and in parliament before acceding to governmental office.[3] In the United Kingdom, for example, since 1945, ministers have, on average, spent some fifteen years and Prime Ministers some twenty-five years in parliament before attaining office. However, on occasion a non-parliamentarian may be appointed to government in these countries (although in the United Kingdom such a minister will either be awarded a peerage, or will fight an early by-election in order to enter parliament).

The composition of governments also reproduces the 'unrepresentative' character of the parliamentary membership. This is most striking in respect of the under-representation of women in government. The few women ministers, moreover, have largely been confined to areas such as health, consumer affairs and women's rights. However, since 1979, the United

Kingdom has been led by a woman Prime Minister and in August 1980 in Iceland Ms Viadis Finnbogadottir became the first directly-elected woman head of state.

(b) Leadership succession and the composition of governments

Leadership succession in western Europe follows several contrasting patterns. Where the party systems and electoral systems have given rise to stable governments the issue of who will head the government, as well as the party composition of the government, will effectively be settled by the electorate – in conjunction with the internal procedures of the major parties for selecting their leaders. In the case of stable coalition governments, this will also depend on the parties making clear their alliance commitments in advance of the elections.

In both the United Kingdom and West Germany legislative elections have thus come to focus increasingly on the choice between two main candidates for the offices of Prime Minister and Chancellor. These elections therefore assume a similar function, in confirming the authority of these leadership positions, to that of direct presidential elections in France. However, on two occasions in West Germany there has been a change in the party composition of the government between elections: in 1966, when the SDP first entered government in the Grand Coalition, and in 1982, when the FDP decided to change coalition partners (see below).

In recent years, elections in a few other countries have been focused in a similar way on deciding who will lead the next government, as well as the party composition of that government. For example, both Austria since 1966 and Greece since 1977 have had one-party governments. Similarly, the electorate in Sweden in the three elections held since 1976 has been presented with a clear choice between Olaf Palme's Social Democrats and a three-party centre–right alliance led by Fälldin (of the Centre Party).

In France it is the President who effectively heads the government. Here the electorate's role in settling the issue of **leadership succession at the five direct presidential elections held** since 1965 has, however, only been effective on the second ballot, where voters are faced with a choice between two candidates only. (Each election to date has had two ballots, since no candidate has won an absolute majority of votes on the first ballot; and at the first ballot the candidates and their parties have not always made clear their alliance intentions for the second ballot.)

In a number of countries, however, the electorate rarely plays a direct role in determining either who will lead the government or even its party composition. Repeated changes of government may occur between elections, and appeal to the electorate through frequent early dissolutions may be avoided. Italy provides the most striking example of this pattern. There, forty-three governments have taken office since 1945 but only ten legislative elections have been held. Similarly in France, under the Fourth Republic, there were twenty-five governments between 1946 and 1958 but only three elections to the lower house. Somewhat more modestly, Finland has had thirty-seven governments and thirteen legislative elections since 1945, while there have been thirty-six governments in Belgium and fifteen legislative elections.

Moreover, in these countries the alliance intentions of parties are often not made clear during electoral campaigns and, even when elections do record significant shifts in the electorate's party preferences, these will not necessarily be reflected in the party composition of the government. Instead, both in the aftermath of elections and between elections, leadership succession is resolved by complex, and sometimes extremely protracted negotiations within a limited circle of party leaders drawn both from the parliamentary party groups and their extra-parliamentary party organisations.

The Italian republic has exemplified this pattern since 1948, despite the presence of a dominant party of government, the Christian Democrat Party. This has been in government throughout the period, with varying coalition partners and, on occasion, as a minority one-party government. It provided the Prime Minister of each government from 1946 until June 1981. Most changes of government have taken place between elections, through the resignation of the cabinet as a result of internal factional struggles within the Christian Democrat Party (votes of no confidence in the government by parliament have not been common). Erosion of the Christian Democrats' electoral base and increasing support for the Communist Party in the 1970s did not, however, lead to the latter's inclusion in government, even after

1977 when it advocated an 'historic compromise' (see chapter 3). Moreover, in the resolution of government crises successive presidents have come to play a role of some importance, deciding the order in which they will invite the leading contenders for the Prime Ministership to attempt to form a government and present it to parliament. Partly because of this, leadership succession at the presidential level has itself become the object of protracted disputes, with twenty-three ballots being required, for example, to elect Leone in December 1971.

Finland provides a distinctive variant on this pattern. With an average government duration of one year since the foundation of the republic in 1919, it has been the presidency, held by Urho Kekkonen from 1956 to 1981, which has assumed a decisive role, nominating the Prime Minister and determining which parties will participate in government. Kekkonen avoided recourse to the early dissolution of parliament and sustained a pattern of centre–left coalitions from 1966, on occasion resorting to civil service-based caretaker governments. He thus confined the Conservatives to permanent opposition despite their growing electoral support in the 1970s, and ensured an enhanced role for the Centre Party which he formerly led (even conferring the Prime Ministership on the party in 1970 following its worst-ever electoral performance).

Even where, as in the Netherlands, coalition governments have achieved greater stability, there may be little direct relationship between government formation and the electorate. The May 1977 elections in the Netherlands, for example, were followed by a record nine-month period of party negotiations before the junior partner (the Christian Democrats) of the previous Social Democrat-led coalition were able to form a government with the Liberals, excluding the Social Democrats who had been the only party to make major electoral gains. Again in 1981, months of inter-party negotiations were required between the elections and the formation of a new three-party government (this time including the Social Democrats).

In contrast, one country, Denmark, has consistently resorted to dissolution in recent years in an attempt to provide a direct linkage between the electorate and government. However, despite holding five elections at two-yearly intervals from 1971 to 1979, the parties were unable to organise alliances for the electorate to choose between, and the result has been a succession of one-party minority governments (with only one, short-lived attempt at a majority-based coalition in 1978 – between elections).

(c) The formation of governments

In all the western European countries the *formal* power to nominate the other members of government (subject usually to confirmation by parliament) lies with the Prime Minister.[4] However, even where governmental stability and the importance conferred on the party or coalition leaders by the electoral process have served to enhance the weight of the Prime Minister in relation to other ministers, the Prime Minister's choice of ministerial colleagues has been subject to certain constraints. Apart from the need to appoint ministers from amongst the membership of parliament, taking into account the previous ministerial and parliamentary experience of individual politicians, the heads of government in these countries will also need to ensure a balance between the different political tendencies within the party of government (as in the United Kingdom) or between the coalition partners and the tendencies within these parties. In the case of coalition governments the head of government also has to engage in what may be lengthy negotiations with leading members of the coalition parties in order to establish an agreed programme of government.

In France, where successive Presidents have acquired a predominant role in allocating ministerial posts (in spite of the constitutional provision for the Prime Minister to nominate the members of government), Presidents have, in practice, been subject to noticeably fewer constraints in their choice of leading ministers than have the heads of the West German and United Kingdom governments – in part because French Presidents are able to bring in non-parliamentarians and other non-party technicians. A somewhat similar situation has obtained in Finland.

Elsewhere, where there has been a pattern of relatively unstable coalition governments, Prime Ministers are subject to considerable restrictions in deciding on their choice of ministerial colleagues. In Italy, the intervention of the President has been an additional factor, with successive Presidents imposing restrictions as to the party composition of the government and its policy programme, while Belgian Prime Ministers have to appoint equal numbers of French and Flemish speakers to their cabinets. In some countries one or two parties play a pivotal role in government, their participation being vital to successive coalitions with varying partners, and this is reflected in the incoming Prime Ministers' need to include many of the leading personnel of the preceding cabinet in their own government. This has been the case with the Catholic Party in the Netherlands, the Social Christians in Belgium until 1974, and it was true, for certain periods under the Fourth French Republic, of some leading members of the Radical Party and the MRP. The leading figures of such parties thus become permanent fixtures of government – in some cases retaining the same ministries through several changes of government. Luns, for example, retained the Ministry of Foreign Affairs in the Netherlands from 1953 to 1971; in Belgium Eyskens figured in most governments from 1947 to 1972; while in France Schumann of the MRP, for example, was in office virtually continuously as Minister of Finance, Prime Minister and Minister of Foreign Affairs from 1946 to 1952.

In such cases, prime ministers are reduced to acting as political brokers between leading 'ministrables' who can expect to continue in office after the fall of the current government. The position of the dominant party of government in Italy, the Christian Democrats, has been similar in this respect, with a number of leading figures from the different tendencies in the party (Andreotti, Colombo, Fanfani, Moro and Rumor) in office almost continuously. These, however, have tended to move from one ministry to another (the ministries with the greatest stability of personnel being defence, economy and the interior but these, too, changed hands every two or three years on average).

(d) Patterns of governmental stability

It is commonplace to contrast the experience of governmental stability which a limited number of countries in western Europe have enjoyed (the United Kingdom, West Germany, Sweden, and more recently France) with the instability of others (Belgium, Finland, France under the Fourth Republic, Italy and, more recently, Ireland and Denmark). Certainly the first group of states may be distinguished from the second in terms of the relative infrequency of changes in their (effective) head of government and their governments' control of a disciplined majority in the parliament. However, the drama of frequent, and often prolonged governmental crises in the second group of states has in some cases, as has been shown, co-existed with a considerable continuity of government personnel (most notably in Italy). In contrast, within the first group the relative stability of governments has not precluded a quite considerable turnover of ministerial personnel in the United Kingdom and in France under the Fifth Republic. In both these countries government reshuffles between elections have been an accepted practice, as has the early dissolution of parliament, usually for tactical electoral reasons. In the United Kingdom, of thirteen elections since 1945, only three fell at the end of a full five-year parliamentary term, while in France four of the nine elections held since 1958 were called early. On the other hand, in West Germany there have only been two early elections (in 1972 and 1983) and changes in ministerial personnel between elections have been much less frequent than in the United Kingdom or in France.

Studies of cabinets in the period 1955 to 1970 have indeed shown that the total number of individuals holding cabinet office was greater in the United Kingdom than in Italy. When individual ministries are compared, the most marked differences between these two countries arise with Prime Ministerial office (with an average period in office of forty-five months in the United Kingdom compared to eighteen months in Italy) while for other major ministries the average periods were much closer (just over two years in each country for Chancellor of the Exchequer, Ministers of the Treasury and for Ministers of Defence; thirty months for Home Secretaries as against 22½ months for Ministers of the Interior; 22½ months for Foreign Secretaries as against 16½ months for Ministers of Foreign Affairs).[5] Moreover, Italian ministers have, on average, had considerably longer experience of cabinet office than have their counterparts in the United Kingdom (where the two major parties have alternated in government), a number of leading Christian Democrat politicians having been, for twenty or more years, almost continuously in office. These two countries therefore offer important contrasts in the way in which differing rates of turnover for Prime Ministers and ministers may combine to affect both the balance of power within the political executive, the issue which will be considered in the next section, and also relations between the political executive and the administration, the subject of the final section of this chapter.

The balance of power within the political executive

The principle of the collective responsibility of cabinet ministers for the actions of government operates in all west European states in the sense that when parliament passes a vote of no confidence it is the whole cabinet which then goes out of office. This is an arrangement which implies a measure of political equality among all the members of the cabinet in their deliberations on policy.

As against this, however, it can be argued that certain ministries are generally regarded in all these countries as senior ministries (notably the Treasury/Ministry of Finance; Home Office/Ministry of the Interior; Foreign Office/Ministry of Foreign Affairs), while others are considered to be second-ranking (such as Trade, Transport, Education, Health), and that ministers have a different political weight in the cabinet's proceedings accordingly. Furthermore, as has been seen, western European states vary considerably in terms of the balance of power within the political executive.

In particular, the pattern of relatively long-serving heads of government in West Germany and the United Kingdom backed by secure and disciplined majorities in parliament, together with the case of the interventionist French Presidents directly elected for a seven-year term of office, stand in contrast to that other range of Prime Ministers who enter office with no real expectation of holding their cabinet together for more than a year or two, and who may be flanked in office by a group of senior politicians with long experience of government who owe a primary allegiance to the interests of their own party or party faction. However, in at least one case – the Netherlands, where ministers are required to resign their parliamentary seats after three months in office – the Prime Minister's position has been strengthened by a loosening of ties between ministers and their parliamentary party groups, the parliamentarians seeking to sustain their party's distinctive identity and electoral appeal, while the members who accept office are prepared to subordinate these to the interests of effective national government.

Beyond these kinds of difference, many political analysts have identified other factors which have worked towards a concentration of power within the political executive. How far these are new trends may be debatable. However, it will be useful to summarise these arguments briefly here, before proceeding to an examination of current trends in the United Kingdom, West Germany and France.

1. It is argued that the traditional combination of *general leadership* (provided by a collectively responsible cabinet) and *specialised leadership* (provided by individual ministers with departmental responsibilities) has been ill-suited to cope with the vast increase in state activity and the highly technical issues raised by much policy debate. These developments, it is suggested, have put a premium on the need for medium- and long-term *policy co-ordination* and for a substantial new input of leadership skills in order to ensure clear *arbitration* between the conflicting claims of different policy sectors.

2. It is also argued that the growing interdependence of states within the western bloc in the fields of defence and economic affairs, has encouraged the emergence of *national leaders able to claim an undisputed mandate* to act on behalf of their own state when participating in international discussions and negotiations. A particularly clear example of this has been the regular meetings ('summits') of the heads of government and heads of state of the member states of the European Community (see chapter 11).

3. Finally, it has also been suggested that the mass media have exacerbated trends towards mass politics (see chapter 1) and contributed to a greater '*personalisation*' of politics both at election times and between elections, political choices being posed increasingly in terms of support for the individual contenders for government leadership.

(a) 'Prime Ministerial government' in the United Kingdom

From the early 1960s, much debate has been generated over the proposition that cabinet government in this country has been superseded by 'prime ministerial government'.[6] The proponents of this thesis have, in part, been concerned with developments in the United Kingdom which have reflected the three general trends in western governments noted above. Examples include the growing importance within the cabinet of small committees whose decisions are then 'rubber-stamped' by the cabinet as a whole (with the Prime Minister appointing the chair of all such committees and having a decisive voice in settling their membership); a tendency for the cabinet office to be used as the personal staff of the Prime Minister of the day; and the establishment of a high-powered policy unit at no. 10 in 1972 – the Central Policy Review Staff (the 'think-tank') under the Prime Minister's control. In addition, the relatively high ministerial turnover suggests that many members of government may be preoccupied with mastering their departmental responsibilities.

Offsetting these developments, however, one could point to the weight of various senior politicians in the cabinet, pursuing their own interests and policy priorities; to both major parties' need to sustain broad political bases in order to maximise their electoral appeal and the impact this has on the Prime Minister's choice of ministerial personnel and on the policy output of the government; to the ability of the departments to defend their own interests; and, in particular, to the importance of the Treasury and its views on the economy. Moreover, Prime Ministers themselves have only stayed in office for four years on average. Mrs Thatcher's Prime Ministership since 1979 has, however, been noteworthy for a marked shift from the pragmatic mould adopted by previous Conservative governments in the post-war period, for her retention throughout her period in office to date of Chancellors of the Exchequer who have followed her prescriptions for the economy, and for new moves to strengthen her personal staff, notably in the foreign policy field.

More generally, there are certain particularities of the political system in the United Kingdom which, it is argued, have worked against the principle that the Prime Minister is merely first among equals. Firstly, there is the context provided by stable one-party government, with Prime Ministers able to rely on a disciplined majority in parliament. Although Labour Prime Ministers have in recent times faced some challenges over policy from their party organisations, the structure of neither major party has allowed for a strong party leadership to develop, separate from the parliamentary leadership, as has happened in some other west European countries. The position of successive Prime Ministers has been enhanced by the patronage under their control (notably the large number of ministerial appointments which cover a wide range of paid posts and may cover up to one in three of all the majority party's MPs); by their control over the timing, agenda and proceedings of cabinet meetings; by the status and publicity afforded by such parliamentary proceedings as the weekly question time; and by their control over the dissolution of parliament, which has resulted in their acting as their parties' main electoral tacticians. In addition, two further features of government in the United Kingdom – the centralised state administration and the traditional secrecy surrounding much policy-making (although this has been partially offset by 'leaks') – may also be of relevance to this debate.

(b) 'Chancellor democracy' in West Germany

In the Federal Republic of Germany, the chancellor enjoys a certain constitutional pre-eminence over the members of his cabinet. The Chancellor is entrusted with a general responsibility for the government's policy before parliament and it is only the Chancellor who is voted into office by the Bundestag (although the composition of his cabinet is known, and he presents to parliament the programme agreed with his coalition partners). Moreover, his security of tenure is enhanced by the 'constructive vote of no confidence' required to remove him from office.

The term 'Chancellor democracy', was coined primarily to characterise the quite particular pre-eminence over policy formulation achieved by Konrad Adenauer during his tenure of the office. However, the Adenauer period may be regarded as rather exceptional. In a period of considerable uncertainty for the new republic, he held the office continuously for fourteen years (from 1949 to 1963). The major party of government, the Christian Democrats, felt itself to be dependent on the chancellor for its electoral popularity, and Adenauer himself held the chairmanship of the party as well as the Chancellorship for a long period. Moreover, the limited electoral support enjoyed by the CDU's coalition partners meant these could exercise little political leverage in government.

Subsequently a number of developments have reflected the general trends referred to previously. In particular, under Brandt the role of the Chancellor's office was very considerably strengthened. Ministers were required to keep the office informed of all new policy proposals from an early stage, with specialist staff in the office covering all policy sectors. New staff were also introduced from 1967 to undertake longer-term planning of the government's legislative programme. This, however, met with considerable resistance from the individual departments seeking to preserve their own autonomy, and from the Ministry of Finance, in particular, which already assumed a co-ordinating role through its control of the budget, which determines the allocation of funds to spending ministries. This more ambitious role for the Chancellor's office was abandoned after the 1972 elections, but nevertheless the office has acquired a certain importance from its co-ordinating work.

At the same time, elections have largely focused on the choice between alternative Chancellor candidates. Both Brandt (through his 'Ostpolitik') and Schmidt (who played an increasingly prominent part in EEC and other western summits) were spokesmen for the Federal Republic in international negotiations, which undoubtedly served to enhance their leadership of the government. However, Brandt did not use this to develop a distinctive stance, separate from the SDP programme, whereas Schmidt developed a distinct political image in his own right and used the FDP's weight in the coalition to gain a certain autonomy from his own party.

The balance of the relationship between Chancellors in West Germany and their ministers is partly redressed by the fact that ministers are normally experts in the policy sector of their department (through their pre-political careers or parliamentary experience) and there is usually little rotation of offices among ministerial personnel. In addition, Chancellors are faced with other particularly influential figures within their own party organisation – the party chairman and the chairman of the parliamentary party group.

The party of the West German Chancellor has only once enjoyed a majority of seats in the Bundestag. Chancellors, therefore, have usually come into office by negotiating an agreed programme between at least two parties. Important decisions on policy have had to be settled, not in the cabinet, but through direct inter-party negotiations; and during the SPD–FDP coalitions from 1969 to 1982 the FDP was, in return for its parliamentary votes, able to exact major ministries and a disproportionate weight in such inter-party negotiations. Furthermore, the federal structure of the state requires an additional dimension of bargaining and concessions between the federal and the *Land* governments and their representatives in the Bundesrat.

(c) *'Presidentialism' under the Fifth French Republic*

The Fifth French Republic has provided the clearest example in western Europe of the concentration of political power in one office, with the term 'presidentialism' being used to denote the imbalance in favour of the head of state which currently characterises France's political institutions. As was noted in the previous chapter, these developments can in part be traced back to the 'hybrid' provisions of the 1958 constitution, and to the ambiguous formulation of several of its key provisions.

The constitution conferred on the presidency new authority as the 'arbiter' of the political system.[7] To this end, the constitution added the power to appoint the Prime Minister and certain reserve powers to the tasks which have traditionally been entrusted to French Presidents, for example in the foreign and defence policy sectors and in resolving governmental crises. The President's new powers included the right to dissolve parliament (to be exercised only once, however, in any twelve month period; this has been used four times, in 1962, 1968, 1981 and 1988); the right to submit a policy for decision by the French people by referendum (to date five referenda have been held: in 1961, April and October 1962, 1969 and 1972); and the right to assume full powers by proclaiming an emergency (as de Gaulle did in 1961, for six months, following an army rebellion led by four generals opposed to Algerian independence).

The circumstances in which de Gaulle returned to power in 1958 undoubtedly favoured the emergence of a dominant national leader. De Gaulle was invested as the last Prime Minister of the Fourth Republic with special powers to draw up a new constitution following the May 1958 uprising of European settlers and a section of the French army in Algiers. The issue of Algerian independence was one which deeply divided French public opinion, the political parties, parliament and the army, and it continued to dominate French domestic politics until an independence settlement was negotiated in 1962. In this period de Gaulle achieved a personal ascendancy over the members of his government, and over the party formed to support him, somewhat similar to that achieved by Adenauer in the Federal Republic of West Germany. This enabled him, like Adenauer, to remain in office for a particularly long period (1958–69).

However, in contrast to West Germany, other developments in France served to consolidate and sustain this new balance of power within the political executive after de Gaulle's resignation. Most notably, the introduction of direct elections for the presidency in 1962 acted as a catalyst for changes in the party system and in electoral behaviour, because a successful candidate has had to win an absolute majority of votes and has needed to maintain a coherent alliance of parties in parliament and at legislative elections to back him throughout his seven-year period of office. It is at presidential elections that the electorate chooses the effective head of government. Presidents can claim a special mandate as 'l'élu de la nation' and candidates present detailed policy programmes for governments formed by them to carry out. (Legislative elections have been correspondingly marginalised, serving to confirm the incumbent President's coalition.)[8]

As has been noted, presidential dominance has been reflected in the relatively free hand enjoyed by successive Presidents in choosing their Prime Ministers and making ministerial appointments. Within the cabinet their position has been enhanced by the presence of technician-ministers (particularly at the Ministry of Foreign Affairs) and by their own lengthy mandate (seven years) compared to the average period of under four years which ministers spend in government. The pre-eminent position of the President has also been embodied in the procedures which have developed for policy-making. Presidents have been able to use their own large staff of specialists at the Elysée Palace to maintain close liaison with the individual ministries. At governmental level there is a hierarchy of committees bringing together ministers and top civil servants to prepare and co-ordinate policies. While the majority of these are organised by the Prime Minister and his personal staff, the most important are convened at the Elysée by the President, with either the President or one of his personal staff in the chair. In addition, Giscard d'Estaing introduced a new procedure during his period of office, sending presidential directives to his Prime Ministers, setting out the timetable for the government's business for the next six months, and to individual ministers, giving detailed instructions concerning policies which he invited them to prepare.

Finally, the impact of France's party system on the powers of the presidency has also been double-edged. The policies pursued by French Presidents have been constrained by the parties represented in their governments and which provide their majority in parliament (Giscard d'Estaing, for example, was forced to modify his capital gains tax in face of Gaullist opposition in 1976). Nevertheless, the breadth of the electoral coalition which a successful presidential candidate must put together in order to win over fifty per cent of the vote, has, in the final analysis, served to strengthen the position of the presidency. The French system is one in which the parties of the governing coalition have competing electoral interests, but it has also established the President as the unchallenged arbiter of such policy disputes within his coalition.

Relations between the political executive and the rest of the executive branch

The relationship between governments and their state administrations has long been of interest to political analysts. In the liberal democracies of western Europe it is the provisions for electoral representation and a competitive party system which serve to legitimise the laws and regulations which make up the policy output of these political systems. But how possible is it for the members of the political executive, who are elected and therefore hold office on a temporary basis, to control the activities of the permanent, appointed personnel of the rest of the executive branch?

This is a problem which has been exacerbated in nearly all these countries since the second world war by substantial increases in the numbers of those employed by the state and by extensions to the range of activities in which they are engaged. Indeed some would contend that the preoccupation of much political analysis with major policy changes is misplaced. Arguably, the experience of most citizens is more directly shaped by the myriad of 'small' decisions at various levels of the state administration through which policy is converted into detailed regulations and is then implemented[9].

A more specific issue of concern has been the relationship between ministers and those who comprise the upper echelons of the state administration: *the state administrative elite*. As has been noted, studies of the role of top civil servants have underlined the extent to which political and administrative tasks are blurred together in their work, belying the sharp differentiation of function which is suggested by the terms 'civil servant' and 'administrator' on the one hand, as against 'politician' and 'minister' on the other. This section will therefore need to explore both sides of this relationship.

The states of western Europe can be contrasted with other political systems which have developed particular methods for ensuring political control over the state administration. In the single-party system of the Soviet Union the ruling party's own bureaucracy parallels that of the state, and exercises special controls over appointments to the state administration at all levels. Moreover, it is the leading bodies of the party – the Politburo and Central Committee – which monopolise policy-making, rather than party members holding ministerial posts. In the United States, what is often termed the 'spoils system' provides for a large number of posts which would be filled by permanent civil servants in western Europe to be subject to a change of personnel at the periodic presidential, state and local elections.

While the west European states do not have recourse to either of these methods, in some countries parties of government, and individual ministers, do exercise considerable powers of patronage in respect of appointments to and promotions within the civil service (see below). Three countries, however, have adopted a specific mechanism for strengthening the minister's control over his department: *the ministerial 'cabinet'*. In Belgium, France and Italy, incoming ministers appoint their own personal staff who may be civil servants, political activists or outside 'experts' (academics, journalists, etc.). They are paid from public funds and assist with formulating policy and supervisng the work of the department, as well as liaising with other ministries, parliament, the press and the public. (In the United Kingdom there have been small-scale attempts to introduce this system; a number of ministers have appointed personal political aides since the Wilson government.) In France ninety per cent of 'cabinet' personnel under the Fifth Republic have, however, been drawn from the upper echelons of the civil service. It could therefore be argued that they provide an additional mechanism for the state administrative elite to influence its political masters, rather than ensuring ministerial primacy.

France, Italy and Spain also have a system of *prefects*, under the authority of the Ministry of the Interior, who act as agents of the government at the local level. Those prefects have a quasi-political role as well as an administrative one, even where, as in France, they are drawn from a specialist corps of permanent civil servants. In France, in particular, where the prefects co-ordinate the work of many of the central ministries' field services (as well as supervising local elected authorities – see chapter 10), this system has afforded an additional mechanism for central political control over local units of the state administration.

More generally, the average duration of governments and the average tenure of individual ministers in office in the different countries of western Europe are also factors which influence the effectiveness of political control. Certainly there are numerous examples where one party has achieved a continuous presence in government over a relatively long period: the Social Democrats in Sweden from 1932 to 1976, the Christian Democrats in Italy since 1945, Fianna Fail in the Republic of Ireland until 1973, the CDU in West Germany from 1949 to 1969, the Gaullist Party in France from 1959 to 1981, and the Conservative Party in the United Kingdom from 1951 to 1964. The pattern of ministerial tenure, however, ranges from examples of individual politicians holding a ministry for many years through numerous changes of coalition government, to the United Kingdom experience of ministers surviving, on average, little more than two years in any one department of government.

Where one party has been dominant in government for a long period, a different problem may arise, with ministers using their powers of patronage to 'colonise' their ministry and related agencies with members of their own party or party faction. This kind of *politicisation* has been characteristic of the Italian state administration at all levels. In Belgium, too, there has been a high degree of politicisation and the segmentation of society on religious, linguistic and regional as well as political lines has resulted in such factors affecting procedures for recruitment and promotion, and has served to link individual civil servants, through their career prospects, to the interests of the major parties and trade unions. In France the phrase 'l'Etat-UDR' was used by critics to designate similar trends that had developed by the early 1970s. However, in neither the Italian nor the Belgian case has such politicisation of the state administration enhanced the ability of governments to exercise strong leadership. On the contrary, factional struggle within the Italian Christian Democrat Party and social segmentation in Belgium have served to fragment political control and to reproduce this political fragmentation within the state administration, increasing its size rather than its effectiveness.

Where politicisation of this kind takes place, civil servants – and not only those at the highest levels – use their role in the making and implementation of policy to promote specific party political interests. A rather different pattern of politicisation may occur where the right of civil service personnel to stand for elective office is safeguarded. In the United Kingdom the rights of many public employees (both in the departments of central government and in local government) to participate in party politics have been effectively restricted. In many west European countries, on the contrary, state employees enjoy positive rights in this regard, being able to take leave to stand in elections and having the right to return to an equivalent posting on leaving an elective office. In both France and West Germany such a system has fostered an interchange of political and administrative personnel and has led to an overrepresentation of certain types of public employees among the parliamentary representatives of the main parties (see chapter 8.

In France this interchange of political and administrative personnel has gone further, since a preliminary career in the upper echelons of the civil service, followed by a period in ministerial 'cabinets', has become an increasingly common pathway to ministerial office. (This has been termed the *fonctionnarisation* of the political executive, *fonctionnaires* being the French term for civil servants.) In West Germany a somewhat different issue has arisen. Political loyalty to the state has been made a condition of state employment. This was confirmed by a Constitutional Court ruling in 1975 which sanctioned what is often referred to as a *Berufsverbot* (occupational ban), since it has operated to debar Communist Party members and other radical critics of the state from the whole range of public employment (including teaching, the railways and post office).

More generally, concern about the type of inputs which the state administrative elite may be in a position to feed into the policy-making process has centred on their recruitment and training and on their subsequent contacts with organised interests. In a number of west European countries new entrants to posts equivalent to the administrative class in the United Kingdom are drawn disproportionately from the upper middle classes. This is the case both where the state has established its own competitive entry specialist schools to train recruits to the top levels of the civil service (as in France, with its various *Grandes Ecoles* for different specialist corps) and where the state draws its recruits from the university sector (as in the United Kingdom, where candidates with public school and Oxbridge backgrounds still dominate the competitive examinations for the administrative class, and in West Germany, where successful applicants normally have a law degree and are often the sons of upper civil servants). In these cases, the state administrative elite that results is one 'which reflects the distribution of power in wider society'.[10] In as far as such recruitment and training procedures may also be associated with specific patterns of shared values, the state administrative elite may provide a distinctive policy input which persists not only through changes of government but also through changes of regime.

How accurate, however, is it to talk of a cohesive state administrative elite in each country? Does not the division of this personnel into separate departments and agencies and between different tiers of central and local government make for a degree of fragmentation and conflicts of interest among members of the state administrative elite? In the United Kingdom the civil service is both highly centralised and, in terms of recruitment and training, the most highly unified. In contrast, in West Germany the organisation of the state administration is considerably decentralised, yet the system of pre-entry legal training and probationary practical training affords a degree of cohesion. France has traditionally had a more highly compartmentalised system with a number of separate prestigious corps each with its own specialist training and career structure. However, here, the establishment of the Ecole Nationale d'Administration (ENA) immediately after the war has provided a new cohesion, its graduates sharing, in particular, a 'technocratic' commitment to state intervention to achieve economic growth and modernisation.

Nevertheless, the strength of distinctive and conflicting 'departmental views' is a common theme of studies of the state administrations of western Europe. Beyond a concern to defend and, where possible, extend their share of national expenditure, some studies have also suggested that the policy priorities of leading civil servants may come to reflect the concerns of those organised interests with which they have developed a close working relationship. In addition, in the case of politicised state administrations, like those of Italy and Belgium, certain organised interests (Catholic Action, for example, in Italy and the major pressure groups linked to the Social Catholic and Socialist parties in Belgium) may 'colonise' parts of the state administration.

In France, provision for members of the main specialist corps to take periods of leave from their corps has facilitated their movement into top positions in both the public and private sectors of the economy, as well as into political careers. In the United Kingdom wider work experience of this type was advocated by the Fulton Report on the civil service in 1968, but greater interchange of personnel between the economic and administrative elites has, in recent years, often taken the form of leading civil servants moving into related industrial and commercial concerns or pressure group organisations on retirement from state service. This trend itself raises questions as to the nature of the working relations which develop between civil servants and the organised interests which are closely affected by their departments' policies.

The issue of political control over the state administration is one which thus raises complex questions about the relative merits of different methods of recruitment and training and about the policy inputs with which state administrative elites may associate themselves. These questions are of increasing concern as the scale of state intervention has come to be regarded as of critical importance for the performance of the national economies of western Europe.

Notes

1. See, for example, the published diaries of two former British Labour Party ministers; R. H. S. Crossman, *The Diaries of a Cabinet Minister*, 3 vols. (London, Hamish Hamilton, 1975, 1976, 1977), and B. Castle, *The Castle Diaries, 1974–76* (London, Weidenfeld and Nicolson, 1980).

For a wider discussion of the structures of a number of west European state administrations, see F. F. Ridley (ed.) *Government and Administration in Western Europe* (London, Martin Robertson, 1979).

2. However, in France, the third Mauroy government, formed in March 1983, included only fifteen ministers of cabinet rank. In West Germany, since the mid-1960s, Chancellors have in addition appointed a number of parliamentary state secretaries, who do not rank as ministers.

3. It has also been not uncommon for a limited number of ministerial posts to be held by civil servants and other 'experts' in both the Netherlands and Belgium.

4. The major exception is Switzerland where the seven members of the federal government are elected by the Federal Assembly to reflect both the strength of the main parties in the lower house and the linguistic and religious balance between cantons. The chairmanship of the council of ministers rotates.

5. See R. Rose, 'The making of cabinet ministers', *British Journal of Political Science*, October 1971, and P. Allum, *Italy – Republic without Government?* (London, Weidenfeld and Nicolson, 1973), pp. 119–21.

6. See in particular the introduction by Richard Crossman to W. Bagehot, *The English Constitution* (London, Collins, 1963) and G. Jones, 'The prime minister's power', *Parliamentary Affairs*, XVIII, no. 1, spring 1965, pp. 167–88.

7. Article 5 of the 1958 Constitution states: 'The President of the Republic sees that the Constitution of the Republic is respected, ensures by his arbitration the regular functioning of the organs of government and the continuity of the State. He is the protector of national independence, of territorial integrity, and of respect for agreements with the French Community.'

8. With the exception of those held in 1986.

9. See, for example, F. F. Ridley (ed.), *op. cit.*, Introduction.

10. G. Smith, *Politics in Western Europe* (London, Heinemann, 1980), p. 184.

FEDERALISM, DEVOLUTION AND LOCAL GOVERNMENT

Patterns of government organisation

Though all democratic states resemble each other in many important ways, there are differences in the manner in which they can be organised. One such set of differences relates to the distribution of powers within central government: the respective roles of the legislature, head of state and executive government, discussed in chapters 7, 8 and 9 (above). Another important difference is concerned with the degree to which political power in the state is centralised or diffused: the Federal Republic of Germany, Austria and Switzerland all have a diffused pattern of organisation, like the USA, India and Canada, which qualifies them as *federal* states, whilst the other states of western Europe, such as Italy, France and the United Kingdom, are *unitary* states, with a more centralised pattern of organisation. Briefly, federal states possess two quite distinct levels of sovereign authority: the central, federal government and the various separate provincial governments. Each level possesses its own powers, as laid down by a written constitution, and some means, such as a constitutional court, is provided for resolving disputes between the central and provincial levels of government concerning competence to exercise authority. In unitary states, only one level of authority exists: provincial, regional or local government may be provided, but the powers which such governments exercise are always subject to the superior authority of the central government.

Why should two such different patterns of state organisation exist? Which, if either, is to be considered 'normal' and which 'exceptional'? To answer the second question first, it is probably correct to consider the unitary pattern as normal. Certainly it is more usual, and better corresponds to ideas about states possessing a single, undisputed and unrestricted source of ultimate authority: the 'sovereign power'. Federal states exist because of the special historical circumstances which were the context within which the state was called into being, when, for geographic or political reasons, some looser, more flexible arrangement of power than exists in centralised states was thought to be necessary or desirable. An interesting modern parallel to the formation of such states is the European Community, an association of 12 states in which certain powers are exercised by the Community institutions under the Treaty of Rome, whilst others are preserved as powers of the member-states (see below, chapter 11).

Federalism can give rise to disputes that would not exist, or would be easier to resolve in a unitary state. It can appear cumbersome, and can provoke seemingly unnecessary and inefficient regional variations (e.g., the different school curricula which exist in the various *Länder* of West Germany, causing problems when a child is moved from one *Land* to another). But it is also an attractive solution to the problem of how best to delegate power from the centre, so that local or regional problems can be dealt with swiftly, so that the needs and aspirations of regionally distinct groups can be satisfied, so that responsiveness of government can match the democratic expectations of the citizen. This chapter will first examine the way in which federalism operates in West Germany and Switzerland (the federal arrangements in Austria tend to resemble those in West Germany to a considerable extent), and then, in contrast, how unitary states such as the United Kingdom, France, Italy, Belgium and Spain cope with the problems of the delegation and diffusion of governmental power. Since such delegation and diffusion of power in both federal and unitary states involves the structures of local government, the chapter will conclude by surveying the functions and organisation of local government in the United Kingdom, France and West Germany, and will draw attention to recent or proposed reforms of local government in those countries.

The federal model

West Germany
A federal form of state organisation was adopted for the new West German state in 1949 for three main reasons:

the western occupying authorities (the UK, France and the USA) agreed that this arrangement of state power would be the most likely to obstruct any possible re-establishment of a dictatorial regime and would also be the most favourable to the development of democratic attitudes and behaviour;

the period between the end of the second world war and the establishment of a West German state had seen the growth of democratic government in the provinces (the *Länder*) of each western occupation zone, and these provinces were not prepared to surrender their autonomy completely to a new central government;

Germany had been united as a *federal* state in 1871, and the federal principle, though weakened under the Weimar republic and practically extinguished as a political force by the Nazis, could be regarded as part of the German political culture.

So the Basic Law (the West German constitution) enshrines the principle of federalism as an unamendable part of the constitution. It sets out the powers which shall be exercised by the federal government in Bonn, over such matters as defence, foreign affairs, the national budget, social security and international trade, as well as those powers specifically reserved to the *Länder*: such as the police, education (including university education), broadcasting, many aspects of justice and the courts, local transport, local government and industrial development policy. The Basic Law also lists certain areas in which either or both the central and provincial governments may exercise authority. It lays down arrangements for securing financial resources for the *Länder* free from central control. It provides for disputes between the federal government and the *Länder*, between two *Länder*, or between a citizen and the government of the federation or a *Land*, to be settled by a constitutional court as final arbiter of the Basic Law.

Such a federal arrangement needs more than a constitutional basis in order to function successfully. It requires both the institution of co-ordinating arrangements (in order to ensure co-operation), and the ability of the *Länder* to participate in national politics (in order to ensure integration). Such co-operation and integration in West Germany are provided through the Bundesrat, the 'second chamber' of the national legislature in which representatives of the governments of the *Länder* participate, with powers to discuss legislation, to veto any legislation that affects the constitutional powers or political responsibilities of the *Länder*, and to delay other legislation, or amend it. The composition of the Bundesrat is outlined in chapter 8. Disputes between the two chambers of the West German parliament are often settled through the use of the 'mediation committee' of representatives of both the Bundestag and the Bundesrat, drawn proportionately from each chamber according to party strength. In addition, the administration of many aspects of federal policy, though under the control of Bonn, is delegated to the *Länder* to put into effect, which again involves them in national policy. Some matters, such as the planning of higher education or aid to marginal rural areas of the country in need of special measures of economic development, are dealt with by committees composed jointly of representatives of all the *Länder* and of the central government, under the provisions of treaties signed by all the governments involved.

Each *Land* has its own constitution, and its own government and legislature. The *Land* parliament is normally elected every four years (except for the Saarland and North Rhine-Westphalia, elected at five-year intervals). With very minor exceptions, the party systems in all the *Länder* reflect the party systems in the national context. Indeed, *Land* elections are increasingly contested as trial runs for national elections, and the results seen as indicative of the national popularity of parties. West Berlin has a special status, not being part of the Federal Republic as such, but adopting for itself the laws passed by the Bonn legislature, and otherwise possessing the structure, powers and political system of a *Land*.

Problems arise because of the differences among the *Länder*. Though each has responsibility for the same range of functions, the *Länder* vary in size from the small city-states of Bremen and Hamburg to the vast territories of Bavaria and North Rhine-Westphalia; some, like Baden-Württemberg and Hamburg, are relatively prosperous, whilst others, such as the Saarland and Lower Saxony, have fewer resources per head of population. Many proposals have been made to remedy the situation. There is a form of 'pooling' of some revenues from taxation, whereby the wealthier *Länder* supplement the income of those with below-average financial resources, but this has only limited effect. Suggestions that the northern and central *Länder* be amalgamated to produce fewer, more equally sized and uniformly wealthy *Länder* have been rejected because the smaller *Länder* have not wished to lose their status and identity.

Figure 3   West Germany and Berlin, showing Länder boundaries and capitals

Table 14   The Länder of the Federal Republic of Germany

Land	Population (million)	Area (sq. km)	Current Government	Votes in Bundesrat
Baden-Württemberg	9.3	35,751	CDU	5
Bavaria	11.0	70,549	CSU	5
Bremen	0.7	404	SPD	3
Hamburg	1.6	753	SPD & FDP	3
Hesse	5.5	21,110	CDU & FDP	4
Lower Saxony	7.2	47,430	CDU & FDP	5
North Rhine-Westphalia	16.8	34,045	SPD	5
Rhineland-Pfalz	3.6	19,831	CDU & FDP	4
Saarland	1.0	2,568	SPD	3
Schleswig-Holstein	2.6	15,680	SPD	4

Switzerland

The origins of the Swiss state can be traced back to a defence pact entered into by three cantons in the thirteenth century, but the modern federation really dates from the peace settlement following the Napoleonic wars and the constitutions of 1848. So, like West Germany, federalism in Switzerland is a way of accommodating historical differences among regions wishing to form a single state. Unlike West Germany, those differences are reinforced by differences of religion and language (some cantons have a majority of French speakers, others of German speakers, and one of Italian speakers). There are now twenty-six cantons (counting the 'half-cantons' – where a former canton has been divided into two – separately).

The neutrality of Switzerland and its relative unimportance in international relations has meant that domestic, rather than foreign politics and policies have been all-important, and domestic political issues very often involve local differences – again reinforcing the political significance of the cantons rather than that of the federal state. Identification with the canton is still very strong, and the use of the referendum to settle important local, as well as national issues helps to preserve the significance of the local political focus.

The Swiss constitution reserves a limited range of functions for the federal government (among these are foreign affairs, defence policy, banking and coinage, immigration and the railway system), while all other functions belong to the cantons, including local transport, policing, education, cultural affairs, tourism and environmental planning. In addition (as in West Germany) the cantons take responsibility for the administration of many of the federal government's policies.

The institutions of the political system reflect the dominance of the cantons in Swiss politics. The National Council (Nationalrat) is elected by the people directly, but the second chamber, the Council of the States (Ständerat) consists of nominees of the cantons, each of which may decide on the method of choice and term of office of its two representatives (the 'half cantons' have only one representative each). The equivalent of the cabinet is the federal council (Bundesrat) consisting of seven members, who must be drawn from seven different cantons, and who are elected by a joint assembly of both chambers of the legislature. The cantons have their own sources of finance protected by constitutional provision.

Although from time to time suggestions are made concerning the revision of cantonal boundaries, the only successful example of the creation of a new canton for many years was in 1979, when Jura became a canton following a referendum. In general, neither the number of cantons nor the differences which exist in their size, wealth and population, are serious matters of political concern. Yet the differences can be considerable: in area, for instance, Graubunden has 7109 square kilometres and Bern 6887, yet Basel City has only 37 and Zug 239.

Federalism seems to suit the Swiss, and is certainly not itself an issue of political debate. There has been, inevitably, a gradual strengthening of the centre in recent years, but the deep differences in the social, cultural and economic composition of the cantons means that local autonomy is still regarded as the most efficient, and the most democratic, method of conducting politics within a national framework.

Unitary states: regional devolution

Although they all have a single, unchallenged central source of sovereign authority, unitary states display a variety of arrangements for devolving and delegating power from the central government to subordinate territorial units. Unitary states are more flexible than federal states in this respect, for they can introduce, amend or abandon patterns of devolved or delegated power usually without the need for a long and involved procedure of constitutional amendment.

Several west European states have experienced special problems relating to claims for local autonomy or regional devolution in recent years, and they have produced a variety of different responses. In addition, there has been a generalised tendency to decentralise political power in the name of more responsive government and as a counter to the extension of centralised bureaucratic control over the economy and other aspects of public life.

The United Kingdom

In some ways, it is surprising that the United Kingdom has not transformed itself into a federal state. Certainly, given the distinctiveness of the peoples of Scotland, Wales and Northern Ireland (not to speak of the Isle of Man and the Channel Islands) the case for a federal pattern of government would seem to be as strong as it was for, say, Austria or West Germany. The Royal Commission on the Constitution (the Kilbrandon Report) of 1973 did go some way toward suggesting a system of elected regional authorities, including the areas of Wales and Scotland, but these proposals were not adopted by the government either at the time or later. Legislation was, however, eventually produced by the government and, with some amendment, passed by parliament. This entailed referenda being held in 1979 in Wales and Scotland with a view to the creation of elected assemblies for those areas, but the electorate in those referenda did not support the proposals in sufficient numbers for them to be adopted. In Northern Ireland, the semi-autonomous parliament for the province, Stormont, was placed in abeyance in 1972, and Northern Ireland became subject to direct rule from London. Attempts to devise a new form of self-rule, involving a dilution of the Protestant majority through some form of power-sharing with Catholics, were defeated by the non-cooperation of the Protestants, sometimes extending to illegal forms of direct action. However, an election for an Assembly took place in autumn 1982.

Scotland and Wales do have a limited form of special status

within the United Kingdom. Scotland still has devolved powers of executive government exercised by the Secretary of State for Scotland and the Scottish Law Officers, and many laws passed by parliament have to be duplicated so that they apply also to Scotland (e.g., in local government, education, policing, criminal justice and local transport). Wales, too, now has its own Secretary of State, and there is a Welsh Office in Cardiff, with substantial powers concerning matters such as housing, planning and education. Both Scotland and Wales have their own special committees in the House of Commons.

France

France has often been held up as the prime example of a centralised unitary state, in which decisions about the erection of a set of traffic lights in Strasbourg have to be ratified first in Paris, taking perhaps three or four years in the process. The Napoleonic organisation of France into Departments (of which there are now ninety-six, plus six overseas Departments), in each of which the Prefect exercises the delegated authority of the government in Paris, came increasingly to be questioned in the Fifth Republic. President de Gaulle attempted, in an unsuccessful referendum in 1969, to introduce an element of regional autonomy, after the Departments had been grouped into twenty-two regions, each with its own Regional Prefect, in 1964. The growth of dissatisfaction with the effectiveness and responsiveness of central government, in particular in Brittany and Corsica, revived demands for some form of regional government elected by the people, to supplement the regional councils and regional economic and social committees, both indirectly-elected bodies, that were established in 1972. Under Mitterrand's presidency, new legislation, was adopted by the National Assembly in 1982, introducing direct elections on the basis of proportional representation for the regional councils and enlarging their powers. The first such direct regional elections took place in 1986. In addition, a new statute has been adopted for Corsica, providing the island with a measure of autonomy.

Other forms of regional devolution

Several other unitary states in western Europe have developed some form of regional devolution and autonomy.

In *Italy*, twenty regions were designated by 1970, extending over the whole of the country, after regional authorities had first been introduced for the poorer, less-developed areas of southern Italy. Each region has an elected assembly, which in turn chooses an executive council from among its membership. The regions have powers over agricultural development, the police, tourism, housing, education and some aspects of industrial development. Elections are keenly contested by the parties, which see regional power as something well worth striving for. To an extent, this regional structure makes Italy a quasi-federal state; certainly, the regions have more powers than do the provinces of the formally federal Austrian republic. But, unlike a genuine federal state, in Italy regions do not possess entrenched powers independent of the decisions and desires of the central government.

The deepening linguistic cleavages in *Belgium*, reinforced by differences of economic structure and resources, led in 1970 to the designation of the two language areas of Wallonia and Flanders (with Brussels as a special region) and nominated cultural councils were appointed in 1971. It is intended to introduce directly-elected councils for Wallonia and Flanders, which will have responsibility for matters of regional significance, such as education, culture, roads and regional economic development, and which will control about ten per cent of the national budget. However, progress has been slow on this matter, which is a policy subject to political pressure and developments at a national level. The trend in the Belgian party system toward linguistic-based parties (see chapter 5) is a complicating factor which may well further delay progress toward a satisfactory and acceptable regional structure.

A similar development has occurred in *Spain*, where local particularism in the Basque region and Catalonia led to violence and tensions within the democratised post-Franco regime. A system of autonomous regions was introduced from 1980, with regional governments responsible to elected regional legislatures having authority over policing, education, banking, transport, energy, local government and language and cultural policy. These arrangements initially covered the Basque Country. Andalusia, Catalonia and Galicia, but were subsequently extended to the rest of Spain. Regional elections in the thirteen additional regions were held in May 1983 and again in June 1987.

Local government

Whether a state is organised on a federal or a unitary pattern, there will still be a requirement for a structure of local government to deal with matters of local importance, under authority delegated either by the central government or by provincial governments. The general purposes of local government are to administer matters such as street lighting, refuse disposal, housing provision, public libraries, road maintenance, schools and local public transport, according to the wishes of the community expressed through elections to local councils and in other ways. The structure of local government authorities varies from country to country (indeed, as in West Germany and the United Kingdom, it can vary within the same country), but in general, there is a two- or three-tier arrangement, with the larger unit responsible for services and obligations which are best carried out on an area basis, and sub-divided into smaller units which are responsible for more localised services. Finance for local government is provided in a variety of ways: property taxes, government grants both of a general and a function-specific nature, charges for services, and the automatic allocation of shares of certain taxes, are the most usual methods.

The *United Kingdom* local government system was developed in stages in the nineteenth century, though counties, boroughs and parishes had long before then possessed a variety of rights and obligations concerning relief of the poor, regulation of markets, maintenance of roads and the administration of justice. The current structure dates from major reforms of local government in London (which took effect in 1965), and elsewhere (with effect from 1974). The country is divided into administrative counties, such as Cheshire, Surrey and Gwent, and into regions (such as Strathclyde) in Scotland. Each of these, in turn, is divided into districts. Both of these two tiers, or levels, have their own elected councils. Elections occur periodically, with councillors serving four-year terms, and are contested by the national political parties, as well as by independents and representatives of local groupings, such as the ratepayers' associations. Turnout is extraordinarily low (usually no more than thirty to forty per cent of registered voters), compared either to turnout at national elections of around seventy per cent, or to the turnout recorded at local elections in other west European countries.

The counties are responsible for education, policing, social services, libraries, major roads, fire and ambulance services and local public transport. The districts deal with the provision of public housing, planning control of building projects, refuse collection, sports and recreation facilities, car parks and other local services, as well as acting as the agent of the county in administering some of its services.

Revenue comes from two main sources: rates levied on property, such as houses, shops and factories, and grants from central government. There is currently great dissatisfaction with the inequities and uncertainties produced by this system of financing, and various governments in the past twenty years have promised to find a substitute for the rating system.

In *France*, the Departments are divided into some 36,400 communities, each with its own elected municipal council and its own mayor, who acts both as the head of the local government authority and, under the prefect, as the agent of the central government. Paris was an exception to this arrangement until 1977, when its council elected its own mayor for the first time. These communities (called 'municipalities') vary in size, but only about ten per cent have more than two thousand inhabitants, whilst ten per cent have fewer than a hundred! Municipal councils are elected for six years, and the council chooses its mayor from amongst its elected members. The mayor is responsible for the main functions of the municipality, which include the control of public order and safety, public sanitation, and such other functions as may from time to time be delegated to it by higher authorities (such as the Department). Elections are held for departmental councils on a cantonal basis: each canton (which may consist of a group of small municipalities, or even one part of a very large municipality) elects one member to serve for a six-year term (though elections are held in half the cantons every three years). Departmental councils deal with the administration of state services, such as roads and schools, and have only restricted powers of initiation of policy. Previously the Departmental Prefect had acted as the executive officer of the Department, but the 1982 reforms provided for an elected president of the Department to fulfil this role.

Local authorities in France have very few financial resources of their own, being dependent upon loans and subsidies from the central government for much of their revenue. Despite their lack of powers and disposable finances, local government authorities are regarded by the population as being politically important, and elections are keenly contested, with a relatively high turnout of voters.

The *West German* system of local government was influenced by the fact that it developed locally within the zones of military occupation after the war, before the organs of central or *Land* government were established. Consequently, the structure of local government still varies in certain respects from region to region. The city-states of Bremen and Hamburg (and also West Berlin) are simultaneously units of local government and *Land* government. They are subdivided into districts.[1] In other *Länder*, there are three levels of local government competence: the region (e.g., in North Rhine-Westphalia there are six regions); the district (equivalent to a county or county borough in Britain); and the local community. Some larger cities have the status, and exercise the powers both of a community and of a district.

The community, besides carrying out tasks delegated to it by the *Länder*, is responsible for school building, refuse collection, hospitals and old people's homes, child welfare, cultural institutions and some public utilities, such as municipal bus services and water supply. It is financed by a share of the income tax, calculated on the basis of the amount raised in its area, by a share of the tax on petrol, by subsidies from the *Land*, and by local taxes. The chief executive (e.g., the mayor) is directly elected in some areas (such as Baden-Württemberg) and indirectly in others (such as Hamburg), while in some cases there is a collective chief executive.

The district, which, like the community, has a directly elected council, mainly operates as an aggregate of its constituent communities, dealing with matters which the communities wish to undertake collectively, such as the provision and construction of hospitals, certain welfare services, perhaps a swimming pool, which it is more economical to provide on a district basis. The finances of the district are derived from payments from the communities and from some local taxes. The region acts as an administrative sub-division of the *Land*.

Local government reform has been a pressing political issue in several west European states in the past twenty years or so. In part, this is because of the 'nationalisation' of politics, which makes local differences and distinctions less valid, and the struggle between major parties even at the local level acquires national importance. In part, it has occurred because of the relative importance of local government expenditure, both absolutely and in relation to national economic policy. In part, local government reform has been demanded as a means of improving the responsiveness of government to the wishes of the electorate.

Reform has concentrated upon two main topics: the structure of local government, and its financing. In terms of structural reform, in the United Kingdom the types of authority and their number were 'rationalised' by the Local Government Acts of 1963 and 1972. In West Germany, most of the *Länder* have completed a process of reduction of the number of independent communities by amalgamation and by the extension of the boundaries of major cities, such as Köln, so that there are now only about 7,500 communities instead of over 22,000. In France, the Guichard Report of 1976 pressed the case for the creation of a powerful district authority above the level of the municipality, with its own sources of finance, but so far nothing has been done to implement those recommendations.

Little of note has been achieved with regard to the reform of financing of local government. The problem is to find a system which is equitable with regard to those who pay, inexpensive to operate, yet sufficiently flexible to accommodate changing levels of local government expenditure. Reliance on central government grants is seen as a restriction of the autonomy of local government, yet the dictates of national economic policy demand that local government expenditure be linked to national monetary and fiscal controls to some extent. The reforms of local government financing sought by Mr Heseltine when Secretary of

State for the Environment in Britain, as part of the Conservative government's policy of monetary control, have highlighted the conflict between central control of local government on the one hand, and local democracy on the other, and for that reason have been opposed by local government authorities of all political persuasions. This problem, affecting many of the states of western Europe, seems to admit of no easy solution.

Note

1. The situation in Bremen is complicated by the fact that the *Land* includes the town of Bremerhaven, which has its own town council. The Bremen *Land* parliament, excluding the Bremerhaven representatives, forms the Bremen town council.

11

POLITICS AND THE EUROPEAN COMMUNITY

The European Community is a novel political arrangement, being one of the most important and successful examples of supranational political co-operation that can be found in the modern world. It is also of considerable significance in the ways that it impinges upon the politics of its member-states, and even on the politics of potential members and non-members. It is of interest also because it is an important variation of the *federal* pattern of political arrangements.

In chapter 10, the concept of federalism was presented as being a means of providing a form of common central authority whilst retaining a considerable degree of local independence and autonomy for the constituent provinces or regions. An extension of this idea is the concept of *supranationalism*, in which there is provision of some limited form of common institutions and common political authority on behalf of a group of states, which voluntarily agree to accept the exercise of such authority as binding (provided it is restricted to such matters as were originally intended), but which retain for their own national governments and parliaments authority over all other affairs. This is more than is involved in membership either of military alliances (such as NATO: the North Atlantic Treaty Organisation) or of international organisations such as the Organisation for Economic Cooperation and Development (OECD) or the Council of Europe. Such organisations have, normally, extremely restricted and quite clearly-defined goals. A supranational organisation, on the other hand, may have open-ended, developmental and quite wide-ranging purposes.

The *European Community* (EC) – often referred to as the Common Market' – is one of the few existing examples of such a supranational organisation. It was created by the Treaty of Rome in 1957. The Treaty, in its preamble, refers to the goal of promoting 'an ever-closer union among the peoples of Europe', and, in article 2, states that

The Community shall have as its task, by establishing a common market and progressively approximating the economic policies of the Member States, to promote throughout the Community a harmonious development of economic activities, a continuous and balanced expansion, an increase in stability, an accelerated raising of the standard of living and closer relations between the States belonging to it.

Such a task can, in these terms, never be regarded as completed, hence the 'developmental' and open-ended quality of the Community.

This chapter will trace briefly the historical evolution of the European Community, examine the institutions and processes which constitute its political system, and, in conclusion, consider some of the fundamental problems which face the Community and its member-states.

The evolution of the European Community

The European Community, as it exists today, is the product of two important ideas that found expression in the immediate post-war period in western Europe. One of these ideas was that of European co-operation, and even of European integration, based on the hope that closer links among the peoples and nations of Europe would prevent any repetition of the two world wars that had in the twentieth century been triggered by European quarrels. The other, more practical and immediate idea was that of economic co-operation, to accomplish the pressing tasks of post-war reconstruction more swiftly and more effectively.

It was this wish for economic co-operation, stimulated particularly by the need to resolve the problem of control of the coal and steel resources in the Ruhr district in West Germany, that led to the first stage in the evolution of the Community. Encouraged by the USA, upon whom western Europe depended for its security and for economic assistance, six west European states founded the *European Coal and Steel Community* (ECSC) in 1951, to regulate the production, pricing and marketing of coal and steel products of the member-states (West Germany, France, Italy and the Benelux countries). A more ambitious plan to create a *European Defence Community* in the early 1950s failed, because of the sensitivity of the issue and, especially, because of the reluctance of some political parties in France and West Germany to countenance German rearmament for any reason whatsoever. The North Atlantic Treaty Organisation, formed in 1949 and extended to include armed forces from the German Federal Republic in 1954, was a much larger alliance than that envisaged by the plan for a European Defence Community, and included several states not comprehended by plans for west European integration, such as the USA, Canada and the United Kingdom.

The success of the ECSC, the progress toward a stable democratic political system in West Germany, and the increasing rigidity of the east–west division of Europe encouraged politicians to plan a much more ambitious and comprehensive scheme of economic co-operation: the *European Economic Community* (EEC). The six member-states of the ECSC signed the Treaty of Rome in March 1957, which provided for the development of a common market for industrial and agricultural products, for the free movement of capital and labour within the territories of the member-states, and, as a corollary to the elimination of customs duties between member-states, for the creation of a common set of customs duties for the import of goods from non-member-states. In the same year, a treaty to create a parallel organisation to coordinate nuclear energy development in the six member-states was signed (EURATOM). In 1965, the executives of these three European institutions (EEC, ECSC and EURATOM) were merged, though the legal identities of the organisations remained separate.

The institutional development of the EEC was swifter than even the most optimistic 'Europeanists' had hoped. Customs duties were harmonised ahead of schedule. Policies to realise the goals of a common market through the elimination of barriers to trade, the creation of a price-support scheme for several key agricultural products and schemes for regional development were promoted by the Commission in Brussels and accepted – though sometimes not without political difficulties – on behalf of member-states by the Council of Ministers. Those who saw

economic integration as but a preliminary to political integration
in western Europe were encouraged, despite clear warnings from
some politicians, and especially from President de Gaulle, that,
for them, economic union was the destination, not merely a
staging-post on the road to political union.

The success of the Common Market encouraged the United
Kingdom – which had stood aloof in the earlier period of
European integration – to seek admission to the EEC. Twice –
under the Conservative government of Macmillan and the Labour
government of Wilson – France's veto blocked the UK's
admission. Under the premiership of Edward Heath, however,
and in changed political circumstances in western Europe,
negotiations were commenced and the UK, together with Eire
and Denmark, became a member in 1973. Norway, which had
simultaneously negotiated terms for admission, decided in a
referendum not to become a member. The enlargement of the
EEC to nine members brought problems in its wake. Some were
internal and institutional, such as the rearrangement of staffing in
the Commission to provide new members with an equitable share
of posts (including new commissioners (see below)) and
extension of translation facilities; others were political, such as the
matter of the UK's trading links with its dominions, and the
long-running saga of United Kingdom contributions to an
ever-increasing Community budget because of the Common
Agricultural Policy. Greece became the tenth member in 1981.
Spain and Portugal became members in 1986, though France and
the UK both expressed reluctance, for different reasons, concerning the admission of Spain.

The political system of the European Community

The Commission
The most visible and best-known of the institutions of the
European Community is the Commission. It is located in Brussels,
which therefore has the strongest claim to the status of being the
'capital city' of the Community. Televised news reports
concerning the Community usually have as a background the
Berlaymont building, which houses most of the staff of the
Commission and which is the site for the meetings of the
commissioners themselves.

There are now seventeen commissioners: two each from France, Italy, West Germany, the United Kingdom and Spain, and one each from the Netherlands, Belgium, Luxemburg, Eire, Denmark, Greece and Portugal. One commissioner is chosen as President. Each of the other commissioners exercises responsibility for one (or more) of the functional divisions of the Commission: for example, the Community budget, external affairs or agriculture. Within each of these functional divisions, the staff of the Commission, drawn on an approximately proportional basis from the member-states, prepare *proposals* to be presented to the Council of Ministers. The Commission has responsibility for the *execution* of the Community policy, though principally this takes the form of monitoring the administration of policy by national governments and their civil services. To enable the Commission to undertake these duties, a large staff of translators and secretaries, as well as bureaucrats, is employed.

Though drawn from the member-states by government nomination, the commissioners are not subject to instruction by their national governments, nor subject to recall by governments. Commissioners do not necessarily even belong to the party in government at the time of their nomination: in the case of the UK, for instance, the practice has been for one of the commissioners to be a Conservative politician, the other to come from the ranks of the Labour Party. Commissioners serve for a four-year term, but there is no bar to renomination.

The responsibility of the Commission is to develop and foster a 'Community interest', to counter the national interests which are the responsibility of national governments. Their success in so doing depends in part on the qualities and determination of the commissioners. However, it also depends on the extent to which governments of member-states are prepared to modify their national interests for the benefit of the Community as a whole.

The Council of Ministers

The central decision-making institution of the Community is undoubtedly the Council of Ministers. It alone has the authority to take decisions concerning implementation of the proposals of the Commission.

The Council consists of one appropriate ministerial representative from each member-state. For example, when the annual price-support schedules for agricultural products are being considered for adoption, the Council will be composed of Ministers of Agriculture. On other matters, for example, the Foreign Ministers, Finance Ministers or Transport Ministers may constitute the Council. The seat of the Council is also in Brussels, where its small permanent staff is located.

Meetings of the Council are chaired by its President. This office is held by the appropriate minister of each of the member-states in rotation, for a six-month period. The President of the Council has responsibility for drawing up the agenda, convening all meetings of the Council and its expert groups, and generally expediting the business of the Council. The period of the presidency provides each member-state in turn with the opportunity (should it so desire) to press ahead with particular objectives, to settle a contentious matter outstanding from an earlier period, to change the direction or alter the pace of Community development, or to affect the style and efficiency of the handling of Community business.

The Council must work in close co-operation with the Commission. Without a proposal from the Commission, the Council cannot act; without a decision from the Council, the Commission has no power to implementation. Decisions of the Council take the form of:

(*a*) *regulations*: these are immediately and directly applicable throughout the Community, and require no additional sanctioning by national governments or legislatures; much of the Common Agricultural Policy takes this form.

(*b*) *directives*: these are binding on all member-states, but require national legislation to be passed in order to take effect; the introduction of tachometers (the 'spy-in-the-cab') required legislation by the United Kingdom parliament, for instance, before taking effect in the UK.

(*c*) *decisions*: like regulations, these also require no implementing national legislation, but are usually very specific and require a particular form of action, for instance the termination of discriminatory business practices by a firm or group of firms.

Depending on the type of business, decisions in the Council of

Ministers are subject to a variety of voting rules, as set out in the treaties which founded the Community institutions. Fairly minor matters require only a simple majority vote. More contentious or significant issues need to be settled by a qualified majority, based on weighted votes designed to reflect the differences in the size of member-states. At present, the weighted votes are distributed as follows:

France, West Germany, Italy United Kingdom	10 votes each
Spain	8 votes
Belgium, Netherland, Greece and Portugal	5 votes each
Denmark, Eire	3 votes each
Luxemburg	2 votes

On especially sensitive matters (such as the admission of new members) unanimity is required. The extension of majority voting to issues affecting the internal market took effect from 1 July 1987, in preparation for the creation of a single internal market by 1992.

Despite these treaty provisions, despite the progress made in terms of economic harmonisation and integration, and despite the efforts of the Commission and the hopes of the 'Europeanists', majority voting is still the exception, not the rule, in Council business. National interests have been safeguarded through insistence on unanimity and the protection of what is therefore a national veto. Even the very exceptional refusal of other states to respect a UK veto on the agricultural price supports in 1982 was accompanied by strident insistence by some states that the convention of respect for the national veto had not been breached or weakened thereby. Consequently, meetings of the Council are often prolonged and acrimonious, and result more often than not in compromise decisions which allow only slow progress along the prescribed path of increased economic and political integration.

COREPER and the European Council

Both the prominence of national interests, and their protection, in EC affairs are reinforced by two other institutions which operate as auxiliary to the Council of Ministers.

The Committee of Permanent Representatives (COREPER) consists of the ambassadors to the EC of each of the member-states. Together with their staffs of experts, they represent the interests of their governments on a permanent basis in Brussels. The main task of this committee is to prepare for every meeting of the Council of Ministers, first by isolating the more contentious issues on the agenda, and then by attempting to secure agreement, at least at the level of the officials most concerned, on as many of these issues as possible. Given the volume of work which each session of the Council of Ministers is expected to complete, this preparatory role of COREPER is vital. It compensates, to some extent, for the otherwise extremely fragmented administrative and political network of decision-making of Community matters which is dispersed among the capitals of the member-states. The Commission, though, takes a less sanguine view of the increasing prominence of the COREPER role. It sees it as an unwelcome intruder into what the Commission would prefer to regard as an intimate Commission–Council of Ministers dialogue, and as an element that is less predictable and less open to Commission influence than the Council itself.

The *European Council* is an institution which had no formal basis in the treaties, but which has developed as a useful adjunct to other Community institutions. The label 'European Council' has been attached to the series of 'summit meetings' of the heads of government and of state of member-states. These have occurred at regular intervals since 1974. These highly-publicised meetings, in a variety of locations, have sometimes managed to produce agreements on difficult issues where solutions at a lower political level have not been forthcoming, such as the UK's budget disputes in June 1984 and February 1988. In other cases, however, little more than pious generalities have resulted. In such cases, where hopes have been raised only to be dashed, where high expectations of progress on contentious issues have been frustrated, harm rather than benefit can result. A three-day series of 'fireside chats' among pre-occupied political leaders, especially on matters involving complex detail, is an inappropriate forum for international decision-making. As with COREPER, the Commission is similarly suspicious about the role of the European Council, and sees it as an additional complication in the process of securing cross-national agreements beneficial to the 'Community process'.

The European parliament

Though limited to little more than a consultative role by the Treaty of Rome, the European parliament has developed many of the formal procedures of a national legislature, such as a committee system for the scrutiny of Community policies, attempts to impose a measure of accountability on the Commission and the Council of Ministers by the use of written and oral questions and debates, and cross-national party groupings.

Members of the European parliament were, until the first direct elections were held in June 1979, appointed from their national legislatures, with the number of members drawn from each country allocated by a formula which took account of the differences in population. Such a formula still applies, but now the 518 members are elected by the voters in each member-state.[1] Thus far, elections have used versions of the several national electoral systems in force at the time, but the intention is to agree upon a uniform electoral system.

The powers of the parliament have gradually increased over the years. In 1970, reform of the budgetary procedures of the Community gave the parliament a limited power of amendment over a part of the Community budget, and in 1975, it acquired the right to approve or reject the whole of the Community budget (but *not* the right to amend the major proportion of it). It also has developed – especially with the new dignity of being a directly-elected parliament – a representative function, by which it hopes to air grievances effectively and influence both the Commission and the Council of Ministers.

However, its role is still very restricted. It has no legislative function. Its views on proposed legislation, though well-researched and often vociferous, can be ignored by the Council of Ministers and national governments. True, it can remove the Commission *en bloc* from office, by a two-thirds majority vote, but has not yet tried to use this sanction, and in any case lacks the power to appoint a successor Commission. Accountability in the EC still flows via *national* channels to national parliaments. The influence of the European parliament may increase, but, as things stand, it is difficult to see how its formal powers can increase until a far greater degree of political integration in the Community has been attained – and that will only exist when the power of national governments in the politics of the EC has been reduced.

The Court of Justice

The Court of Justice, located in Luxemburg, consists of thirteen judges from each of the member-states. It is responsible for ensuring that the legal obligations laid down in the Community treaties and those subsequently created by Community legislation are adhered to throughout the Community. The court has a unique status, created by the provision that Community law (mainly applicable to commercial and economic activity) supersedes national laws wherever these conflict with Community principles. For example, the Community provision for the complete free movement of goods throughout the Common Market area would render inoperable any national law allowing discrimination against imports of any kind from another member-state.

Although the court might appear a distant and rather aloof institution, it is nevertheless accessible to a variety of groups within the Community. Community institutions may initiate cases before the court, but may themselves be brought before the court for failure to carry out obligations required by the treaties. The governments of member-states can bring complaints against each other to the court, as the United Kingdom did against France, whom they accused of flouting Community rules in the 'lamb war' of 1980. Individuals or firms can bring cases under Community law, though usually only via the national courts in their own country.

The role of the court is important – as in nation-states and especially in federal states (see above, chapter 10) – both as an authoritative interpreter of the law and as arbitrator between complainants. As the number of decisions reached by the court increases, so does its schedule of precedents upon which it can draw. The court provides an interesting example of the indivisibility of politics and law in systems of government.

The Economic and Social Committee

In recognition of the fact that national governments may not necessarily provide effective representation of all the major interests within the Community, the Economic and Social

Committee was set up in 1957. It consists of representatives of interest groups in the Community, such as consumers, trade unions and business organisations. The members are drawn on a proportional basis from member-states, and are consulted by the Commission or the Council of Ministers when proposals for new legislation are under consideration. The role of the committee is purely advisory, though it has developed a thorough and well-organised system for co-ordinating the views of the range of sectional interests which it represents.

The Court of Auditors

The newest of all the institutions of the Community, the Court of Auditors was created in 1977 because of concern, especially on the part of the European parliament, about the lack of effective monitoring of Community expenditure. Expenditure on Community policies essentially eludes the normal national accounting processes, and already the Court of Auditors, working closely with the Budget Committee of the European parliament, has managed to stimulate a tightening-up of financial control procedures within Community institutions. Ironically, one of its most publicised investigations has been concerned with the expenses payments made to members of the European parliament itself!

The role of national governments

The political role is performed through the Council of Ministers, COREPER and the European Council, but governments influence and constrain the behaviour of Community institutions in other ways.

Because the decision-making process of the Community itself relies upon a continuous input from national governments, orchestrated especially through the Council of Ministers, each national government has had to organise itself internally, both at the ministerial and the official level, so that a coherent national viewpoint can be presented in Brussels. Because so many Community issues, such as the budget, economic and regional policy, or relations with 'third world' countries, cross departmental boundaries within national administrative structures, national governments have been forced to acquire or adapt co-ordinating machinery to enable them to present an effective case in Brussels. The French, for example – in accordance with national political and administrative traditions – have used a high-powered and efficient 'clearing-house' mechanism in the form of a co-ordinating secretariat reporting directly to the Prime Minister; this unit takes responsibility for monitoring and co-ordinating all official contacts between the French government and Community institutions. The United Kingdom's system relies on a less centralised pattern, with co-ordination responsibilities shared between the Foreign Office and the Cabinet Office. In the Netherlands, Italy and West Germany, the more fragmented structure of the executive and the exigiencies of coalition politics have made centralised co-ordination of policy-making on Community matters more difficult, though the increasing importance and complexity of recent Community issues (such as reform of the Common Agricultural Policy and increased co-operation on monetary policy) have persuaded the Dutch and West German governments to make efforts to develop a more rigorous and effective approach to the organisation of policy co-ordination.

Some member-states also have used the specialised committee systems of their legislatures to deal with Community issues, either by creating new, specialist European Community committees or sub-committees or by allocating Community matters to foreign affairs committees. Both chambers of the United Kingdom parliament have specialised committees to deal with Community affairs; the Lords committee has been the more industrious and successful, in part because the Commons is divided, more or less along party lines, on the fundamental issue of Community membership. The Danish legislature has a special Market Relations committee, composed of leading members of various political parties, which keeps a close scrutiny over Danish ministerial activity in the EC. On the whole, though, national parliaments are ill-equipped to influence the actions of governments in Community negotiations, which are often of a highly complex and confidential nature. They can usually do little more than exercise a retrospective monitoring role, unless a treaty amendment or the accession of a new member-state gives them an opportunity to play a direct part in the ratification process.

The overriding of the United Kingdom veto on farm prices in June 1982 was but one in a long series of conflicts within the

Community which have revealed either the incompatibility of national interests and the 'Community interest' or, more nakedly, competition among different national interests of member-states. This problem of the persistence of national, rather than Community perspectives is reinforced by political parties and public opinion, both of which in a democracy set definite limits to what governments may do, or concede in international negotiations. In some countries (notably the United Kingdom, Greece and – on some issues – Denmark) certain political parties are opposed to the European Community. In France and Italy, opposition by some parties to particular aspects of Community development has also been apparent, particularly where client groups (such as steelworkers or wine growers) feel that their interests are threatened by Community policy. At a less specific level, public opinion in member-states is divided about the benefits of Community policy or Community membership. In only a few states – the UK, Greece, Denmark – is the issue of membership itself of political importance; in some states, such as the Netherlands, Luxemburg and West Germany, public opinion is broadly in favour of the Community. But the lack of any very strong stream of opinion in favour of expanding the competence of Community institutions at the expense of national authority is a major obstacle to further integration among the member states.

The European Community: a political system?

It is helpful to apply the framework of David Easton's model of the political system (chapter 2) to the institutions and processes of the European Community.

There are complications, particularly the multilayered structure of the decision-making process, involving as it does national (and even local) government levels, as well as the Community level, and the complexity of the feedback process. But, in a simplified form, the Community political system may be perceived as involving the conversion of *inputs* into *outputs*, which are then, through *feedback*, influential in the shaping and stimulation of new inputs.

Inputs come from the public, via members of the European parliament, the interests represented on the Economic and Social Committee, other national and supranational interest groups and through national channels of representation, such as political parties, legislatures and national governments. The Commission and the Council of Ministers, in their respective roles, then convert the demands into *outputs*: reform of the Common Agricultural Policy, greater financial and administrative efficiency within Community institutions, economic sanctions against Argentina during the Falklands crisis, or a common negotiating stance over steel exports to the United States. The mass media, national governments and information from the Community itself then supply *feedback* information to the general public and to groups directly affected by such outputs (e.g. sheep farmers, transport firms, holidaymakers). Such outputs and feedback then may lead to further demands, and so on.

The European Community: problems and opportunities

The European Community is beset by problems. Many of these problems relate to the ambitious and exceedingly complicated process of more closely integrating the economies, administrations and legal systems of the member-states: in matters such as monetary union, the reduction of barriers to competition among business enterprises, the provision of assistance to less-developed regions in the EC, or the alignment of external relations. No single one of these problems would be likely so to damage the Community as to necessitate its termination or even its radical revision. There are, though, four major areas of difficulty which conceivably could, alone or in combination, change the nature of the EC or bring about its breakdown.

1. The most obvious of these is the problem of *the budget* of the EC. This is another way of referring to the problem of the Common Agricultural Policy (CAP), for it is the CAP which devours by far the largest portion of the Community budget, and has, on at least three occasions, triggered a crisis about the net contributions made by the UK (which, like the German Federal Republic, pays the Community substantially more than it receives). Calls have been made several times for a revision of the CAP, which subsidises the production of agricultural commodities and then has to pay to store unsold surpluses of

butter, milk powder and wine. But the farmers who benefit financially from the policy are politically important in France, Italy, Ireland and West Germany and the governments in those countries dare not risk electoral defeat by acceptance of a less costly system of price supports. The overriding of the UK's veto of the 1982 price-support levels has called into question both the willingness of the UK to continue to provide increasing sums of money for the Community budget, and the convention that, on crucial issues, member-states must find a consensus before changes are made.

2. The matter of *further enlargement* of the Community has already called into question the ability of the EC to go on absorbing new members, especially when they are primarily agricultural countries (such as Greece, Spain and Portugal) whose products would be in competition with those of, say, Italy and France, and whose surpluses would add to the costs of the Common Agricultural Policy. In addition, workers from those countries could, as of right, compete for scarce jobs with the growing numbers of the unemployed in existing member-states. Greece has already joined, but with special and costly interim provisions for her benefit. France has indicated hostility to the application of Spain for membership. Certainly, were Spain and Portugal to be admitted, the voices heard in favour of a 'two-tier' Community – in which new members, plus perhaps the UK, would have a different status from other member-states – would grow louder and more persuasive.

3. Plans to attain longer-term objectives, such as *closer political union*, have not made progress. Without such a move to closer political harmonisation, other aspects of further integration will hardly be feasible (such as the introduction of a common currency or even of common passports), and there will be nothing to sustain interest in the Community as national political pressures in a period of economic crisis force politicians to focus increasingly on domestic problems.

4. The *institutional patterns* of the EC seem neither to be properly efficient nor sufficiently adaptable to enable the Community to cope even with its more immediate policy problems. Aside from the problem of translation of an increasing

number of Community languages, the image of the Community is too closely associated with the Brussels bureaucrat, the jet-setting Euro-MP or the unbending Council of Ministers to engender much optimism or enthusiasm about the ability of the institutions of the EC to lead the Community forward.

All is not gloom and doom, though. The Euro-optimist would point to the survival and development of the EC through a quarter of a century of crises and problems, to the effective functioning of the common market and customs union, to the progress made in co-ordinating some aspects of the external policies of member-states, to the positive features of the agricultural policy and the new commitments in the Single European Act signed in 1986. Last, but by no means least, and whatever the share of the credit that should go to the Community, there has been not the slightest hint of a war breaking out again between western European states. In that, at least, the pro-Europeans have been proved correct.

Note

1. For details of the 1984 direct elections, see 'The European Community' in the appendix. Spain and Portugal were not members at the time of those elections, so sent appointed members.

12

POLITICAL CHANGE IN WESTERN EUROPE

In considering the issue of political change we will be concerned both with assessing what have been the most important *sources of change* that have been at work in the countries of western Europe and with analysing *the different levels* at which change has taken place in their political systems. This final chapter will therefore return to some of the broader propositions concerning the nature of liberal democracy that were raised in the first three chapters and will offer, in the conclusion, a general appraisal of the ways in which liberal democracy has evolved as a system of government in western Europe since 1945, paying particular attention to the most recent developments in this period.

Introduction

For purposes of analysis it is possible to distinguish a range of separate, although inter-related, levels at which changes may occur in any political system. It will be useful to consider four such levels at which changes may take place:

(*a*) at the level of specific *policies*;

(*b*) at the level of *political leadership*, that is involving changes in the personnel of government and in the government's political orientation;

(*c*) at the level of the *political regime*, with alterations in the 'rules of the game'. Such changes may be of a formal, constitutional kind; equally, informal changes may occur in the practice of established institutions, effectively altering the way in which they operate;

(*d*) at the level of the *political community*, where the bases on which individuals and groups have hitherto identified themselves as belonging to a distinctive unit – in this case, to one of the established 'nation-states' of western Europe – may be subject to change over time.

In principle, the political institutions of the liberal democratic states of western Europe are peculiarly well adapted to allow for changes to take place at the levels of *policy* and *political leadership*. Indeed, this is central to the legitimacy of such states, to their claims to provide 'representative and responsive governments'. Periodic elections contested by competing parties, it is argued, provide the best available mechanism for ensuring that, over time, changing values and needs in society will be reflected in alterations in the political composition of both parliament and the government of the day; periodic elections should also encourage those with responsibilities for policy-making to be responsive between elections to shifts in the balance of public opinion.

If this electoral mechanism works effectively to allow adaptation of policy and renewal of government, then such states might be expected to develop a contrasting pattern of *stability* at the level of their *political regime*. However, on this reading of liberal democracy the particular patterns of change that occur at these first three levels – of policy, government and regime – may ultimately depend on developments arising at the fourth level, that of *political community*. It is at this level that we should expect significant *sources of political change* in the states of western Europe to be generated, in the form of new perceptions of individual, group and national interest emerging from the interplay between developments in domestic circumstances on the one hand, and a changing international environment on the other.

Formal changes of regime

A notable characteristic of the experience of nearly all of the western European countries since the late 1940s has been the virtual absence of change at the level of *political regime* – at least as far as *formal* changes in institutions have been concerned.

This pattern of regime stability and political continuity is in striking contrast to the turbulence and upheavals of the inter-war years. Then the institutions of representative democracy were overturned by political forces of the extreme right in a number of countries, and elsewhere were challenged by forces both on the left and the right. After the second world war, liberal democratic principles formed the basis of state institutions in all except two of the countries considered here. An important factor contributing to the political stability of this period has been the widespread acceptance of the principles of representative democracy and a competitive electoral system; these principles are now embraced by virtually all significant political forces in these countries.

Leaving aside the quite distinct cases of Portugal and Spain, where changes of regime in the 1970s re-established liberal democratic institutions, only France and Greece have undergone a change of regime in this period. The colonels' coup in Greece in 1967 was the only case of a successful outright challenge to the norms of liberal democracy in western Europe; the ensuing military dictatorship, however, collapsed in 1974 (see chapter 8). The change of regime which took place nearly a decade earlier in France was of a more limited and a more ambiguous character. Here, too, the crisis originated, in May 1958, with a challenge to the country's parliamentary institutions from elements in the army. However, a solution was found through constitutional procedures, General de Gaulle being invested as the last prime minister of the Fourth Republic with powers to draw up a new constitution, to be ratified by a national referendum. This new constitution, although respecting the formal norms of parliamentary democracy, significantly reduced the effective powers of the French parliament while increasing those of the presidency, leading to an unusual concentration and personalisation of power in this office.

In both cases differing views of how the national political community itself was constituted generated tensions about 'the political rules of the game'. Moreover, it was elements within the military, who had developed a distinctive perception of the national community, who played a decisive role in challenging each country's parliamentary institutions. In Greece, the colonels mounted their coup in order to forestall parliamentary elections which were expected to bring Papandreou's Centre Union into government.[1] In France, the military rebels in Algeria allied themselves with European settlers in an attempt to block the formation of a new government which might seek to negotiate independence for Algeria. In a number of other countries in western Europe issues about the composition of the national political community have similarly been raised in the post-war period by the process of decolonisation (such issues continue to be raised in the case of Northern Ireland's relationship to the United Kingdom), without this leading directly to a political rupture as it did in France. The only other country in which this did happen was Portugal and there, unlike in France, those most politically active among the military acted as a force for democratisation.

The other major movements of this period which have contested the way in which the existing political communities of western Europe are constituted have not for the most part mounted any direct challenge to the principles of representative democracy. Both the movements which have sought closer supranational integration and those which have campaigned to devolve powers to regional units, have, of course, opposed the existing pattern of nation-state units (and the 'nation-state' is the organisational form which liberal democracy has historically assumed as a system of government). Nevertheless, they have been concerned to reproduce the institutions of representative democracy at other levels, rather than to challenge its underlying principles.

Apart from France and Greece, there have been very few cases where established institutional arrangements have been subject to any formal alterations at all in this period in western Europe. Where such alternations have been made they have been designed to consolidate the principle of electoral representation. Examples include the abolition of the upper chambers of parliament in Denmark and Sweden, the provisions to confine the Swedish monarchy to purely ceremonial duties, and the Belgian decision to devolve certain powers to elected authorities for that country's main linguistic communities.

Patterns of governmental change

In contrast to the general pattern of regime stability which most of the countries of western Europe have shared since the war, their experience of *change at the level of government* has been much more varied. However, the patterns of governmental change seem to point to the existence of a range of common problems which all the western European states face, in attempting to secure *government by consent* through *the government of a majority*.

Two aspects of the process of governmental change need to be considered to understand the varied patterns found in western Europe and the problems to which they give rise – the duration of governments and their party composition. Table 15 combines these two aspects, providing two contrasting positions along the horizontal axis *A* (representing frequency of change over time) and three separate positions along the vertical axis *B* (representing party political change). Six distinct patterns of governmental change are thus set out, all of which can be illustrated from the experience of western European states since 1945.

Table 15   Patterns of governmental change in western Europe

A. Duration of Governments

		(*i*) Frequent turnover	(*ii*) Relative stability
B. Party composition of governments	(*iii*) Alternation between major parties	France, Fourth Republic Eire (recently)	United Kingdom West Germany more recently: Sweden Greece Spain
	(*ii*) Substantial continuity with right- to left-of-centre coalition	Belgium	Austria (before 1966) Netherlands
	(*i*) Substantial continuity with dominant parties of left or right	Italy Finland more recently: Denmark Portugal	France, Fifth Republic (until 1974) Sweden (until 1976)

A. *The duration of governments*

The left hand and right hand columns of Table 15 distinguish between countries where governments have normally survived for only one or at most two years (this has usually been without resort to the verdict of the electorate, through dissolution) and those where governments have usually lasted for at least three to four years (although not necessarily for the full terms of their legislatures). It is perhaps surprising that the experiences of most European states are adequately covered by this simple dichotomy, although Eire and France, for example, figure in both columns, for different phases within this period.

The main issues raised concern the effectiveness of governments in the countries listed in the left-hand column, and whether public perception of ineffectiveness may not, over time, undermine the credibility of liberal democracy as a system of government in states which have been characterised by chronic governmental instability over a prolonged period. This has been the case, for example, in Finland, virtually since the foundation of its republic in 1919, and in Italy since 1948. In some of these cases, as was seen in chapter 9, governmental instability has, however, masked a very substantial continuity of ministerial personnel.

Important questions are raised by this pattern of governmental instability, in particular as to whether this could produce an underlying disaffection with the institutions of representative democracy among their populations and enhance the potential appeal of alternative styles of political leadership, of an authoritarian or technocratic kind. Certainly, in the case of Finland, it has served to reinforce the political authority of the president, at the expense of the government which is responsible to parliament. Likewise in France it could be argued that the Fourth Republic's history of governmental instability probably made the subsequent downgrading of parliament's role as a representative mediator, under the Fifth Republic, more acceptable to the general public.

B. *The party composition of governments*

The differing patterns of party participation in government set out in Table 15 also raise important issues about the way in which liberal democratic institutions function in practice in western Europe today. As was noted earlier in this chapter, through the provisions for periodic, contested elections western European states seem to have an in-built capacity for change at the levels of political leadership and policy. Indeed, some change in the party composition of government may be regarded as a necessary condition for sustaining the legitimacy of such states' institutions. Yet the extent to which changes of government in the different states of western Europe have, in practice, led to changes in the party composition and overall political orientation of their governments has varied very considerably.

While no country in western Europe has experienced a complete absence of party alternation in government since 1945, there are two distinct sets of cases where the same party or parties have remained in government continuously for a prolonged period. The first category (*B*i) involves countries where lack of party alternation has been caused by one major party, of the right or left, securing a dominant position in government. In all these cases, the dominance of one party has resulted in the consignment of one or more other parties, enjoying the support of a substantial part of the electorate, to a position of permanent opposition, effectively excluded from any direct influence over the national policy-making process.

It is this pattern of party government which would seem to pose the clearest problems for the legitimacy of liberal democratic institutions. For, while the ability of one party to secure a dominant position in government could be taken to testify to a broad degree of consensus in society, a notable feature of each of these cases has, on the contrary, been the existence of entrenched lines of cleavage within the national political community. These cases, then, may point to a certain 'mismatch' between actual social structures and liberal democratic institutions, which would seem to require a more open and pluralist form of society. They also raise questions as to the continuing attachment to liberal democracy of minorities who have been denied the prospect of representation in national government over a very long period. However, two of these countries, France and Sweden, have recently experienced a new pattern of party alternation, while in Italy the exclusion of the large Communist Party from national government has to some extent been offset by its strength at local and regional levels of government.

A second, and quite distinct case involving a virtual absence of party alternation in government is found in countries (*B*ii) where the major political forces within a spectrum ranging from left-of-centre to right-of-centre have been able to sustain a series of broadly-based coalition governments. The most notable examples here are the Netherlands, where between 1952 and 1977 governments were formed by varying permutations of the three main religious parties, the Socialists and the Liberals, and Belgium, where both the Christian Democrats and the Socialists were present in most governments formed in the 1960s and for periods in the 1970s.

A third pattern is provided by those countries (*B*iii) which have experienced alternation between major parties or coalitions of parties over some period of time. This group includes the United Kingdom and West Germany, although in both these countries the years since 1945 have included a period of virtual one-party dominance (with the British Conservatives in government from 1951 to 1964, and the West German Christian Democrats in office, with various junior coalition partners, from 1949 to 1966). Further examples are provided in the very recent period by the Republic of Ireland, where Fianna Fail and Fine Gael have alternated in a series of short-lived coalition and minority governments, and by Sweden, where a right-of-centre alliance was in government for six years before the Social Democrats returned to office in October 1982. Greece and Spain may also, provisionally, be cited as examples of this pattern, although in these countries only one change of parties in government has so far taken place since their changes of regime (in both cases the change being from conservatives to socialists).

Many of the countries in these second and third groups have faced a common problem in their lack of a coherently organised political majority within the electorate. This problem again seems to derive from the existence of entrenched lines of cleavage within the electorate. In some cases, the absence of an electoral majority is reflected in persistent governmental instability, as in both Ireland and Denmark recently; in France under the Fourth Republic; and in Belgium for much of the period. However in other cases, this pattern of governmental instability has been obviated through the emergence at the parliamentary level of a majority able to sustain governments in office. Such a situation has arisen either where parties construct alliances after elections (which the electorate were not given the opportunity to sanction), or where, as in the United Kingdom and France, the electoral system enables a single party or alliances of parties to gain a clear majority of seats in parliament without needing to win the support of a majority of the electorate. In the third group of countries, moreover, relatively minor shifts in the distribution of votes may result in major alterations in the party composition of government.

However, this issue is a complex one, for it is possible that the problem resides at the level of their party systems rather than at the level of their social structures. The particular patterns of division within their party systems may testify not so much to the entrenched nature of a range of conflicts of interest within the political communities of these states as to the ways in which the electorates' choices have been structured by the combined effects of the different electoral laws and the inherent interest which parties may have in maximising their electoral support by emphasising a distinct political identity.

However, while each of the patterns of governmental change found among the west European states has been shown to raise certain problems for the legitimacy and effectiveness of liberal democratic institutions, it is also true that in this period liberal democracy as an ideal has not faced any significant, direct challenge from movements championing an alternative system of government.

Changing political communities

While the territorial boundaries of the different states of western Europe have been subject to virtually no alterations since the war, the populations inhabiting these territories have changed in a number of important respects.[2] For example, there have been quite substantial movements of population between and into these states and the populations *within* many of these states have been redistributed geographically both between different regions and, more generally, between rural and urban areas. Many of these population movements have been closely bound up with considerable changes in the distribution of the working population between different occupational categories. This period has seen important changes in the socio-economic and age structuring of European populations.

Changes of these kinds raise questions concerning, firstly, the ways in which they may generate altered perceptions of individual, group and national identities and, secondly, the forms in which these changes may then be fed into the political process. Although in this section it will only be possible to comment on some of these issues quite briefly, it will become clear that we are concerned with changing *political communities*. The changes that have occurred in many cases either arose from, or were indirectly associated with, economic developments. The first part of this section will consider the changes occurring in the three decades of sustained economic growth, up to the mid-1970s; the second part will comment on the developments and issues that have arisen during the period of international economic recession in the last decade.

The experience of rising prosperity from the 1950s to the early 1970s almost certainly offset, in a number of ways, the varied problems which many of the states of western Europe faced in sustaining effective government in the absence of clear, and coherently organised electoral majorities. However, the performances of the different national economies varied considerably in this period, and the benefits of economic growth were, in any case, unequally distributed within the populations of each of these states. Moreover, in other ways the pursuit of economic growth and modernisation further complicated the political task of constructing a negotiated consensus at the electoral, parliamentary and governmental levels, out of the conflicting interests present. Growth and modernisation entailed a major restructuring of economic activities in western European states and so brought new patterns of expectations and opportunities, at the same time as engendering grievances and resistance to change.

While rising expectations in this period of economic growth were in large part concerned with achieving higher levels of income and new patterns of personal and family consumption, they also came to be focused on educational opportunities and the possibilities which these opened up for social mobility. These, in turn, were linked to one of the most notable features of the changing pattern of employment in this period: the growth of what has often been termed 'white-collar employment, though this category embraces widely varying levels of status and remuneration. Some of these workers became particularly associated with new political themes concerning the quality of life and the protection of the environment, which received a new prominence in western Europe (see chapter 3). At the same time employment opportunities were shrinking in other economic sectors, most visibly – and most dramatically in the case of France and Italy – for small farmers, for skilled and semi-skilled manual workers in a variety of traditional industries from coal to textiles, and for various groups of the self-employed, both in small-scale commercial and artisanal activities and in the liberal professions. These three categories constituted important electoral clienteles for major parties of the right or left in most west European states, and this on occasion gave rise to difficulties for these parties when in government, as well as contributing to a fluidity of electoral support for different parties of protest (see chapter 5).

With changes in the pattern of employment opportunities and labour mobility came new patterns of economic differentiation between regions; the issue of population decline in many areas being reinforced by concern about the ageing structure of the population. Developments of this kind therefore often gave a new depth to older, historically-rooted cleavages (of an ethnic, linguistic or religious as well as of a class nature) in the political communities of the western European states, or sometimes raised new issues, over-laying or cross-cutting these longer standing lines of division. The awakening of distinctive forms of what may be termed 'ethno-regionalism' became an important feature of western European politics, most notably in Belgium, France, Spain and the United Kingdom. But broad changes in patterns of education, employment and personal consumption also contributed to the emergence of other kinds of group identity in this period. New patterns of intergenerational differences in attitudes and values, in particular, arose with the emergence of distinctive 'youth cultures'. At the same time, and associated with the rising numbers of women drawn into paid employment in this period, many women began to raise specific policy demands (some of them deeply controversial, since they challenged established attitudes and relationships in society) to enable them to play a fuller and more equal role in society both within and outside the sphere of the individual family household.

A number of broad socio-economic changes in this period thus had an unsettling impact on the political communities of western Europe, as different kinds of local, regional and social group identities emerged to prominence, and this created additional sources of tension for the working of liberal democratic institutions in these states. Regionalist movements have posed a challenge to the idea of a common interest operating at the level of the nation-state unit. So too have the issues of class and the redistribution of wealth, which have remained central political issues in most of these states, and towards the end of this period more combative forms of working-class action emerged in a number of countries – in France in the events of 1968, in Italy in the autumn of 1969, in the United Kingdom in 1974, when the miners' strike precipitated a general election and change of government, and also in Portugal, following the change of regime in 1974.

The substantial movements of population that took place between states in this period provided another important development. To meet labour shortages, large numbers of immigrant workers were drawn into many of these states both from the poorer countries of southern Europe and from overseas dependencies and former colonies.[3] Only in a limited number of countries – notably in the United Kingdom and, for a period, in the Netherlands – were large numbers of these immigrant workers able to bring their families and to enjoy formal citizenship rights, but even here they found themselves to be, in important respects, second-class citizens. In other cases, such as France, Switzerland and West Germany, where immigrant workers also came to form an important part of the total workforce, the notable contribution which they made to these countries' economic performance was not matched by the conferment of rights of political participation. A significant section of the labour force has thus effectively been excluded from the national political communities of these states. Their presence has provided the basis for new multiracial definitions of political community, but in several western European states a major response to their presence has been the generation of racialist definitions of national identity.

Certain developments in inter-state relations in this period also had an unsettling impact on perceptions of national interest and national identity. In a number of states, as has been noted, the process of decolonisation generated conflicting perceptions of national interest. Only in France and in Portugal (see pages 204–5) were these conflicts of such severity as to precipitate a major political crisis and change of regime. Continuing conflict over the maintenance of the six counties of Northern Ireland in the United Kingdom has, however, put considerable strains on the operation of liberal democratic institutions and principles in this state. The new patterns of trading links that were forged in this period also affected different sectors of public opinion in a number of ways. On the one hand, the rapid growth in trade among western European states – particularly within the Scandinavian grouping of countries and among EC member-states – gave rise to an awareness of economic interdependence which led many to see themselves as belonging to a broader community of interests, beyond that of their own nation-state. However, only limited steps towards supranational institutional arrangements were taken (see chapter 11) and within the EC, the process of achieving major common policies in many cases engendered a reassertion of national interests and served to reaffirm national identities. On the other hand, the penetration of 'national economies' by 'foreign firms' – for the most part US-based multinationals – led in some quarters to an erosion of that idea of a broader Atlantic community of interests which was so much a part of the liberal democratic consensus constructed in post-war western Europe (see chapter 3). Hostility towards a particular pattern of 'Atlanticism', however, has become much more strongly focused in the last decade with the growing debate over nuclear arms and NATO's nuclear strategy.

Public perceptions of the national political community in each of these western European states were therefore subject to a variety of strains and tensions in the long phase of economic growth which lasted until the early 1970s. Nevertheless, governments in this period generally subscribed to certain patterns of policy commitments which were seen as an expression of, and served to sustain, a sense of societal interdependence and commonality of interest at the level of each nation-state. This pattern of policy commitment to full employment, to fairly extensive welfare-state provisions and to the expansion of educational opportunities – commitments underpinned by public ownership, in some form, of a substantial sector of the economy in most of these states – has come under challenge, decisively, in the subsequent period of international economic recession. A fundamental development in this period of recession has therefore been the disruption of that broadly consensual framework of politics which had previously been constructed in many of these states, and in which a particular perception of political community, informed by a commitment to some measure of equity and social justice, had played such a crucial role.

In the last decade a common governmental response to the recession has been the introduction of measures which, to varying degrees, will serve to restrict social welfare and educational provisions or to dismantle parts of the public sector. In a number of these countries public expenditure cutbacks will most directly affect the living standards of the poorest sections of the community, those who are often least well organised to defend their interests through the channels available, while some governments have also sought to weaken trade union powers. Above all, governments have abandoned, at least in the short and medium term, their previous commitment to maintaining high levels of employment. In seeking to defend this change in the direction of policy, not only governments to the right of centre but also, in some cases, those belonging to a left-of-centre tradition have become involved in a new and critical task. Increasingly they have attempted to recast public perceptions of what constitutes the 'community of interests' which binds together the different social groupings within their respective nation-states, and of what the proper expectations of individual members of these political communities should be. The changed economic climate has undoubtedly engendered a certain fatalism and sense of resignation in the face of growing social and economic inequalities and the prospect of continuing high levels of unemployment. Yet the riots in major cities in the United Kingdom in the summer of 1981 also testified to the presence of explosive social tensions and to the ways in which the prospect of long-term unemployment (particularly when compounded with the experience of racial discrimination) may lead a younger generation to reject any sense of belonging to a broader national community of interests.

Liberal democracy at a crossroads in western Europe?

While the period since the war has been remarkable for the degree of continuity and stability that has characterised the formal 'rules of the political game' in force in most of the western European states, the preceding chapters have nevertheless pointed to a range of problems which have arisen in the practice of institutional arrangements formally embodying liberal democratic principles.

For example, although electoral turnout is generally high in these states (certainly in comparison to the United States), voting in periodic elections constitutes a limited form of political participation (particularly when the level of information possessed by much of the electorate about key policy issues may also be quite limited, as opinion polling in several countries has suggested is the case). Only a minority of the citizens of these states seek to extend their involvement in political affairs by being active in a political party. Elections in any case raise difficult issues, as was seen in chapter 4, concerning the proper basis on which elective representation should be secured.

Those elected to national parliamentary bodies, moreover, in most cases play only a somewhat restricted role in terms of making policy and controlling and scrutinising the actions of the executive branch. Parliaments in most of these states have retained their importance as bodies legitimising the exercise of state power, yet this too has been encroached upon by the increasingly close links established between governments and administrations, and a range of pressure groups. The role of pressure groups also raises serious issues concerning, for example, their representativeness and the varying resources and sanctions which different organised interests in society can bring into play in attempting to influence policy outcomes and the implementation of policy.

Finally, when we turn to the arena of government itself, the west European states have faced a number of problems in this period in securing governments that are seen to be both representative and effective, while the relationship between those holding elective political office and the permanent civil service also raises important issues. Moreover, the question of securing a proper balance between central and local levels of elected authority is one that has not proved easy to resolve in a number of these states. For those states which are members of the EC there has been the additional problem of evolving acceptable and effective policy-making procedures at the Community level and determining what balance there should be between these and the existing national policy-making procedures based on elective representation.

In addition, this period has seen, with the emergence of mass access to television in those states from the 1950s and 1960s, the development of a remarkably powerful means of communication. While it has not been possible, within the format of this book, to discuss the complex issues that are raised by the varied kinds of television practice which have developed in western Europe and the different combinations of state-controlled and commercially-sponsored networks which have emerged, some comment should be made on the differing institutional arrangements through which broadcasting is regulated in these states.[4] As was stressed in chapters 1 and 2, for liberal democratic institutions to operate effectively, much hinges on the availability of a plurality of means of expression and easy access to a wide variety of sources of information and opinion.

While it has been common practice in all the western European countries for the state to intervene to regulate the organisation of broadcasting services, there have been wide variations in the opportunities for the government of the day, or for political parties more generally, to exercise a direct influence over the management of the most politically sensitive areas, such as news, current affairs and documentary programmes. An example of such intervention by the dominant party of government is provided by France under the Fifth Republic, and this situation has given rise to considerable public controversy and debate. In contrast, the predominant influence in Italy achieved by the major party of government since the war has been offset under recent reforms, which have enabled a broad range of parties to be directly involved in controlling the state broadcasting authority. In West Germany, a degree of party political involvement in the management of television services is also provided for, but this operates at the *Land* level, since there are no broadcasting services controlled by the federal government, and therefore allows for varying patterns of party influence to affect the different television channels and regional broadcasting services.

It is certainly not an easy task to assess the full impact which television has had on politics in the western European states. Nevertheless, if television does have a considerable potential for influencing the formation of public opinion, then critical questions need to be asked about the range of information and experiences which television services make available to the individual citizen, and about the ways in which television contributes to setting the terms of current political debate. This is particularly important since television in many of these states presents what is claimed to be an authoritative and impartial source of news, in contrast to the explicit associations between newspapers and party political stances.

There would therefore seem to be a number of respects in which institutional practices in western Europe since 1945 have not always corresponded to the principles of participation and representation from which the institutions draw their legitimacy. Moreover, despite some of the reforms which were instituted during the period of sustained economic growth lasting until the early 1970s, the west European states also face a further problem. One of their founding principles is political equality, yet questions could still legitimately be raised as to the efficacy of this principle in conditions of economic and other inequalities such as are present within the states of western Europe.

It remains to be seen what the long-term effect of economic recession and high levels of unemployment will be. Certainly, in the last decade governments have needed to become involved in the difficult task of securing a shift in the terms of debate as to what is politically both possible and desirable. Governments have become centrally concerned with limiting the expectations which they deem it appropriate for most sections of their populations to entertain. Even the recently-elected socialist governments in France, Greece and Spain have faced this same problem.

This altered economic context could create considerable strains on the political systems of western Europe. The institutional procedures of liberal democracy do ultimately depend on broad sections of the population feeling that they have a positive stake in their state's prevailing economic and social, as well as political arrangements. The coming years could therefore witness a process of party-political and ideological polarisation around national and class identities and growing international rivalries, as in the inter-war years. However, even though institutional practices may now be changing in a number of respects there are, as yet, few signs of the assertion of alternative 'rules of the political game' which directly challenge the claims and norms of liberal democracy.

Notes

1. The coup was supported by the American Central Intelligence Agency.

2. The former territory of Germany was divided into two separate state units after the war (while the Saar, which France sought to control, was reintegrated into the new west German state in 1955). Two major disputes concerning territorial boundaries remain, Spain contesting UK sovereignty over Gibraltar, while Eire and part of the population of Northern Ireland contest UK sovereignty over 'the six counties'.

3. For further details on patterns of immigration in western Europe and the political status of migrant workers, see J. Power, *Western Europe's Migrant Workers*, Minority Rights Group Report, no. 28 (revised edition, 1978).

4. See in particular, Anthony Smith (ed.), *Television and Political Life: Studies in Six European Countries* (Macmillan, London, 1979), covering France, West Germany, Italy, the Netherlands, Sweden and the United Kingdom.

APPENDIX

Countries and international organisations in western Europe

Austria
Belgium
Denmark
Finland
France
Greece
Iceland
Ireland
Italy
Luxemburg

Malta
The Netherlands
Norway
Portugal
Spain
Sweden
Switzerland
United Kingdom
West Germany

Council of Europe
European Community
North Atlantic Treaty Organisation

Austria

Population	7.6 million (1985 est.)
Capital	Vienna
Territory	83,855 sq. km.
State form	Republic, based on Austrian State Treaty (signed by USA, USSR, the UK and France as occupying powers and by Austria) in force 27 July 1955.
	Current head of state: *President Dr Kurt Waidheim* (born 1918, elected 8 June 1986).
State structure	Federation: each of 9 provinces has its own elected Assembly. Provincial governments have relatively little autonomy.

Form of government	President appoints Chancellor, who forms government.
	Current government: Socialist and People's Party coalition, under Chancellor Dr F. Vranitzky, formed January 1987.
	Legislature: bicameral. *Nationalrat* (183 seats) and *Bundesrat* (58 seats). Limited veto of Bundesrat over legislation can be overturned by simple majority in Nationalrat.
Electoral systems	1. *President* Directly-elected. Term of office: 6 years.
	2. *Nationalrat* Proportional representation based on national party lists. Term of office: 4 years.
	3. *Bundesrat* No election. Members appointed by provincial councils in proportion to party strength.
Party system	2 major parties: Socialists and Christian Democratic People's Party. There is also a small liberal Freedom Party and an alliance of Green parties. The Communist Party has negligible electoral strength.

Table 16   Election results: November 1986

	Votes (%)	Seats
Socialists	43.1	80
People's Party	41.3	77
Freedom Party	9.7	18
Greens	4.8	8

Belgium

Population	9.84 million (1980)
Capital	Brussels
Territory	30,519 sq. km.
State form	Constitutional monarchy
	Constitution adopted 1831

Current head of state: *King Baudouin* (born 1930, crowned 17 July 1951, on abdication of father, Leopold III).

State structure   Originally unitary; constitution amended in 1970, providing for considerable decentralisation to three economic and linguistic regions: Flanders, Wallonia, Brussels. (Implementing laws finally voted for first two regions in 1980.)

Form of government   Monarch nominates senior politician as 'informateur', who consults parties and recommends prime ministerial candidate ('formateur') to form government and seek vote of confidence on its programme (from the lower house of parliament).

Governments can be dismissed by vote of censure.

Cabinet of about 25 ministers and Secretaries of State is presided over by Prime Minister. Ministers are normally members of parliament but non-party 'technicians' may be appointed.

Legislature: bicameral. *House of Representatives* (212 members) and *Senate* (181 members) have virtually co-equal powers of legislation.

36 governments since 1945 under 13 different Prime Ministers. Currently, W. Martens, Social Christian; government – his eighth – formed in May 1988, a coalition of the Flemish and Walloon wings of both the Social Christian and the Socialist Parties.

Electoral systems   1. *House of Representatives* Proportional representation (d'Hondt system based on local and 9 provincial constituencies); voting is compulsory. Term of office: 4 years. 15 elections since 1945; last election held in December 1987.

2. *Senate* 106 directly elected members (plus 50 members chosen by provisional councils, and 25 co-opted members). Term of office: 4 years; last elections held in November 1985.

Party system	3 major parties, Social Christians, Socialist and Liberals all now have separate Flemish and Walloon organisations. The Flemish nationalist Volksunie and 2 Francophone parties (in Wallonia and Brussels) took over 20% of the vote between them in the early 1970s but have subsequently declined somewhat, as has the small Communist Party. In 1981 2 ecology parties won 1 seat each in the lower house of parliament for the first time.

Last election results given in chapter 5 (p. 87).

Denmark

Population	5.124 million (1987 est.)
Capital	Copenhagen
Territory	43,074 sq. km. (excluding Faroes: 1399 sq. km. and Greenland: 2,175,600 sq. km.)
State form	Constitutional monarchy, based on constitution of 5 June 1953.
	Current head of state: *Queen Margrethe II* (born 16 April 1940, accession 14 January 1972).
	The Evangelical-Lutheran Church is the official church of the state.
State structure	Unitary: the Faroes and Greenland have devolved legislature and executive for local matters.
Form of government	Monarch appoints Prime Minister and, on Prime Minister's recommendation, other ministers.
	Current government: coalition of Conservative People's Party, Liberals, Centre Democrats and Christian People's Party, under Prime Minister P. Schluter (formed September 1987).
	Legislature: single-chamber *Folketing* (maximum 179 members including 2 from Faroes and 2 from Greenland). Monarch has power to dissolve *Folketing*.

Referendum introduced by 1953 constitution. Constitutional amendments must be approved by referendum.

Electoral system   *Folketing* Proportional representation based on constituency lists, with allocation of 'additional members' from lists on a regional basis to ensure proportionality. Minimum of 2 per cent of the vote is required for a party to be allocated seats. Terms of office: 4 years.

Party system   Social Democrats are the largest party; Conservative People's Party is its closest rival; the left-wing Socialist People's Party and liberal Venstre (Liberal Democratic) Party each obtained over 10 per cent at the 1984 election. 5 smaller parties also obtained seats at that election.

Table 17   *Election results: September 1987**

	Votes (%)	*Seats*
Social Democrats	29.3	54
Conservative People's	20.8	38
Liberals (Venstre)	10.5	19
Socialist People's	14.6	27
Progress	4.8	9
Centre Democrats	4.8	9
Radicals	6.2	11
Others	8.9	8

* Excluding Faroes and Greenland members.

Finland

Population   4.79 million (1980)

Capital   Helsinki

Territory   305,475 sq. km.

State form   Republic
Constitution adopted July 1919 (following civil war. Previously autonomous Grand Duchy of Tsarist Russia, from 1809).

Current head of state: *Dr M. Koivisto* (Social Democrat, born 1924, first elected 27 January 1982).

State structure

Unitary

Form of government

President appoints prime minister and other ministers. Governments do not need, and do not normally seek, vote of confidence from parliament. Governments can be dismissed by a vote of confidence.

Cabinet of 15–20 members is chaired by president. Ministers are normally members of parliament, but need not be.

Legislature: unicameral. *Eduskunta* (200 members). Legislation passed by parliament may be vetoed by president (but this can be overriden if, after dissolution, new parliament repasses bill). President, not prime minister, has power of dissolution.

3 presidents since 1945 (J. Paasikavi, 1946–55; U. Kekkonen, 1956–81; M. Koivisto, 1982–   ) and 37 governments headed by 19 different Prime Ministers, currently H. Holkeri, National coalition party (conservative); government – his first – formed in March 1987.

Electoral systems

President Electoral colleges of 301 members, chosen by universal suffrage. Term of office: 6 years. Most recent election: February 1988.

Parliament Direct proportional representation. 4 year term; 13 elections since 1945, most recently in March 1987.

Party system

Of the 4 major parties, the Centre (ex-Agrarian) Party has been in office virtually throughout the period since 1945, usually in coalitions with the Social Democrats (and sometimes also with two smaller centre-right parties, the Liberal and the Swedish People's Parties). The Communists (SKDL) have also participated in a number of governments since the late 1960s, while the Conservatives formed the main opposition party until they won office in 1987. The party system has become more fragmented, the Rural Party splitting from the Centre party in the late 1960s, 2 new conservative parties being established in the 1970s (the Finnish Constitutional People's Party and the Finnish Christian Union), and the Democratic Alternative (Deva) splitting from the Centre Party.

Table 18   Election results: March 1983

	Votes (%)	Seats (no.)
Social Democrats	24.1	6
Conservatives	23.1	53
Centre Party	17.6	40
Communists	9.4	16
Swedish People's Party	5.3	12
Deva	4.2	10
Rural Party	6.3	9
Christian Union	2.6	5
Ecologists	4	4

France

Population	53.28 million (1979)
Capital	Paris
Territory	543,814 sq. km.*
State form	Republic

Constitution of current Fifth Republic was adopted by national referendum in September 1958; revised by referendum October 1962.

Current head of state: *President F. Mitterrand* (Socialist; born 1916; first elected 10 May 1981).

Fourth Republic, established in 1946, ended by vote of parliament following May 1958 army revolt in Algiers.

Form of government   President appoints Prime Minister and (in conjunction with latter) other ministers. Governments do not need a vote of confidence from lower chamber to enter office, but normally seek one; governments may be dismissed by vote of censure in lower chamber.

Cabinet, comprised of 25–30 senior ministers, is chaired by President. Ministers may not be members of parliament.

Legislature: bicameral. *Assemblée Nationale* (577 members) and *Sénat* (314 members). In certain policy areas, specified in the constitution, legislation must be passed by both chambers (and signed by the President who may send bills back for reconsideration); in other areas, governments have decree-making powers. The President has the power at his own discretion, to dissolve parliament (once in twelve months), to submit an issue for decision by national referendum and to declare an emergency.

4 Presidents of the Fifth Republic: General de Gaulle (1958–69); G. Pompidou (1969–74); V. Giscard d'Estaing (1974–81); F. Mitterrand (1981–).

11 Prime Ministers have headed 21 governments since 1958, currently M. Rocard, Socialist; government – his second – a minority government (formed June 1988 following inconclusive legislative elections).

Electoral systems

1. *President* Direct universal suffrage (since 1962). Second ballot between 2 leading candidates, if no candidate receives absolute majority on first ballot. Term of office: 7 years. 6 elections since 1958.

2. *Assembly* Single member constituencies. Second ballot if no candidate receives absolute majority on first. 5 year mandate: 9 elections since 1958, most recently on 5 and 12 June 1988.

3. *Senate* Multi-member constituencies (the departments). Electoral college comprises all departmental councillors, some local councillors, and deputies. 9 year mandate; 1/3 of seats renewed every three years.

Party system	5 major parties: Gaullist, Giscardian (a confederation of several smaller parties of centre and right), Socialist, Communist and National Front Electoral alliances have operated at legislative and local elections between the first two, and between the last two (together with small Left Radicals) until 1986. The National Front first emerged as a major force in the 1984 European elections.

Last election results given in chapter 5 (p. 82).

* Metropolitan France only. In addition 5 overseas departments and 4 overseas territories are directly represented in the French parliament.

Greece

Population	9.45 million (1979)
Capital	Athens
Territory	131,986 sq. km.
State form	Republic, established by referendum December 1974.
	Constitution adopted by constituent assembly, June 1975.
	Current head of state: *C. Sartzetakis* (Pasok; born 1907, elected March 1985).
	Previous constitutional monarchy (re-established after second world war following civil war) overthrown by military coup in 1967. Military dictatorship collapsed in 1974 following Turkish invasion of Cyprus.
State structure	Unitary

Form of government	President appoints Prime Minister who forms government which must seek a vote of confidence from parliament. Government may be dismissed by a vote of no confidence passed by an absolute majority of members of the parliament.

Form of government

President appoints Prime Minister who forms government which must seek a vote of confidence from parliament. Government may be dismissed by a vote of no confidence passed by an absolute majority of members of the parliament.

Cabinet of about 20 ministers, is chaired by Prime Minister. Ministers are normally members of parliament.

Legislature: unicameral. *Parliament of the Republic* (300 members). Legislation passed by parliament may be referred back by President and then needs the support of an absolute majority in parliament to become law. The President has the right to dissolve parliament, to call a referendum on major issues of national policy and to proclaim a period of martial law, at his own discretion.

3 Presidents since 1975: K. Tsatsos (1975–80); C. Karamanlis (1980–5). C. Sartzetakis (1985–).

4 civilian governments headed by 3 different Prime Ministers since 1974, currently A. Papandreou, Socialist, (Government – his second – formed in June 1985).

Electoral systems

1. *President* Elected by parliament (2/3 majority needed). 5 year mandate; 3 elections since 1975.

2. *Parliament* Elected by a form of weighted proportional representation. 4 year mandate: 3 elections held since 1975, most recently on 2 June 1985.

Party system

Two major parties of government: the right of centre New Democracy Party (founded by Karamanlis) and the Socialist Party (PASOK) led by A. Papandreou. In addition, the Greek Communist Party (Exterior), closely aligned with the Soviet Union, received 10 per cent of the votes cast in 1985 while the Communist Party (Interior), with a Eurocommunist stance, and a range of other small parties on the right, left and centre have received very limited electoral support.

Table 19   Election results: June 1985

	Votes (%)	Seats (no.)
Pasok	46	161
New Democracy	41	125
Communists (Exterior)	10	13
Communists (Interior)	2	1
Others	1	0

Iceland

Population	229,187 (1980)
Capital	Reykjavik
Territory	103,000 sq. km.
State form	Republic

Constitution adopted in 1944.

Current head of state: *President V. Finnbogadottir* (non-party Left; first elected 29 June 1980).

State structure	Unitary
Form of government	President nominates candidate Prime Minister to form government and seek vote of confidence from parliament on its programme.

Cabinet of about eight members share 12 ministerial portfolios; can be dismissed by parliament.

Legislature: bicameral. *Althing* (60 members, they elect 20 of their number to form upper house, remaining 40 forming lower house). Both houses have legislative functions, but sit as a single chamber to vote on no-confidence motions.

4 presidents since 1944 (S. Bjornsson (1944–52); A. Asgeirsson (1952–68); K. Eldjarn (1968–80); Ms V. Finnbogadottir (1980–   ).

17 governments since 1944 under 12 prime ministers; currently, M. Palsson, Independent Party, leads a coalition with the Progressive and People's Parties, formed in 1987.

Electoral systems

President direct universal suffrage. Term of office: 4 years. Most recent election: June 1988.

Parliament proportional representation (49 seats for 8 constituencies; 11 seats filled from party lists). Term of office: 4 years.

Party system

4 main parties: conservative Independent Party, centrist Progressive Party, Social Democrats (currently in opposition) and People's Alliance (led by communists and opposed to NATO membership). Social Democrats split early in 1983, when a new feminist grouping stood for the first time.

Table 20   Election results: April 1987

	Votes (%)	Seats (no.)
Independent Party	27.2	18
Progressive Party	18.9	13
People's Party	15.2	10
People's Alliance	13.3	8
Citizens' Party	10.9	7
Women's Alliance	10.1	6
Others	1.2	1

Republic of Ireland (Eire)

Population   3.54 million (1986)

Capital   Dublin

Territory   70,283 sq. km.

State form   Republic (following separation from United Kingdom in 1922) based on constitution of 29 December 1937.

Current head of state: *Patrick Hillery* (elected 3 December 1976 re-elected 3 December 1983).

State structure	Unitary state
Form of government	President appoints Prime Minister, who selects his cabinet.

Current government: Fianna Fail government under Prime Minister C. J. Haughey, (formed February 1987).

Legislature: bicameral. *House of Representatives* (166 members) and *Senate* (60 members). Senate has no power of veto over legislation. President may dissolve House of Representatives.

Referendum required for constitutional amendments, and may be used for other issues.

Electoral systems	1. *President* Direct universal suffrage. Term of office: 7 years.

2. *House of Representatives* Single transferable vote in multi-member constituencies (see above, pp. 66–7). Term of office: 5 years maximum.

3. *Senate* Nominated members and members elected by universities and a special electoral college representing cultural, economic and administrative interests.

Party system	2 main parties: Fine Gael and Fianna Fail. The smaller Labour Party and Progressive Democratic Party have importance particularly where, as recently, neither major party can secure an overall majority in the legislature.

Last election results given in chapter 5 (p. 84).

Italy

Population	57 million (1979)
Capital	Rome
Territory	301,263 sq. km.
State form	Republic

Constitution came into force January 1948.

Current head of state: *President F. Cossiga* (Christian Democrat; born 1928, elected July 1985).

Previous constitutional monarchy (which had provided the framework in which Mussolini established a fascist dictatorship, after being appointed as prime minister in 1922) was terminated by national referendum, held in June 1946.

State structure Unitary, but some devolution of powers to 20 regions with directly elected assemblies.

Form of government President nominates candidate Prime Minister to form a government, which must seek vote of confidence within 10 days and may be dismissed by vote of no confidence in *either* chamber.

Cabinet of about 30 senior ministers, is chaired by Prime Minister. Ministers are normally members of parliament.

Legislature: bicameral. *Chamber of Deputies* (630 members) and *Senate* (315 members) with co-equal powers of legislation and executive control. Legislation passed by both houses is subject to judicial review by constitutional court.

The President has a suspensive veto over legislation and may dismiss parliament (on advice of Presidents of *both* chambers of parliament).

8 Presidents since June 1946, 48 governments headed by 18 different Prime Ministers, currently C. De Mita, Christian Democrat, heads 5-party coalition.

Electoral systems 1. *President* Electoral college comprised of members of both chambers plus 58 representatives from the regions. 2/3 majority required on first 3 ballots, single majority thereafter. Candidates must be 50 years old. Term of office: 7 years, 8 elections since 1946.

2. *Chamber of deputies* Proportional representation. Candidates must be 25 years old. 5 year mandate: 11 elections since 1946, most recently in May 1987.

        3. *Senate* Proportional representation, on a regional basis (plus some life members – all former Presidents of the republic and 5 members appointed by the President for services to the nation). Candidates must be 40 years old. 5 year mandate since 1965, with elections on same day for both chambers.

Party system   One dominant party of government since 1946, the Christian Democrats. Major pole of opposition formed by the second largest party, the Communist Party. Several small parties: Social Democrats, Republicans, Liberals and Socialists have participated in coalition governments, the latter's leader, Crati, being Premier from 1983 to 1987. Neo-fascist Italian Social Movement gained nearly 6 per cent of votes in 1987.

Last election results given in chapter 5 (p. 85).

Luxemburg

Population   365,100 (1980)

Capital   Luxemburg

Territory   2,586 sq. km.

State form   Constitutional monarchy

Constitution adopted 1890

Current head of state: *Grand Duke Jean* (born 1921; crowned 12 November 1964).

State structure   Unitary

Form of government   Monarch nominates candidate Prime Minister who seeks vote of confidence from parliament.

Cabinet of 8–10 members share 19 ministerial portfolios. May be dismissed by parliament, but this has been rare.

Legislature: unicameral. *Chamber of Deputies* (58 members). Legislation must be adopted a second time, after a 3 months delay, unless advisory Council of State waives this requirement.

10 governments under 6 Prime Ministers since 1945. Currently, J. Santer, Social Christian in a coalition with the Socialist Party, formed July 1984.

Electoral system   *Chamber of Deputies:* proportional representation based on 4 districts. Voting is compulsory. Term of office: 5 years (since 1959). Last elections held 10 June 1979.

Party system   3 principal parties: Social Christian, which has been in nearly all governments since 1945, with either the Socialist or Democratic (liberal) parties. In addition, there is a small communist party and a social-democratic split from the Socialists.

Table 21   Election results: June 1984

	Votes (%)	Seats (no.)
Christian Social	36.6	25
Socialist	31.8	21
Democratic	20.4	14
Communists	4.4	2
Others	6.8	2

Malta

Population   315,974 (1980)

Capital   Valletta

Territory   316 sq. km.

Form of state   Republic (from December 1974, remaining within the British Commonwealth).

Constitution adopted 1964; amended January 1987 to ensure party with majority of votes forms government and to protect Malta's neutrality.

Current head of state: *President A. Barbara* (first elected February 1983).

State structure   Unitary

Form of government   President appoints Prime Minister, and, on advice of latter, other ministers.

Cabinet of about 15 members can be dismissed by parliament.

Legislature: unicameral. *House of Representatives* (65 members).

5 heads of state since republic formed (Sir A. Mamo (1974–76); A. Buttigieg (1976–81); A. V. Hyzler, (1981–83); A. Barbara (1983–). 7 governments since full independence in 1964 under 4 different Prime Ministers, currently, F. Adami, Nationalist Party; government formed in May 1987.

Electoral systems   *President* elected by House of Representatives. Term of office: 5 years.

Parliament proportional representation by single transferable vote system, based on 13 constituencies. Term of office: 5 years; 5 elections held since 1964; most recently on 9 May 1987.

Party system   2 major parties, Labour Party (in government 1971 to 1987) and the Nationalist Party.

Table 22   Election results: May 1987

	Votes (%)	Seats (no.)
Nationalist Party	50.9	35*
Labour Party	48.9	34

*including 4 members co-opted to reflect party's overall majority of votes, under 1987 Constitutional Amendment.

The Netherlands

Population   14.48 million (1985 est.)

Capital   The Hague

Territory   40,844 sq. km.

State form   Constitutional monarchy, based on constitution of 1814 and later revisions.

Current head of state: *Queen Beatrix* (born 31 January 1938; succeeded her mother, Queen

Juliana, who abdicated in her favour, on 30 May 1980).

State structure	Unitary
Form of government	Monarch appoints senior politician to explore possibilities for coalition formation (which may take several weeks); monarch then appoints Prime Minister. Ministers may not hold seats in legislature.

Current government: centre-right coalition of Christian Democrats and Liberals, under Prime Minister R. Lubbers (formed November 1982).

Legislature: bicameral. *States-General* (lower chamber has 150 seats, upper chamber has 75 seats). Upper chamber may reject legislation, but not amend it.

Constitution can only be revised by legislation, which has to be confirmed by a newly-elected parliament with a two-thirds majority.

Electoral systems   1. *Lower chamber* Proportional representation based on national party lists. Term of office: 4 years.

2. *Upper chamber* Elected by members of provincial councils. Term of office: 6 years (one half retire every three years).

Party system   Three main parties: Labour, Christian Democrat and Liberals. Left-wing liberal 'Democrats '66' is largest of several smaller parties which gain representation in the legislature.

Table 23   Election results: May 1986

	Votes (%)	Seats (no.)
Labour	33.3	52
Christian Democrats	34.6	54
People's Party for Freedom & Democracy (Liberal)	17.4	27
Democrats '66	6.1	9
Others	8.6	8

Norway

Population	4.16 million (1986 est.)
Capital	Oslo
Territory	386,638 sq. km.
State form	Constitutional monarchy, following termination of personal union with Sweden (under which Norway had the same monarch as Sweden) in 1905. Constitution dates from 17 May 1814.

Current head of state: *King Olav V*, born 2 July 1903, accession 21 September 1957.

The Lutheran Church is the national, state-endowed church.

State structure	Unitary.
Form of government	King appoints Prime Minister, who then chooses cabinet. Ministers must not be members of the legislature, though they can attend and speak there.

Current government: minority Labour government under G. Brundtland (formed May 1986).

Legislature: bicameral. The *Storting* (parliament), with 155 members is elected *en bloc*, but meets to choose one-quarter of its membership to form the upper house (*Lagting*); the remaining three-quarters of members form the lower house (*Odelsting*). The king can veto legislation, but if legislation is passed by three successively-elected Stortings, it becomes law despite the veto. Laws require the consent of both houses, but, if the two houses disagree, can be passed by a joint session by a two-thirds majority. This two-thirds majority of a joint session is also required to pass constitutional amendments.

Referenda can be used to consult the electorate directly on constitutional issues; a referendum rejected proposed membership of the European Community in September 1972.

Electoral system	*Storting* Elected by proportional representation based on district party lists. Terms of office: 4 years.
Party system	Main parties are Labour, Conservative, Agrarian and Christian Democratic Christian People's parties. A left-wing Progressive Party and extreme left-wing Socialist Left Party also obtain seats in the legislature.

Table 24   Election results: September 1985

	Votes (%)	Seats (no.)
Labour	40.8	71
Conservative	30.4	50
Christian People's	8.3	16
Centre (Agrarian)	6.6	12
Socialist Left Party	5.5	6
Progressive	3.7	2
Others	4.2	

Portugal

Population	9.58 million (1977)
Capital	Lisbon
Territory	88,860 sq. km.* (In addition the Azores and Madeira Islands are directly represented in the Portuguese parliament.)
State form	Republic

Constitution promulgated April 1976. Revised by parliament, August 1982.

Current head of state: M. Saores (Socialist; elected 26 January 1986).

Dictatorship established in 1932 by Dr Salazar (who was succeeded as Prime Minister in 1968 by

Dr Caetano), overthrown by military
intervention in April 1974 revolution.

State structure   Unitary.

Form of government   President designates Prime Minister who forms
government which must seek vote of confidence
from parliament on its programme within 10
days. Government may be dismissed by vote of
no confidence in Assembly (and, until 1982
revision, by President).

Cabinet of 15–20 ministers, is chaired by Prime
Minister. Ministers are normally drawn from
parliament but need not be.

Parliament: unicameral. *Assembly of the
Republic* (250 members). Legislation passed by
Assembly is subject to review by a constitutional
commission (and until 1982 could be blocked by
veto of now disbanded Supreme Council of the
Revolution, chaired by the president). President
has the power to dissolve parliament.

4 presidents since April 1974: General A.
Spinola (April–Sept. 1974), General Costa
Gomez (Sept. 1974–76), General R. Eanes
(1976–86), M. Saores (Jan. 1986–   ).

13 governments since April 1976, headed by 8
different Prime Ministers, currently A. Cavaco e
Silva, Social Democrat Party; government – his
second – formed in July 1987.

Electoral systems   1. *Presidency*. Direct universal suffrage.
Candidates expected to be members of armed
forces. 5-year mandate; 3 elections held since
1976 (most recently on 26th January 1986).

2. *Assembly*. 4-year mandate. 6 elections held
since April 1976, most recently in July 1987.

Party system   Four major parties have now established themselves, the Social Democratic Party dominating
the right-of-centre (at the expense of the more
traditional, clerical CDS), since 1985, while
on the left former President Eaves new party,
(Democratic Renewal) has won a modest base in

a period of declining support for both the Socialist and Communist parties.

Table 25   Election results: July 1987

	Votes (%)	Seats (no.)
Social Democrats	50.2	146
Socialist Party	22.3	59
Communist Party	12.2	30
Democratic Renewal Party	5.0	7
Centre Social Democrats	4.3	4

Spain

Population	36.3 million (1977)
Capital	Madrid
Territory	490,774 sq. km. (Excluding two enclaves on the Moroccan coast and the Balearic and Canary Islands, which are represented in the *Cortes*. In addition, Spain claims sovereignty over Gibraltar.)
State form	Constitutional monarchy

Constitution adopted by national referendum, December 1978. Current head of state: *King Juan Carlos 1* (of Bourbon, born 1938, sworn in on 22 November 1975).

Previous dictatorship of General Franco, established in 1939 following 3 year civil war against Popular Front forces of the Republic (founded in 1931), ended on his death in November 1975.

State structure — Unitary, but with considerable devolution of powers to elected regional assemblies.

Form of government   Monarch nominates candidate Prime Minister,
who must gain vote of confidence in the lower
house of parliament before designating members
of government. Governments may be dismissed
by the lower house.

Cabinet, of 20–25 members, is chaired by Prime
Minister. Ministers are normally members of
parliament.

Legislature (*Cortes*): bicameral. *Congress of
Deputies* (350 members) and *Senate* (249
members). Legislation passed by *Cortes* is subject
to judicial review by a constitutional court. Prime
Minister may dissolve parliament (once within
twelve months).

7 governments under 4 different Prime Ministers
since November 1975, currently F. González,
Socialist; government – his second – formed in
June 1986.

Electoral systems   1. *Congress of Deputies*. Proportional
representation on a regional basis. 4-year
mandate; 4 elections held since 1977, most
recently on 22 June 1986.

2. *Senate*. 208 members elected by majority
system on a provincial basis (with 4 senators for
each mainland province). In addition, monarch
appoints 41 senators. Elections held on same day
for both houses.

Party system   In the October 1982 elections the Spanish
Socialist Workers' Party (PSOE) emerged as the
country's dominant political force, the main
opposition being formed, on the right, by M.
Fraga's Popular Coalition. The previous
governing alliance from 1977, the Union of the
Democratic Centre, split in 1981–82, ex-PM
Suárez leading a new reformist party, the Democratic and Social Centre Party. The electoral base
of the Communist Party, which has a eurocommunist stance, has also been much reduced.
Several regionally-based parties retain significant
support primarily in the Basque and Catalan
provinces.

Table 26   Election results: June 1986

	Votes (%)	Seats (no.)
PSOE	44.1	184
Popular Coalition	26.0	105
Democratic and Social Centre	9.2	19
Communists	4.6	7
Convergence and Union (Catalonian)	5.0	18
3 Basque Parties*	3.2	13

* These parties stood separately.

Sweden

Population	8.358 million (1985 est.)
Capital	Stockholm
Territory	449,964 sq. km.
State form	Constitutional monarchy, based on constitution of 1975 (which replaced that of 1809). King must be a member of Lutheran church, which is the established national church.

Current head of state: *King Carl XVI* (born 30 April 1946, accession 15 September 1973).

State structure   Unitary

Form of government   Monarch appoints Prime Minister, and, on his nomination, the Council of State (cabinet). In a political crisis, power of appointment belongs to the Speaker of the *Riksdag*. Ministries prepare and present legislative proposals, but main administration is carried out by central boards.

Current government: Social Democrat government, under premiership of I. Carlsson (formed October 1982).

Legislature: unicameral. *Riksdag*: 349 members.

Consultative referendum can be used on constitutional and other issues.

Electoral system   *Riksdag* proportional representation in districts. Term of office: 3 years. Parties must secure 4 per cent of total vote or 12 per cent in one district to obtain seats.

Party system   Social Democrats dominant party; moderate Centre Party, Liberals and Conservatives are the other significant parties. The Communists, with about 5 per cent of the vote, also obtain representation.

Last election results given in chapter 5 (p. 86).

Switzerland

Population   6.48 million (1986 est.)

Capital   Bern

Territory   41,293 sq. km.

State form   Republic, based on constitution of 29 May 1874.

Current head of state: office held by rotation for one year term by member of Federal Council, elected to that office by joint session of legislature. Re-election to immediate second term prohibited.

State structure   Federation, consisting of 26 cantons (of which 6 are 'half-cantons').

Form of government   *Bundesrat* is chief executive, consisting of 7 members (each from a different canton) elected by joint session of legislature, which also chooses the President and Vice-President. Members of Federal Council act as ministers.

Legislature: bicameral. *Nationalrat* (200 members) and *Ständerat* (Council of States) (46 members: two from each canton and one from each half-canton).

Frequent use is made of the referendum.

Linguistic and religious, as well as party affiliations play an important role in elections and formation of governments.

Electoral systems   1. *Nationalrat* Proportional representation based on party lists. Term of office: 4 years. Female suffrage for national elections first introduced in 1971.

2. *Ständerat* Method of election varies from canton to canton.

Party system

Four main parties: Social Democrats, Christian Democrats, Agrarian Swiss People's Party and liberal Radical Democrats, plus much smaller conservative Independents' Party and Liberal Democrats, as well as several conservative Green and extreme left-wing parties who each poll less than three per cent nationally.

Table 27   Federal elections: November 1983

	Votes (%)	Seats (no.)
Christian Democrats	20.4	42
Radical Democrats	23.4	54
Social Democrats	22.9	47
Swiss People's Party	11.1	23
Independents Party	4.1	8
Liberal Democrats	2.8	8
Communists	0.9	1
Others	14.6	18

The United Kingdom

Population

56,763 million (1986 est.)

Capital

London

Territory

244,046 sq. km.

State form

Constitutional monarchy, no formal written constitution.

Current head of state: *Queen Elizabeth II* (born 21 April 1926, accession 6 February 1952).

The Church of England is the established church; the Queen is head of the church.

State structure

Unitary, with some administrative devolution to Scotland and Wales. Northern Ireland had devolved powers and a provincial legislature (re-established with direct elections in October 1982) but is currently ruled from Westminster.

Form of government

Monarch appoints the Prime Minister (normally the leader of the largest party in the House of Commons), who then chooses cabinet and other ministers for appointment by the monarch. Ministers normally must have a seat in parliament. Government resigns or calls a general election if defeated on important legislation or vote of confidence.

Prime Ministers since 1945: C. Attlee (1945–51); W. Churchill (1951–5); A. Eden (1955–7); H. Macmillan (1957–63); A. Douglas-Home (1963–4); H. Wilson (1964–70 and 1974–6); E. Heath (1970–4); J. Callaghan (1976–9); M. Thatcher (1979–   ).

Current government: Conservative, since May 1979.

Legislature: bicameral. *House of Commons* (650 members) and *House of Lords* (about 1100 members). Legislation must be passed by both Houses and obtain royal assent. *House of Lords* may delay legislation by maximum of one year. Monarch, on request of Prime Minister, may dissolve parliament at any time.

Electoral system

1. *House of Commons* Simple majority system of voting in single-member constituencies. Universal suffrage. Term of office: 5 years. There have been 12 general elections since 1945; the most recent was in June 1987.

2. *House of Lords* No election. Members are (a) hereditary and non-hereditary peers appointed by monarch; (b) archbishops and certain bishops of the Church of England; (c) Law Lords (who conduct functions of House of Lords as final Court of Appeal).

Party system

Four major national parties: Labour, Conservative, Social and Liberal Democrats and a Social Democratic Party. Scottish and Welsh

Nationalist parties have regional support. In Nothern Ireland, protestant Unionist parties and mainly Catholic Social Democratic and Labour Party and Sinn Fein. Communist Party and right-wing extremist National Front have negligible voting support.

Last election results given in chapter 5 (p. 80).

West Germany

Population	61.1 million (1986)
Capital	Bonn
Territory	248,852 sq. km.

State form	Republic

Constitution (Basic Law) ratified by *Länder* in May 1949.

Current head of state: *President* Richard von Weizsäcker (Christian Democrat, born 1920, elected 23 May 1984).

State structure — Federation: Basic Law divides powers between Federation and *Länder*. West Berlin has special and restricted relationship to Federal Republic.

Form of government — President nominates candidate for Chancellor to *Bundestag*, which elects Chancellor. President appoints ministers on nomination of Chancellor. Chancellor may only be dismissed by Bundestag simultaneously electing replacement by 'constructive vote of no confidence'. Cabinet is chaired by Chancellor.

There have been six Chancellors: K. Adenauer (1949–63); L. Erhard (1963–6); K–G. Kiesinger (1966–9); W. Brandt (1969–74); H. Schmidt (1974–82); H. Kohl (1982–   ).

Current government: coalition of Christian Democrats, Christian Social Union and Free Democrats since Oct. 1982.

Legislature: bicameral. *Bundestag* (normally 496 members, plus 22 from W. Berlin) and *Bundesrat* (41 representatives of *Länder* plus 4 from W. Berlin). *Bundesrat* has absolute veto on matters affecting *Länder* interests, conditional veto on other matters. Dissolution of *Bundestag* by President only possible if Chancellor loses majority and if no majority for an alternative Chancellor can be found.

Electoral systems

1. *President* Indirect election by special electoral college consisting of members of *Bundestag* plus equal number of representatives of *Länder* parliaments. Term of office: 5 years (can be re-elected once).

2. *Bundestag* Two-vote system. Half seats filled from single-member constituencies by simple majority, half from *Land* lists so that total number of seats per party is proportional to second votes for each party. Term of office: maximum 4 years.

3. *Bundesrat* No election. Members appointed by *Land* governments as required.

Party system

2 major parties: Social Democrats and Christian Democrats (in Bavaria, separately organised as Christian Social Union). Liberals and new ecological Green Party are the only minor parties with federal representation. No other party obtains over 1 per cent of national vote.

Last election results given in chapter 5 (p. 83).

Council of Europe

Established in Strasbourg, France, following the Congress of Europe held at the Hague, May 1948, to promote common action in economic, cultural, scientific, legal and administrative areas (but not defence) and to protect human rights and freedoms.

10 founding states in May 1949: Belgium, Denmark, France, Ireland, Italy, Luxemburg, the Netherlands, Norway, Sweden and the United Kingdom.

11 subsequent signatories: Greece and Turkey, 1949; Iceland, 1950; Federal Republic of Germany, Austria, 1957; Cyprus, 1961; Switzerland, 1963; Malta, 1965; Portugal, 1976; Spain, 1977; Lichtenstein, 1978.

The Council has an intergovernmental Committee of Ministers (usually foreign ministers, deciding by unanimity) and a consultative parliamentary Assembly (with 170 members drawn from 21 states) meeting 3 times a year.

The European Convention for the Protection of Human Rights and Fundamental Freedoms which was drawn up on the recommendation of the Assembly, came into force in September 1953. Under the convention, the *European Commission of Human Rights* was established in 1954 to investigate violations of human rights, and the *European Court of Human Rights* was set up in 1959.

(Finland is not a member of the Council of Europe)

European Community

Population	322 million (1988 est.)
Territory	12 member-states (see below). 2,240,000 sq. km.
Seats of institutions	Brussels, Luxemburg, Strasbourg
Form of government	Supranational organisation, regulated by Treaty of Rome (25 March 1957) and later accession agreements for new member-states.
	Proposals originate from Commission (current President: *Jacques Delors* (France), took office January 1985) and are passed to Council of Ministers (representing all member-states), who must agree to proposals before they can come into effect. Commission then oversees implementation of decisions of Council of Ministers. European parliament can debate issues, question commissioners and ministers, amend parts of budget, and accept or reject budget as a whole. It can dismiss the Commission *en bloc*.
Electoral system	European parliament: for direct elections in June 1979 and June 1984, modified forms of national electoral systems were used.

Table 28   Results of 1984 direct elections to the European Parliament

	Socialists	Christian Democrat	Liberal	Democratic	Conservative	Communist	Independent	Other	Total
Belgium	9	6	5	–	–	–	2	2	24
Denmark	4	1	2	–	4	1	4	–	16
Eire	–	6	1	8	–	–	–	–	15
France	20	8	13	20	–	10	–	10	81
Greece	10	9	–	–	–	4	–	1	24
Italy	12	27	5	–	–	27	4	6	81
Luxembourg	2	3	1	–	–	–	–	–	6
Netherlands	9	8	5	–	–	–	–	3	25
United Kingdom	33	–	–	1	46	–	–	1	81
West Germany	33	41	–	–	–	–	–	7	81
Total	132	109	32	29	50	42	10	30	434

In addition, Spain sends 60 members (36 Socialists, 13 Democrats, 2 Liberals, 7 Christian Democrats and 2 others), and Portugal sends 24 members (9 Liberals, 6 Socialists, 3 Communists, 2 Christian Democrats, 4 others).

Party system Groupings of national parties have resulted, following co-operation in the European parliament. The main groupings are: Socialists, Christian Democrats (European People's Party), Liberal and Democratic Federation, European Democrats (conservative), and Communists.

North Atlantic Treaty Organisation

Founded with headquarters in Brussels under the North Atlantic Treaty of April 1949 which provided for political and economic as well as military co-operation.

It has an intergovernmental North Atlantic Council, with ministerial meetings twice a year (usually attended by Foreign Ministers, but sometimes held at the level of heads of government and state) and a Defence Planning Committee, with ministerial meetings twice a year (attended by Ministers of Defence).* It also has a parliamentary North Atlantic Assembly, meeting once a year.

12 signatory states in 1949: Belgium, Canada, Denmark, France,* Iceland, Italy, Luxemburg, the Netherlands, Norway, Portugal, the United Kingdom and the United States of America.

4 states have subsequently joined: Greece and Turkey, in 1952; Federal German Republic in 1955; Spain in 1981.

The current secretary-general is M. Wörner (Federal German Republic).

* France, who remains a member of the Atlantic Alliance, is not a member of its integrated military structure and does not attend these meetings.

(Of the west European states, Austria, Finland, Ireland, Malta, Sweden and Switzerland are not members of NATO.)

FURTHER READING

General works on western European politics

Gordon Smith, *Politics in Western Europe* (Heineman, 4th edn, 1983)
A comprehensive interpretation of west European liberal democracy,
political institutions and processes, and contrastive reference to
non-democratic political arrangements. Valuable also for its
chapter-bibliographies.

Derek Urwin, *Western Europe since 1945* (Longman (revised) edn, 1981)
A thorough chronological and thematic coverage of key political
developments in western Europe since the end of the second world war
including the development of western European integration. It includes
a useful bibliography.

B. Kohler, *Political forces in Spain, Greece and Portugal* (Butterworth,
London, 1982)
An interesting account of the contrasting processes by which the
transition to democratic forms of government took place in each of
these countries. Discusses their differing patterns of political forces and
constitutional arrangements, as well as the possible political
implications for each of entry into the European Community.

J. Sallnow and A. John, *An electoral atlas of Europe 1968–81*
(Butterworth, 1982)
A detailed reference work presenting electoral results and data on
electoral systems, together with a brief chronology of recent political
developments in each century.

Studies of national political systems

United Kingdom
D. Kavanagh, *British Politics: Continuity and Change* (Oxford University
Press, Oxford, 1985).
Focusses on the constitutional and historical context of British politics,

and emphasises its distinctive aspects.

Federal Republic of Germany
I. Derbyshire, *Politics in West Germany from Schmidt to Kohl* (Chambers, 1987). A review of recent developments in West German politics, with many useful tables and appendices.

Gordon Smith, *Democracy in Western Germany* (Heinemann, 3rd edn., 1986)
A well-written commentary on the contemporary politics of the Federal Republic, which pays proper attention to the historical background of its modern politics and focuses on the controversies and problems which exist in the political system of West Germany.

France
V. Wright, *The government and politics of France* (Hutchinson, London, 2nd ed. 1983).
A comprehensive and highly readable treatment of institutions and political forces, with a particular focus on the emergence and consolidation of presidentialism.

D. Hanley, A. P. Kerr, and N. H. Waites, *Contemporary France: Politics and Society since 1945* (Routledge & Kegan Paul, London, 1979)
Includes useful coverage of social and economic changes, France's foreign and defence policies and educational system as well as an extensive annotated bibliography.

Political Orientations in Western Europe

R. E. Irving, *The Christian Democratic Parties of Western Europe* (Royal Institute of International Affairs/Allen & Unwin, London, 1979)
A useful reference work, with an extensive bibliography, but covering only the six original member states of the European Community.

Z. Layton-Henry, *Conservative Politics in Western Europe* (Macmillan, London, 1981)
An up-to-date collection of essays covering conservative and christian democrat parties in ten countries.

W. E. Paterson and A. H. Thomas (eds.), *The Social Democratic Parties of Western Europe* (Croom Helm, London, 1977) *and* W. E. Paterson and A. H. Thomas, (eds.), *The Future of Social Democracy* (Clarendon Press, Oxford, 1986)

Two very useful collections of essays, covering nearly all the states dealt with in this book, with details for each party on such issues as membership, electoral base, leadership and organisational structures, and experience in government, and reviews of recent developments.

R. N. Tannahill, *The Communist Parties of Western Europe: a Comparative Study.*
A comprehensive reference work, covering all the states dealt with in this book, and providing details on changes in each party's membership and electoral base, their party organisation, their place in their national party system, and relationship to the Soviet Union.

M. Kolinsky and W. E. Paterson (eds.), *Social and Political Movements in Western Europe* (Croom Helm, London, 1976)
An interesting, if now somewhat dated, volume with essays covering examples from one or more countries of the extreme and nationalist rights, christian democracy, social democracy, communism, the 'new left', and the Europeanist movements.

Electoral systems

S. E. Finer (ed.), *Adversary Politics and Electoral Reform* (Anthony Wigram, 1975)
This book deals with two important themes: the debate concerning electoral reform in the context of British politics (including the argument that a less polarising electoral system would lead to more effective and 'consensual' policies), and the variety of electoral systems in use in countries such as Eire, the Netherlands and the Federal German Republic, as well as in the United Kingdom

D. Butler, H. R. Penniman, A. Ranney (eds.), *Democracy at the Polls: a Comparative study of competitive national elections* (American Enterprise Institute for Public Policy Research, Washington & London, 1981)
Provides comparative and somewhat uneven treatment of such issues as the interplay between electoral systems and party systems, levels of electoral participation, the financing of electoral campaigns, the role of the mass media and opinion polling in elections, together with the role of elections in relation to the formation of governments and the making of policy. Based on twenty-eight countries, including all those in western Europe.

Political parties and pressure groups

S. Henig (ed.), *Political Parties in the European Community* (Allen & Unwin, 1979)
A descriptive overview of the party-systems of the member-states of the European Community, and of the Community-level party organisations which have developed in recent years.

S. Bartolini and P. Moir, eds. *Party Politics in Contemporary Western Europe* (Cass, 1984). A review of developments in party systems in all the principal states of Western Europe.
several of the minor, countries of western Europe, and also has chapters on comparative aspects of their party systems.

P. Schmitter and G. Lehmbruch (eds.), *Trends towards Corporatist Intermediation* (Sage, 1979)
A volume of essays on changing trends in modes of interest representation in western Europe and elsewhere. A rather complex, but important contribution to the understanding of pressure group activity.

Parliaments

D. Coombes (ed.), *The Power of the Purse: the role of European parliaments in budgetary decisions* (Political and Economic Planning/Allen & Unwin, London, 1976)
A volume of essays assessing the budgetary powers of a number of parliaments, paying particular attention to their differing committee structures, and the impact of different systems of parliamentary party organisation. Has separate chapters covering France, West Germany, Italy, the Netherlands, Switzerland and the United Kingdom.

Executive government

R. Rose and E. N. Suleiman, *Presidents and Prime Ministers* (American Enterprise Institute for Policy Research, Washington, 1980)
A survey of contemporary patterns of political leadership, including informative and thorough essays on the United Kingdom, France, West Germany, Italy and Norway (as well as Spain under Franco, and Canada and the United States).

F. F. Ridley (ed.), *Government and Administration in Western Europe* (Martin Robertson, London, 1979)

Covers Belgium, France, West Germany, Italy, the Netherlands and the United Kingdom, providing a succinct description of the main political institutions of each country, but focusing more particularly on the organisation of their central departments of government, their field services, and civil service training and career patterns.

E. C. Browne and J. Dreijmanis (eds.), *Government Coalitions in Western Democracies* (Longmans, London, 1982)
Includes particularly useful tables on coalition partners in government in ten West European states since the war, together with discussion of the problems of coalition formation, although some of the material is concerned with the complications of coalition theory. Extensive bibliographies are also provided.

Subnational and supranational political organisations

K. C. Wheare, *Federal Government* (Oxford University Press, 4th edn, 1963)
Though dated, still a clearly-written and useful guide to federal government, its operation and organisation, with substantial reference to western Europe.

B. Burrows, G. Denton and G. Edwards, *Federal Solutions to European Issues* (Macmillan, 1978)
A discussion of federalism in Europe, especially in the context of its relevance to European problems.

S. Henig, *Power and Decisions in Europe: the Political Institutions of the European Community* (Europotentials, 1980)
A concise description of the major institutions and processes of the European community.

S. George, *Politics and Policy in the European Community* (Oxford University Press, 1985)
A useful study of the relationships between Community institutions and the policy process in the EC.

Journals

A number of specialist journals provide regular coverage of political developments in western Europe, most notably *West European Politics,* the *Journal of Common Market Studies* and also *Scandinavian Political Studies,* while others, for example *Government and Opposition* and *Parliamentary Affairs,* frequently include articles on elections and aspects of policy-making.

In addition, there are several organisations, such as the Association for the Study of Contemporary and Modern France and the Association for the Study of German Politics, which produce newsletters for their members with useful bibliographies and book reviews, while the University Association for Contemporary European Studies arranges regular conferences on policy and institutional developments in the European Community and its member-states.

INDEX

(Pages in bold type refer to the summaries of political systems at the end of the book.)